RELATIONSHIP MARKETING
Text and Cases

S. Shajahan

Professor
ICFAI Business School
ICFAI University
Chennai

Tata McGraw-Hill Publishing Company Limited
NEW DELHI

McGraw-Hill Offices
New Delhi   New York   St Louis   San Francisco   Auckland   Bogotá   Caracas
Kuala Lumpur   Lisbon   London   Madrid   Mexico City   Milan   Montreal
San Juan   Santiago   Singapore   Sydney   Tokyo   Toronto

Tata McGraw-Hill

Copyright © 2004, by Tata McGraw-Hill Publishing Company Limited.

First reprint 2006
RLLCRRCKRZZLD

No part of this publication may be reproduced or distributed in any form or by any means,
electronic, mechanical, photocopying, recording, or otherwise or stored in a database or
retrieval system without the prior written permission of the publishers. The program listings
(if any) may be entered, stored and executed in a computer system, but they may not be
reproduced for publication.

This edition can be exported from India only by the publishers,
Tata McGraw-Hill Publishing Company Limited

ISBN 0-07-058337-4

Published by Tata McGraw-Hill Publishing Company Limited
7 West Patel Nagar, New Delhi 110 008, typeset at Shree Ambaji Laser Teck,
WP-475A, IIIrd Floor, Shiv Market, Ashok Vihar, New Delhi 110 052 and printed at
Sai Printo Pack Pvt. Ltd., Y-56, Okhla Industrial Area, Phase II, New Delhi 110 020

Cover printer: De-Unique

The **McGraw-Hill** Companies

To
my daughter
Heena Shajahan

Foreword

Of late, the Indian corporate has started realising the importance of relationship marketing practices in their marketing strategies. Much of this strategic shift has been ascribed to the converging pressures of geo-political realignment and to the emergence of the Internet technology. Even though such a shift would involve heavy resource commitments, monetary and otherwise, the Indian corporates have taken up this challenge as a part of their survival in a fast moving market-driven economy.

I am very happy to note that Dr. Shajahan has brought a comprehensive book on fundamental concepts in relationship marketing. He has vividly provided the fundamental principles of customer relationship building in the first seven chapters and their applications in the next four. I am confident that this book would be of immense help to both students and marketing professionals alike. The treatment that he has accorded in explaining the concepts of relationship marketing is highly commendable. It is a delight to set that appropriate examples given in the book would give clarity to the concepts described. Similarly, the chapter-end case studies would give ample opportunity to the reader for a thorough understanding of the topics discussed within that chapter.

I am sure that the book will provide a solid foundation to the students and help develop in them an interest in this area. I would like to compliment Dr Shajahan for a job well done and wish him all success.

Prof Jagdish N Sheth
Charles H. Kellstadt Professor of Marketing
Goizeuta Business School
Emory University, Atlanta, USA

Professor Jagdish N. Sheth is widely known as the father of relationship marketing. He is also the founder of the Center for Relationship Marketing (CRM) at Emory University and the Center for Telecommunications Management (CTM) at University of Southern California. Dr Sheth has long associations with several universities like MIT, Columbia University and University of Illinois, to name a few. Dr Sheth is a recipient of the Outstanding Marketing Educator Award given by the Academy of Marketing Sciences in 1989, the Distinguished Fellow Award from the Academy of Marketing Sciences is 1996, the Outstanding Educator Award from the Sales and Marketing Executive International (SMEI), and the P.D. Converse Award from the American Marketing Association. He is also a Fellow of the APA and a Distinguished Fellow of the IEC.

A prolific author, Dr Sheth has written dozens of books, the latest one being *Value Space* (McGraw-Hill). His book, *Handbook of Relationship Marketing* is considered a classic work on the subject. Dr Sheth has also more than 125 international research articles to his credit.

Preface

Preparing a text book on customer relationship marketing has been an exciting and challenging task—the excitement borne out of the potential of the concept that can make sweeping changes across business environment; and the challenge out of incorporating these concepts in the Indian business environment.

The idea for this book originated from experiences both within the academic and other research related assignments. The first hand information that I could gather during my consultancy assignments, both within India and abroad, have also helped in explaining the concepts from a practical point of view, particularly while explaining the realities of undertaking application oriented relationship marketing practices.

The relationship marketing textbooks that I have come across in my academic career have been found inadequate in meeting the needs of both the students and tutors in a complete manner. Either they would have an excessive orientation towards technology-related application, or had their focus completely maintained on American or European market and customers, with relatively lesser emphasis on Indian markets and its consumers. These aspects were particularly kept in mind while I was preparing this book, and attempts have been made to solve these problems to a large extent.

Focus

The focus of the book could be looked upon from three perspectives:

(a) General; (b) Corporate; and (c) Academic.

General Perspective
The concept of relationship marketing has been treated as a relatively new possibility and philosophy in doing business. It involves the process of identifying and creating 'value' with individual customers', and sharing the benefits of this process over a lifetime of association. It also includes management of the ongoing collaboration between suppliers and selected customers for mutual 'value' creation and sharing, through a process of interdependence and organisational alignment.

However, the concept calls for certain fundamental changes from the conventional marketing and selling strategies of business enterprises. These include **(a)** change in the enterprise's marketing mindset; **(b)** closer integration of the enterprise and customer values; **(c)** adopting the principle of mass customisation; and **(d)** creation of a comprehensive customer database.

Corporate Perspective
The book also provides useful tools, methodologies and conceptual approaches for business enterprises that intend to

embark on a relationship marketing path. These include methodologies for: **(1)** calculating lifetime value of the customer; **(2)** creating a customer segmentation portfolio; **(3)** creating data warehouses; **(4)** calculating the profitability potential of current and future customers; **(5)** introducing technological input in enhancing the customer relationship; and **(6)** aligning the various groups of stakeholders within the company for an enhanced relationship strategy. Numerous examples from companies having leading relationship practices have been cited in this regard.

Academic Perspective In a bid to exploit the emerging possibilities in relationship marketing, the subject has been included in the curriculum of various management courses. This book covers the syllabi requirements of MBA, MIB and other post-graduate level management courses of various Indian universities. Moreover, the huge gap that exists in the existing literature and application-oriented relationship marketing techniques in Indian condition have also been particularly taken into consideration while designing the contents of the book .

The syllabus of Anna University has been kept as the framework for preparing the content of this book.

Features

The whole book has been divided into eleven chapters. Additional learning tools like tables, figures and exhibits have been provided for a comprehensive understanding of the subject. Eleven case studies (drawn from global and local contexts) have also been provided for the purpose. These live materials would offer students more ideas, insights and research findings that could stimulate classroom discussion on real marketing issues.

Digital Solutions

The web-based assistance is another supplementary characteristic of this book. The features of this website include: **(a)** Power point slides that condense the important points discussed within the text; **(b)** Chapter-wise case summaries and analyses which provide a guideline for analysing the cases in an effective and systematic manner; **(c)** Chapter-wise multiple choice questions to plot the reader's understanding on a 20-point scale: **(d)** Two multiple choice examination papers; **(e)** A section on relationship accounting matrix—the accounting-based relationship marketing exercise which would be useful both for the students and trainers; and **(f)** Other updates, which include **(1)** latest information on customer-centric organisations, their strategies and ways of managing customer as an asset, and **(2)** the author's latest published works particularly or RFM analysis, life time value (LTV), datamining and the predictive imperatives for maximising the customer value.

The features of this website except the instructor's resources are open for all. The instructor's resources available exclusively to the teachers and trainers contain answers to examination papers and relationship matrix, case analysis and the power point presentation.

I shall welcome suggestions, comments and questions on any topic discussed in the book. It could be addressed either to the publisher or to me at my e-mail address, shaangrila@yahoo.com.

S SHAJAHAN

Acknowledgements

Several of my colleagues, both from the academic and business circles, have helped me in the development of this project. Some of them were directly involved in the project, while others have helped me in developing my thought process on the subject. Although it is impossible to mention all of them, I would like to particularly acknowledge the contribution made by a few: Mr Pacha Muthu (Chairman, SRM Group of Institutions, Chennai), Mr Sharat Kumar (Director, IMT, Ghaziabad), Dr Kumar (Department of Management Studies, Anna University), Dr H Peerumohammed (Asstt. Professor, Department of Management Studies, Anna University), Dr Sahani (Advisor— SRM group), Dr T P Ganesan (Director, SRM College), Prof. N Ranganathan (Former Director, School of Management Studies, CUSAT), Dr K C Sankaranarayanan (Former Dean, Faculty of Social Science, CUSAT), Dr Madhulika Singh (Advisor—CD, AICTE, New Delhi), Prof. Ashok J Chandra (Asstt. Director, ICSSR, New Delhi), Sanjay Banerjee (AIM, Coimbatore), Amit Gupta (Dean, JIMS, New Delhi), Dr Ajay Singh (MDI, Gurgaon), and Ramesh C Gaur (Chief Librarian, IMT Ghaziabad).

I would also like to thank Prof C B Bhattacharya (School of Management, Boston University), Prof Narakesari Narayanadas (Harvard Business School), Prof Jagdish N Sheth (Emory University), and Prof Rajan Varadarajan (Texas A and M University and Chairman, Special Interest Group of the American Marketing Association) for their sincere support to this project.

Mention should also be made of the web portal Rediff.com, and the newspaper dailies—*The Economic Times, Business Line*, and *Financial Express*—for their print and cyber media support. Finally, I would like to thank my publisher Tata McGraw-Hill for their enthusiasm and support they have shown in this project.

S SHAJAHAN

Contents

11. Integrated Relationship Marketing Strategies in the Millennium

AN OVERVIEW OF RELATIONSHIP MARKETING

"Your most unhappy customers are your greatest source of learning."

Bill Gates

Learning Objectives

After reading this chapter you should understand:
- The differences in the marketing strategies of the past and present;
- The concept of relationship marketing—its advantages and how it can be achieved;
- Brand creation; and
- The role of technology in modern marketing;

INTRODUCTION

In the mid-20th century many management philosophers like Peter Drucker, believed that the purpose of a business is to create a satisfied customer. They were of the opinion that profit is not the objective, but the reward. This opinion was formed under the assumption that a satisfied customer is willing to pay the firm well for its products and services as the customer would find 'value' in them. The value will be created for the shareholders in the form of profit, when the customer pays the firm a price that is greater than the entire cost that the firm itself had paid for its product offering. Thus the value is created in the marketplace by customers who perceive value in the firm's product offering.

Prior to the development of the marketing concept, the goal of marketing activity was to produce a sale (and to maximise sales volumes). Profitability was not a major marketing concern then, as the basic assumption was that the sales volume holds the key to profitability. The more the sales and marketing people could sell, the higher the profit the firm could expect as it spread its fixed costs over larger production volume and reduced variable cost per unit as well. Let us examine the current practices in modern marketing management one by one after analysing the gravity of such a paradigm shift.

1.1 PARADIGM SHIFT IN MARKETING

The market place has been undergoing changes under the converging pressures of demographics, global politics, economic upheavals, scientific advancements and social evolutions. Business organisations are not also left apart from this change process. As organisations undergo change, the role of marketing within these organisations also have undergone a transformation. It is very well understood that every business organisation should be organised around the latest information and knowledge oriented systems for its survival in the modern age. Besides they should also be customer-focused, market-driven, networked, and flexible in its ability to deliver superior value to customers who are continuously modifying their definition of value.

In an interview in the *Marketing Science Institute Review* in 1991, Philip Kotler has stated that, "A paradigm shift, as used by Thomas Kuhn..., occurs when a field's practitioners are not satisfied with the field's explanatory variables or breadth...What I think we are witnessing today is a movement away from a focus on exchange—in the narrow sense of transaction— and toward a focus on building value-laden relationships and marketing networks...We start thinking mostly about how to hold on to our existing customers...Our thinking therefore is moving from a marketing mix focus to a relationship focus".

Frederick Webster, another prominent American opinion leader in marketing, has also come to a similar conclusion in an analysis of recent developments in business processes and marketing: "There has been a shift from a *transactions* to a *relationship* focus" and "from an academic or theoretical perspective, the relatively narrow conceptualisation of marketing as a profit-maximization problem, focused on market transactions or series of transactions, seems increasingly out of touch with an emphasis on long-term customer relationships and the formation and management of strategic alliances". The analysis of the above two statements would provide us the marketing concept of the twenty-first century.

The present day marketing concept is radically different from its earlier form as it involves a total organisation commitment, pervasive throughout the firm's operating systems and culture. In other words, the concept of marketing could not be confined to the province of a few specialists. In fact the traditional functional boundaries are disappearing and the boundary between the firm and its environment is increasingly getting blurred.

Three Fundamental Requirements of the Paradigm Shift

This change in the fundamental approach to marketing could be looked upon from three focal points:

> ➤ Focus on customer driven marketing practices
> ➤ Focus on profitability
> ➤ Focus on strategic marketing practices

Focus on Customer Driven Marketing Practices

The commitment to innovation and customer-oriented business decision making is the first step in implementing the modern marketing concept. This commitment establishes the culture of customer orientation that is the foundation of the marketing concept. The attribute of customer orientation is absolutely essential as it is the basis on which all strategic activities should be built. But by itself it is an incomplete business strategy as it does not explain the ways of creating and delivering the customer value profitability.

Focus on Profitability

The next step involves the shifting of focus from sales volume to profitability. When managing for profitability (and not sales volumes), the firm is focusing on the value its products could create for customers in the competitive marketplace. The profit does not come at the expense of the customer. On the contrary, it is the best possible measure of the value that has been created for customers. Declining profitability is a signal that the company's product offering is becoming less effective, relative to substitutes and competitive product offerings, in delivering value and satisfying the customer needs. It may often be the result of aggressive attempts to expand the sales volumes by serving a larger portion of the total market, requiring higher expenditures on promotional activities and low prices. This is where the concept of market segmentation becomes essential to our understanding.

Focus on Strategic Marketing Practices

The market segmentation, market targeting and market positioning constitute the third set of requirements for implementing the paradigm shift in marketing and they deserve special emphasis as they are at the heart of marketing strategy.

The **market segmentation** recognises that the customers have distinct needs, preferences, and buying patterns. It is the process of analysing the market in order to define, in a creative manner, the distinct groupings of customers for whom the firm has the potential to offer superior value. These different groups will respond differently to the firm's product offering and communications.

Market targeting implies the development of products and communications aimed at specific parts of the total market in order to compete in the market in an effective and efficient manner. The market targets should be those segments that offer the best return on marketing investments and the greatest profit opportunities. One of the drivers of the product life-cycle, where the profit margins begin to erode following the early growth stage of the market, is the increased competition from market nichers who selectively target parts of the total market with a superior product offering. The inevitability of the product or market life-cycle brings us back to the centrality of innovation in the marketing concept. The successful firm must continuously improve its product offering in order to remain competitive. The inefficiency and lower profit margins inevitably creep in when the company relies on heavier promotional expenditures and aggressive pricing actions to prop up sales volume for an increasingly obsolete product aimed at multiple market segments.

Positioning is the process of developing the value proposition, which differentiates the product offering from its competitors in the customer's mind. It is implemented through communications—personal selling, advertising, sales promotion, publicity and so on. All brand elements such as company and brand name, logos, packaging, promotional materials and labelling are part of the positioning process. The positioning is critical to the success of the product offering. For many product offerings and market targets, the product positioning is more enduring than the physical product itself. The brand image and positioning may remain constant while the product is continuously refined and improved in response to changing customer preferences and technology.

1.2 THEMES FOR NEW MARKETING

The central theme of marketing has evolved over a number of stages in the past few decades. In the mid-1950s, it was the **marketing mix**, that became the mantra of major business enterprises. The marketing mix otherwise known as the 'the 4ps of marketing' emphasised on four principal aspects viz., product, placement, price, and promotion. (This concept is covered in detail in the subsequent sections)

By 1980, Michael Porter's concept of 'competitive forces' had become the central theme of market strategist. The decade of the 1990s saw the sales and marketing respond to the buyer's demand for more cooperative relationships with the emergence of the concept of relationship marketing. As companies headed towards the twenty-first century, 'solutions' became the buzzword in the marketing lexicon as the concept of 'value' has started replacing products and services in the suppliers' offering.

Similarly, the contribution margin or the bottom-line profitability has usurped the top-line revenue management. Most business improvement ideas seem to be one-dimensional; they propose a business focused on one central idea, such as (a) becoming lean, (b) developing the best competencies (c) becoming competitive or (d) focusing on leadership. While these could help the business organisaton, they often do so in isolation or in a vacuum as they fail to consider (a) the entire supply chain, (b) the extended value chain, or (c) the business ecosystem in which the business is operating.

Business Paradigm and the 'Value' Aspect

The **business paradigm,** according to J Nicholas De Bonis *et al* (2002), is the integration of business strategies, processes, and practices in order to deliver a superior customer value commitment to the chosen target customers, while making a profit. This definition envisions a win-win approach to the conduct of business, with mutual value for both the customer value segments and the supplier. De Bonis defined the concept of 'mutual value' in terms of the difference between a long-term relationship driven by the value exchanged or shared between a buyer and the seller, and the short-term transaction that focus on revenue and costs.

The successful value creation requires an understanding (a) of the basic components of customer value and (b) of the ways by which the resources in a business could be aligned to deliver the value to its chosen value segment. This requires an outside-in, market-focused, customer-driven commitment, which addresses whether the business firm's customer value commitment is the best value for the customer relative to any other factor in the marketplace.

While many business enterprises claim that they are customer-focussed and provide value, the actual corporate behaviour and financial results belie the claim. In fact these businesss firms try to explain the away performance shortfalls as "it's the new economy" or "the global market has become so competitive". These businesses should be prevented from adopting a customer value approach to business. The concepts relating to such corporate pitfalls are explained in detail in Chapter 7.

Many business enterprises have some appreciation of the customer needs, their operating costs, and their products/service benefits and the investor expectations. However, most of the firms, tend to misunderstand which of these factors drives the real performance and which among them follows as an end result. Many studies have reported that the most important aspect of achieving a long-term success lies in providing superior 'customer value'.

The marketing concept requires the specific resource commitments, most of which do not pay off in a short-term period. There is an obvious requirement for information from the marketplace about the customer needs, wants, preferences, buying habits, usage patterns, and about the competitive product offerings. These are long-term investments with long-term payoffs and long-term strategic consequences for the firm. The budgeting for these investments puts the marketing function in direct conflict with other management functions for scarce financial resources.

Developing Market-driven Organisation and Strategies

From a societal point of view, the customer orientation is the strongest source of legitimation for the business as an institution, especially for a business enterprise that has grown too large to be controlled by its owners. Apart from the 'mission' and 'vision' statements, many organisations have very little idea about the type of customers that they should really focus on. As a result, the marketing concept has a nebulous quality about it, which makes it very difficult for the marketing managers and other advocates of customer orientation to defend themselves against other management functions.

Role of Market Research and "Creation" of Markets

A key aspect of customer orientation and integrated marketing is the use of market research to (a) analyse the customer needs and wants and (b) provide feedback to other parts of the business. The implication of this aspect is that marketing has the ability (a) to discover, (b) to understand, and (c) to communicate to others the real essence of customer needs: the even more basic implication is that the customer knows their needs.

The real challenge for a business firm is to create new markets, and not just to serve the existing ones. The legendary success stories of Ford, Disney, IBM, Hewlett Packard, Federal Express, Apple, and AOL have just proven that. They have a vision of a capability to produce a unique product or service that would revolutionise the way the customers solved a problem. They could lead their customers into the future, as they always listened to their customers while developing and refining the features of their product offering. They are committed to leading and educating their customers in the use of their products.

Limitation of Conventional Marketing Definition

A literal interpretation of the marketing concept would suggest that the firm should take information from the marketplace as the sole basis for deciding their operational strategy. Somehow, this belief also implies that the market itself provides not only the information about the customer needs, but also provides the criteria that decides the functional strtegies of the firm. In fact, the market alone cannot provide the whole set of ideas for a firm while designing their operational strategy. Besides, a creative thought process should be put in (a) to observe the market, (b) to understand the potential customer needs and wants, (c) to consider the basic capabilities of the firm, (d) to conceive the potential product offerings based on the present and potential capabilities, (e) to design and develop such products, and (f) to manufacture and deliver the product with the full bundle of supporting services to a clearly defined target market.

In fact the earlier interpretation of market as the sole 'decider' and 'provider' of ideas, has been found an incomplete management philosophy. If the marketing concept was to be a useful management tool, and not just a statement of corporate culture and business purpose, it should be expanded to include a more strategic focus that would make a proper balance between the market needs and the firm's capabilities.

Beyond the conceptual problems associated with the marketing concept, there were a number of problems at the implementation level also. This include:

> Failure to make customer orientation as a primary goal;

> Under-investment in marketing activities;

> Weak performance by the marketing organisation; and

> Creation of a customer-centric organisation and strategies.

However, it should be kept in mind that making resource commitments (a) for marketing information systems, (b) for strategy development, (c) for the process development required for identifying and developing professional marketing, management talent, and organisational structures necessary to keep the total organisation focussed on the customer, is not an easy task. It is even more difficult to develop and maintain (a) a true culture of customer orientation, and (b) a set of values and beliefs that puts the interests of the customer first, ahead of all other constituents and stakeholders served by the organisation. These issues are discussed in detail in Chapter11.

Limitations of the Marketing Mix (4Ps)

Borden has provided the original idea of a list of marketing mix ingredients that have to be considered in every given situation. The items in this list was so extensive. The factors in this list were shortened to four factors (product, placement, price and promotion—otherwise known as the 4Ps) mainly due to two reasons: (a) pedagogical, and (b) a limited number of marketing variables were found representing the "typical situations" observed in the late 1950s and the 1960s which led to the standardisation of these ingredients to a list of four standardised Ps.

Critics of the 4P concept point out that the "typical situations" that led to these standardisation were the consumer packaged goods sector in the North American environment which had (a) huge mass markets, (b) a highly competitive distribution system and (c) a commercial mass media, whereas there were other markets also, where the infrastructure varied in a significant manner, while the consumer packaged goods formed only a part of the products that appeared in these markets. In short, the 4Ps constitute a traditional and fundamental production-oriented definition of marketing, rather than a market-oriented or customer-oriented one.

Even though modern marketing gurus, like McCarthy, recognises the interactive nature of the 4Ps, most of them believe that the model itself does not explicitly include any of the interactive elements. Further, they are also of the view that the 4Ps does not indicate the nature and scope of such interactions.

The problems with the marketing mix are more of theoretical nature, rather than the number or conceptualisation of decision variables involved in it. Originally, the marketing mix was largely based on the empirical induction and the lists of marketing functions of the functional school of marketing. They were developed under the influence of microeconomic theory and especially under the theory of monopolistic competition of the 1930s, which provided more realism to that theory. However, very soon the connection to the microeconomic theory was cut off and subsequently totally forgotten. Theoretically, the marketing mix has become just a list of 4Ps without roots.

Nevertheless, the four Ps of the marketing mix have become the universal marketing model/theory and an almost totally dominating paradigm for most academics. The marketing mix have also made a tremendous impact on the practice of marketing as well. Van Waterschoot and Van den Bulte argued that "...to our knowledge, the classification property(-ies) or rationale for distinguishing the four categories labelled `product', `price', `place' and `promotion' have never been explicated...Though casual observation of practitioners, students, and textbooks suggest a general consensus to classify the marketing mix elements in the same categories, the lack of any formal and precise specification of the properties or characteristics according to which marketing mix elements should be classified is a major flaw".

Van Waterschoot and Van den Bulte has recognised three flaws in the 4P model:

> ➢ Lack of proper identification of the properties or characteristics that have formed the basis for such a classification;
> ➢ Lack of mutually exclusive categories; and
> ➢ Emergence a catch-all sub-category that is continually growing.

Many marketing-related phenomenon have also not been covered under its domain. Similarly, as Johan Arndt has concluded, marketing research remains narrow in scope and even myopic, and the methodological issues become more important than the substance matter.

"Research in marketing gives the impression of being based on a conceptually sterile and unimaginative positivism...The consequence...is that most of the resources are directed towards less significant issues, over explaining what we already know, and toward supporting and legitimising the status quo". Unfortunately, far too little has changed in the mainstream marketing research since this was written over a decade ago.

1.3 MOVING TOWARDS RELATIONSHIP MARKETING

From the academic prospective, it would be fair to say that management science, using the tools of rigorous mathematical and statistical analysis had only limited applications in marketing. This is because of the dynamic nature of business and the vivid consumer responses. Hence, there exists an inherent difficulty in the nature of marketing problems for the manager who wishes to justify the marketing expenditures by establishing the cause-and-effect relationships between marketing actions, and sales and profits results. In a competitive marketplace, where the (a) consumers are exposed to thousands of selling messages from dozens of competing suppliers, or (b) customers have limited ability to process information and a number of other constraints on their decision making, (c) every sale is the result of several complex interactions between the marketing variables and buyer characteristics, it is virtually impossible to find strong casual relationships.

Fallacy of Competition Analysis

Over time, the marketing department has become a distinct organisational entity in many companies, driven in part by the inherent conflict between the sales and marketing viewpoints. The marketing was earlier identified with marketing research and product development, while sales was associated with promotion, distribution, and pricing. When marketing became a function, it was made no longer a focus in many organisations. In some companies, the marketing orientation was even substituted for market or customer orientation.

In most of the organisations, the marketing department is considered the expert on customer, for keeping the rest of the organisation both informed about and focused on the customer.

Another viewpoint regarding marketing is that, the very existence of the concept of marketing rules out the conventional thinking that the main aim of company should be in crushing competition. In fact through proper utilisation of the marketing strategies, the company should try to (a) create value for its chosen customer value segments, (b) make the firms' customers more profitable and thereby gain profitability for the company, and (c) perform all these functions in a manner better than its competitors.

In short, two reasons could be identified for the shift in the company focus from "crushing competition" to value addition: (a) The 'great value creator' (business firm) should understand that it's the customer who is ultimately the final judge of value, and not the competition, and (b) The firm's strategic efforts, thoughts, insights, and actions should be spend on figuring out startegies to win the customers.

Interestingly, the firms are likely to overcome the competition when they deliver the best value to their customer. Every single rupee, every hour of a person's time, and every piece of equipment or relationship with the suppliers and customers should be considered extremely precious, and this approach is getting strengthened everyday. These ideas should be more focused in areas where the company has got the maximum impact and that is while delivering superior customer value (Figure 1.1).

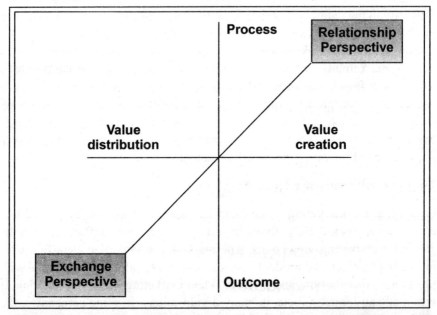

Fig. 1.1 The Paradigm Shift in Marketing Orientation

Source: Jagdish N. Sheth and Atul Parvatiyar (Editors), *Handbook of Relationship Marketing*, Response Book, 2002 with permission.

While the customers would expect more and more value, what they are willing to pay for is another story. Therefore, the marketers should focus on those benefits that have the maximum impact on their customers, and for which their customers would actually pay. Eliminating the lower priority benefits would control costs and this is critical in sustaining the economic profit. While doing so, the business success would attract new customers, even while maintaining a leading edge in the value committed to customers. This would be of particular importance as the firm's success draws the attention of its competitors.

Focus on Value Equity

In the fast-moving consumer good markets, concepts like unprofitability has been exacerbated by the speed of change and the swiftness with which the competitors copy or improve on the firm's offering. This phenomenon is becoming increasingly prevalent in many business-to business (B2B) markets, as protection becomes more difficult and the speed of 'catching up' is proceeding in an accelerated manner. Branding provides one of the most powerful ways of differentiating offerings by linking the core and augmented value offering to the brand. Fundamentally, the brand is a mental representation of the company value. A proactive branding strategy enables the company to assume and exert control over branding to make certain customers' perceptions match up with the firm's objective or even intention. Hence, many business firms tend to focus on:

➢ Providing more value-added quality products/services to customers;

➢ Finding a new point of differentiation with the current products;

➢ Improving cost-efficiencies of current products; and

➢ Creating new products for customers.

While potentially beneficial for the customers, the above perspective puts the focus back on internal thinking, products, and goals. This perspective tends to bind the business from observing the critical value—creating insights that surround the everyday business. Figure 1.2 shows the value chain of customers and its linkage with technology, relationship and consumption.

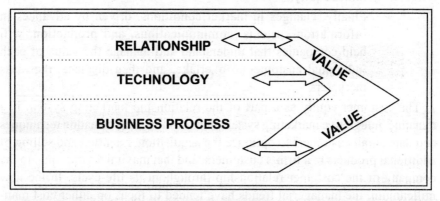

Fig. 1.2 Value Chain : Process of Customers

Source: Jagdish N. Sheth and Atul Parvatiyar (Editors), *Handbook of Relationship Marketing,* Response Book, 2002 with permission.

Many practices, such as the corporate restructuring, customer satisfaction, and six sigma, have become so much a part of the business toolbox that any alternative views would be treated as subversive. In fact these management tools are really beneficial for running the business. However, the focus of most of these tools is in an introspective manner. For example, the customer relationship management (CRM) is often driven first to maximise the firm's profitability with customers. In many cases, the CRM rates the customers on the basis of their profit-stream. The lower rated customers, those with small or no profit are then eliminated from the customer base of the company. It seems to make sense, but it misses the opportunity that might be derived from the real discovery like serving potential customers like the MBA students. Even though they are unprofitable during their study period, the company could evaluate their high potential once they become employable. At that time the cost of serving them may be high or even winning their preference become very difficult. So early associations are definitely of great advantage to the company. (This concept is dealt in detail in the subsequent chapters.)

Managing Customer as an Asset

Managing the customer as an asset is more critical to a firm's success than ever before mainly due to three reasons.

> ➢ First, marketers who take an asset-based view of the customer make better decisions than those who limit themselves to product, brand, or transactions do views.

> ➢ Second, today's computing technology makes precise customer asset management possible. Companies can now efficiently obtain and process the information they need to understand customer equity.

> ➢ Finally, changes in market conditions, driven by advances in information systems, communications, and production, will help companies that understand and manage the value of each individual customer to overtake, and then displace, the mass marketers.

The customer equity as a part of the relationship marketing system is a dynamic, integrative marketing system that uses financial valuation techniques and data about customers to optimise the acquisition, retention and selling of additional products to a firm's customers, and that maximizes the value to the company of the customer relationship throughout its life-cycle. In the new millennium, the managerial trends have tended to focus on either cost management or the revenue growth. The customer equity-based management would balance the two, creating market-based growth, while carefully evaluating the profitability and return on investment (ROI) of marketing investment. We will discuss these concepts in detail in the following chapters.

Focus on Knowledge Management and Experience Marketing

In tune with the present trend, managers should create a business model for their organisations that uses technology for strategic purposes viz., (a) for the addition of value for its customers, and (b) for preparing the organisation more closely to both increasing productivity, and having a positive financial impact on the bottom line. However, the business firm should be watchful of viewing technology as a magic elixir that guarantees successful results.

The technological developments during the last 30 years have had a remarkable impact on the way in which the services are produced and delivered. The developments in telecommunications and computer technology have also led to many innovations in the way services are delivered. Many of the significant changes relate to the use of information technology to improve the supplementary services. One of the most frequently cited service delivery innovations of the past two decades has been the Automated Teller Machine (ATM), which has revolutionised the delivery of retail banking services, making them available 24 hours a day and every day of the year in a wide variety of convenient locations, often far from the traditional retail branches. To expand the geographic area, in which the service could be delivered to their customers, banks have joined regional, national, and even global networks. Figure 1.3 shows the impact of technology on modern marketing approach.

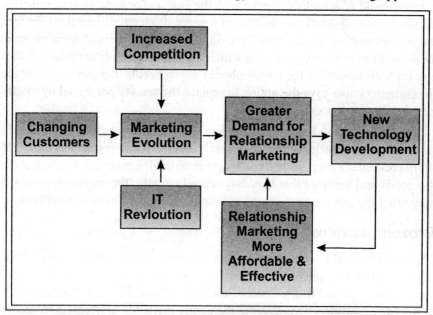

Fig. 1.3 Impact of Technology on Modern Marketing

Source: Jagdish N. Sheth and Atul Parvatiyar (Editors), *Handbook of Relationship Marketing*, Response Book, 2002 with permission

The application of telephone as a medium for selling and ordering goods and services, has increased rapidly during the past few decades. More recently, the entrepreneurs have taken advantage of the Internet to create new services that could be delivered through the electronic channels accessed by computers in customers' homes or offices.

Impact of Electronic Channels

The growth of electronic channels is creating a fundamental change in the nature of marketing. The customers are moving from face-to-face contacts with the suppliers who were earlier located in fixed locations that operate during fixed hours, to remote contacts that operate "anywhere, anytime". More and more services now fall into the category of arm's length relationships rather than the face-to-face interactions. Even then, in some instances, the customers would find it difficult to get rid of the marketplace, for it is the physical environment that attracts them, as in destination resorts. The shopping malls, which earlier had retail stores alone are now being redesigned to create a "total experience". Besides the retail stores, the redesigned malls seeks to provide food services, health clubs, entertainment, exhibitions, and above all a chance to socialise.

The companies that conduct business activities in the market space, by contact, could now replace contact with the physical objects by dissemination of information about those objects (in a paper or electronic catalog). In fact, the information-based services have no inherent requirement for a physical location. Moreover, the context in which the transaction occurs is also different: (a) with on-screen (or on-telephone) contact replacing physical contact; (b) customers also have the option to replace the service personnel by intelligent interactive systems.

Two factors have been found the key driving forces behind such moves: (a) time (which reflects the customer's desire for a faster service), and (b) interest on the part of some customers in obtaining more information about the goods and services that they buy. Paradoxically, the electronic contacts may bring the customers "closer" to manufacturers and service suppliers.

Frozen Services

The technological development has also allowed the benefits of services that formerly had to be delivered by the service personnel in a real-time environment to be captured in a physical product. Richard Norman has coined the term "frozen services" to describe the goods that allow customers to unlock the value through self-services. Many information-based services, for instance, could be captured in some form of storage medium for re-use at a later date. Books are a long-established alternative to lectures in an educational setting. The live performances can be recorded and then brought back to life on demand through the medium of CDs, audiotape, videotape, or film. Expertise in almost any field could be captured on an interactive computer software in the form of CD-ROM or diskettes or even downloaded from the Internet.

Falling prices, greater affluence, and new easy-to-use technologies has also allowed the individual and corporate users to replace the service professionals in a variety of other fields. Thus, washing machines and dryers for home use has replaced laundry services for many types of clothes. As the wheel of progress turns, customers may continue to change the way in which they obtain the valued benefits they seek. The telephone created the need for answering services among the busy people, many of whom solved this need first from services, then from manufactured goods, and most recently from services again.

1.4 INTERGRATING RELATIONSHIP STRATEGIES WITH INFORMATION TECHNOLOGY

It has been realised that the business success is the result of the symbiosis of technology and marketing. Many companies believe that blending technology with customer requirements is an important success element in establishing and developing customer relationships. A partnering of IT, relationship, and marketing holds the key in this direction and following are the emerging practises in this regard:

➢ The company sells directly to customers or uses a multiplayer channel system, direct knowledge of individual customers and their buying behaviours as its lifeblood.

➢ Information-based targeted marketing is becoming more efficient and effective than blanketed mass marketing.

➢ Mass marketing strategies that achieve targeted profits by counting on more-profitable customers to subsidize less profitable ones will fail as the more attractive customers are stolen away by the competitors' targeted acquisition efforts.

➢ As customers gain near-perfect information on their alternatives, switching barriers are dropping dramatically.

➢ Companies that possesss a well-furnished database on customer purchase behavior are acquiring new customers, while retaining existing customers, and cross-selling more effectively than those who do not. These companies can link their insights with cost data to boost up their efficiency as well.

➢ Companies can no longer depend on orderly vertical channel systems to control customers' buying behaviors.

In the present scenario, companies that could understand the asset value of each customer, and that tailor their marketing efforts (and their costs) to acquire and sustain the highest-value assets, would trump the less-focused mass marketers. The free and smooth flow of information about such factors as consumer, product and service performance, operations, logistics, competitive comparisons, suppliers, cost and finance, are becoming crucial in creating, developing, and enhancing the long-term relationships in the IT era.

Generally, it is believed that a strong correlation exists between a proactive company and its profitability. Its average return on assets is usually higher and also integrates the crisis readiness with the TQM and environment. However, a company should be well aware of the purpose of its investment. Research figures from IDC estimates that the total technology spending in India will double by 2005 (nearly Rs 26,000 crore to Rs 54,000 crore)

However initial experience of Indian companies shows that all their investments in IT are not yielding in an expected manner. It has been suggested that an Indian CEO should look at investments in technology as a 'key differentiator', which could provide a fillip to the overall competitiveness of the firm.

The CRM is not always about big money. Companies can start off with simple package like TriVium / Talisma (costs only Rs.5 lakh) at the base of the cost pyramid and then move up the chain as the need increases. When technology is critical to service delivery, it is important to constantly evaluate how customers perceive the service and how it could be improved up on over a period of time. This is possible only with the help of cutting edge technology that would enable the companies to position themselves against intangible competitors.

Technologicalship Marketing

Computerising and electronising relationships could also provide organisations with a powerful tool to profile its existing customer base and to create and retain stronger relationships within it, as well as to find new potential collaborators. The technologicalship marketing is a marketing startegy based on technology tools used by the firms to acquire and manage their relationships. For instance, the online marketing permits for one-to-one marketing which gives the companies the ability to establish an enduring relationship with its individual consumers. In short, the technologicalship is a fully integrated marketing scheme which combines the activities of several marketing tools.

Examples of the technologicalship partners (Benetton, IKEA, McDonald's, NORTEL, Procter & Gamble, etc.) have proven the idea of partnering IT tools and relationship marketing (technologicalship marketing) all over the world. And these organisations believe that the interactivity of IT marketing will make it even easier to build relationships with the consumers.

1.5 ADOPTING RELATIONSHIP MARKETING PRACTICES

Business strategy and planning hold the key to relationship marketing, which has been emerging as the core marketing activity for business enterprises operating in a fiercely competititve environment. The relationship marketing would come naturally to the market-led company, which highlights customer needs to all parts of the organisation, provided the relationship marketing concepts are made the foundation for the business plans, structures, and processes of a business enterprise.

On an average, businesses spend six times more to acquire customers than they do to retain them. Therefore, many firms are now paying more attention to their relationships with the existing customers, to retain them and increase their share of customer's purchases.

Worldwide, the service organisations have been pioneers in developing the customer retention strategies. Banks have relationship managers for select customers, airlines have frequent flyer programmes to reward the loyal customers, credit cards offer redeemable bonus points for increased card usage, telecom service operators provide customised services to their heavy users, and hotels have personalised services for their regular guests.

Advantages of Relationship Marketing

Till recently, most marketers have focussed on attracting customers from its target segments using the tools and techniques developed for mass marketing in the industrial era. In the information era, this is proving to be highly ineffective in most competitive markets. Slowing growth rates, intensifying competition and technological developments have made business organisations to look for ways that would reduce costs and improve their effectiveness.

The business process re-engineering, automation and downsizing have reduced the manpower costs. The financial restructuring and efficient fund management have reduced the financial costs. The production and operation costs have been reduced through total quality management (TQM), just in time (JIT) inventory, flexible manufacturing systems (FMS), and an efficient supply chain management. Studies have also shown that while manufacturing costs have declined from 55 per cent to 30 per cent, while management costs from 25 to 15 per cent, the marketing costs have increased from 20 to 55 per cent. The practice of relationship marketing has the potential to improve marketing productivity through improved marketing efficiencies and effectiveness.

The business firms would adopt relationship marketing only if it has the potential to benefit them. The benefits come through lower costs of retention and increased profits due to lower defection rates. When the customers enter into a relationship with a firm, they are willingly foregoing other options and limiting their choice. Some of the personal motivations to do so result from (a) greater efficiency in decision making, (b) reduction in information processing, (c) achieving more cognitive consistency in decisions and (d) reduction of perceived risks with future decisions.

In the context of service, the relationship marketing has been defined as attracting, maintaining and in multiservice organisations enhancing the customer relationships. Here attracting customers is considered to be an intermediary step in the relationship building process with the ultimate objective of increasing loyalty of profitable customers. This is because of the applicability of the 80-20 rule. According to Market Line Associates, the top 20 per cent of typical bank customers produce as much as 150 per cent of the overall profit, while the bottom 20 per cent of customers drain about 50 per cent from the bank's bottom line and the revenues from the rest just meeting their expenses.

Strategies for Practising Relationship Marketing

Berry (1983) has recommended the following five strategies for practicing relationship marketing:

> ➤ Developing a core service around which to build a customer relationship,
> ➤ Customising the relationship to the individual customer,
> ➤ Augmenting the core service with extra benefits,
> ➤ Pricing services to encourage customer loyalty, and
> ➤ Marketing to employees so that they would perform well for customers.

Developments in information technology, data warehousing and data mining have made it possible for firms to maintain a one-to-one relationship with their customers. Firms could now manage every single contact with the customer from account management personnel, call centers, interactive voice response systems, online dial-up applications, and websites to build lasting relationships. These interactions could be used to glean information and insights about customer needs and their buying behavior to design and develop services, which help create the value for the customers as well as the firms. Successful implementation of relationship marketing practices require a strategic approach, which encompasses developing customer centric processes, selecting and implementing technology solutions, employee empowerment, customer information and knowledge generation capabilities to differentiate them, and the ability to learn from best practices.

CONCLUSION

Relationship marketing has the potential to radically transform the company that adopts the principles and practices it advocates. It involves the ongoing process of identifying and creating new value with individual customers and then sharing the benefits of this over a lifetime of association. It involves the understanding, focusing and management of ongoing collaboration between the suppliers and selected customers for mutual value creation and sharing through interdependence and organisational alignment.

One must realise that the customer requirements are not constant. They change from time to time. The importance of understanding the customer requirements is so great that the companies try innovative ways and means to get close to the customer and hear 'the voice of the customer'. This chapter has given a bird's eye view of the emerging trends, issues and approaches in relationship building and marketing, which in turn form the basis of discussion in the succeeding ten chapters.

CHAPTER REVIEW QUESTIONS

1. Discuss about intangible competitors in Indian context.
2. What do you mean by paradigm shit in marketing? Illustrate with examples of your own choices.
3. Comment on the relationship marketing scenario in the Indian context.
4. Explain how IT would help in building relationship with the customers.
5. Discuss the relevance of customer as an asset in the relationship marketing practices.

CASE STUDY

SOUTHWEST AIRLINES: NETTING PROFITS THROUGH CUSTOMER DRIVEN MARKETING

"Whenever the business enterprise talk about their relationship marketing programmes and what the relevance of such programmes in the affairs of the company, they always tack on the customer database as an afterthought: 'But the most important element is our people.' At Southwest, it pretty much is just the people."

Donna Conovers, Executive VP-Customer Services, S W Airlines

BACKGROUND

The Southwest Airlines flouts all the rules of the airline customer service. They offer no in-flight movies; no miniature pseudo-gourmet dinners; no first-class upgrades and even no reserved seating. They have translated the savings from these areas to their fares, which ranks one of the cheapest in the US airline industry. Besides the monetary factor, the South West also give greater importance to golden rule in customer service. 'Be nice and smile a lot.' "We're in the customer service business that just happens to fly the airplanes," says Ms. Conover. No doubt there are customers who would prefer it to focus first on flying the airlines, but the fact is that the Southwest places a lot of stock in the customer service.

Incidentally, the Southwest was one among the seven airlines that were allowed to take off one week after the WTC tragedy in the US. Besides, the Southwest also survived the economic slump that followed the incident, without even a single retrenchment (against the then industrial trend, which witnessed nearly 70 per cent retrenchment in some sectors). This was a remarkable achievement in the US, where 2.3 million jobs were lost since 2001 due to recession and down sizing of leading corporate house.

SMILES FROM THE HEART

The propagators of the "new order organisation" in the Southwest has realised the fact that if they wanted to raise their customer relationship beyond the aspect of a mere "customer service", they should create a memorable experience with the customer, which in turn, would leave an intangible impact in the mind of the customer. The impact should be like the "feelings" one has about that experience. The impact should not be a pre-empted one, though it should be powerful. It should remain in the mind of the customer and influence the behaviour of the individual and their network of associates. It should be strategic, as establishes the magical and intangible connection between the customer and the enterprise. Going beyond the 'customer service' to 'customer obsession' is a very strategic move, and it will provide any enterprise the distinct and unique competitive advantage, if the firm gets it right and this is true with the Southwest Airlines.

It should be acknowledged that it is the experience of the customer that is really significant, and not just the brand, the product, the facility or the interaction Though all elements are vital (the *product* has to be right from the customer's point of view, the *environment* has to be comfortable for the customer, the *value* has to ring true to the customer, the company people have to be *knowledgeable*) in the regard, the effectiveness of the customer relationship lies in the proper correlation and coordination of all these elements.

Therefore to graduate beyond the aspect of the 'customer service' and achieve a strategic advantage in customer relationship, the firm would have to embrace the new concepts and values and in the process might have to challenge the existing practices of the company. In the Southwest Airlines this aspect has been made a way of life. In other words, the employees are fine tunes to deal with the customers, the employees, and the investors in a positive manner and most important of all, placing all of them at the winning edge. The benefit or satisfaction which precludes at very stage serves as a major source of inspiration for building a longstanding relationship for facing an intangible competitors.

EXHIBIT 1

THE SUCCESS SECRETS OF SOUTH WEST AIRLINES

- ➤ Be nice.
- ➤ Train everyone, including back-office people, to be nice.
- ➤ Hire people with the ability to care and communicate.
- ➤ Treat all customers the same.
- ➤ Encourage and reward good customer service.
- ➤ Give good performance, such as on-time departures–not just good service.
- ➤ Offer a cost-effective product.
- ➤ Empower employees to act in the customer's best interest.

Exhibit 1 shows that the Southwest employee policy has succeeded in winning a long standing relationship with its customer service. The American Consumer Satisfaction Index gives the Southwest a customer satisfaction of 74 (out of 100) for the first quarter of 2003, compared to an industry average of 66. The index has rated the Southwest at the top of the airline customer satisfaction scale (a position it has been enviably holding for a long time).

The airline's customer service starts with its people, whom as Ms Conover claims are hired primarily for their ability to care and communicate. During the selection process, thee candidate are asked questions to gauge these capacities. For instance, they would be asked about a moment they have been proud of themselves. If the candidate answers with a story of the volunteer work or other service, he/she is likely to be a good fit. In a normal organisation, this answer would make sense for the external-facing employees. However in the Southwest it applies the same standards for the internal staff like the IT personnel and the accountants too as the Southwest wants the smiles to be more than skin deep. "If you have a grouchy boss who doesn't give a flip about you, how are you going to give good customer service?" Conover asks. Even those in the Southwest's legal department, she says, have hearts and senses of humour.

NEW PHILOSOPHY

The Southwest stays away from the traditional notions of the airline customer service which showers incentives in those who buy a lot of tickets and frequent travellers, but ignores everyone else. The Southwest goes for a more egalitarian approach. Giving equal preference for both the 'gold-level' frequent fliers and normal/occasional passengers. "We resisted making lines for frequent fliers. You're important to us whether you're occasional or frequent," Conover says. The frequent flier's perks are largely confined to free trips and drink tickets. The universal customer service approach has proven good for the ordinary not-so frequent travellers, but not for the frequent fliers who used to entertain special treatment in other airlines. This illustrates a major limitation of the Southwest's customer-service approach. However, the Southwest has not decided to go out of its way to accommodate the special classes of customers, such as the business travellers seeking more legroom spce, reserved seats, or longer flight segments.

FLYING ABOVE AND BEYOND

Within the Southwest's chosen realm of business, though, its friendly culture has spawned lots of stories of its truly incredible customer service. The Southwest seeks out and rewards the good customer service with mottos life, "If you learn towards the customer, you cannot be wrong." More than once, the Southwest employees have taken the passengers home with them, when they were dropped off at tiny intermediate airports and has to wait until morning to catch a flight. As Conover says, "Our employees are empowered to make those decisions."

The grand example of Southwest customer service goes like this: a customer living in El Paso (Texas) had been notified by his hospital that he could receive an organ transplant if he went to Houston (Texas). The customer called Southwest's reservation line and was quoted the Sunday schedule, not the Saturday schedule he needed. When he showed up at the airport, the last flight of the day had already left. But the couldn't wait overnight to get to Houston. "If you have a problem, we try to solve it," Conover says. " Our employees are empowered to make those decisions." The El Paso weekend duty manager took that seriously, and hired a jet to take the man to Houston. A multi-thousand dollar decision like that would have likely cost the manager his/her job at any other airline.

HIGH TOUCH, LOW-TECH

Whenever the business enterprises talk about their 'whiz-bang' customer friendly systems what they can do for the customers, they always tack the statement, "But the most important elements is our people" as an afterthought. At the Southwest, it is pretty much just the "people". Despite some new systems that help in the proper maintenance of flight schedules—a major component of customer satisfaction—the

Loan Receipt
Liverpool John Moores University
Library Services

Borrower Name: Benitta,Kartika
Borrower ID: **********1110

Relationship marketing :
31111011844196
Due Date: 02/10/2015 23:59

Consumer behavior and marketing action /

31111007469750
Due Date: 02/10/2015 23:59

Consumer behaviour /
31111013287295
Due Date: 02/10/2015 23:59

Total Items: 3
27/07/2015 13:52

Please keep your receipt in case of
dispute.

Southwest takes a pretty "low-tech" approach to its customer service. The company is investigating the relationship building technologies and packages, specifically the systems that would track the customer data, but finds them too expensive for what they deliver. "One thing we examine is its cost-benefit ratio," Conover says. "The question is—what are you going to get back?"

The Southwest has specifically rejected a couple of tools which are of heavy use in the airlines and the associated businesses—the e-mail response systems, and the interactive telephone menus as they found it too impersonal and "intended mostly to take the cost out of customer interactions. The Southwest would rather put a human face on the line a customer would contact a company.

WHY MEMORABLE?

'Good' is the price of admission in any Southwest transaction, whether it is in quality, service, order fulfillment or any measure of satisfaction and performance delivery. But if the price of admission is 'good' in terms of customer service, it cannot be a 'differentiating' or 'strategic' factor if it's the same. Good is merely adequate. Meeting expectations is 'expected.' And 'sameness' is not strategic—it doesn't make a difference in terms out influencing the decision of a customer. This is common belief among the executives in the Southwest Airlines who try harder for excellence through a better offering of customised packages and programmes for every customer.

"We all want to differentiate ourselves, add value and avoid the commodity game. But most of us, most of the time have competitors that can, if they choose, match our quality, match our convenience, match or beat our prices, or otherwise pre-empt us on the tangibles. That is why we invest to build Southwest Airlines brand and the 'share of mind' to move to compete in the realm of the intangible. It is the intangible appeal that ultimately is strategic. True competitive advantage of Southwest Airlines exists only in that magical realm of the intangible. "says Conover".

PIONEERS IN PROGRESS

The Southwest Airlines is making progress in tune with the creation of new services and technologies. It was a pioneer in paperless ticketing and has made a successful push to sell tickets directly to the customer over the Web. Recently, it has turned its notorious cattle-call boarding (in other words no reserved seating and the favourite seats will be provided on a first-cum first-serve basis) into what might be called on orderly cattle call (where instead of everyone boarding at once with the plastic boarding passes, the Southwest's ticketing system now electronically issues the A, B, and C tickets to the customers depending on time they have checked in). The "A" passengers board first, and get a few minutes to breathe before the other groups pour in.

Table 1.1 Southwest by the Numbers	
Revenue, 2003	$ 7.38 billion
Net Income, 2003	$ 611.1 million
Passengers carried, 2003	94,446,773
Average length of passenger haul	815 miles
Trips flown, 2003	940,426
Average passenger fare	$ 82.84
Number of Employees at period-end	33,149
Size of fleet at period-end	366

NETTING PROFIT

Proper customer service is hard to monitor at the Southwest's scale when the customer service executives are doing everything manually. "We've grown and the customers' expectations have changed," says Susan Kirkelie, the Southwest senior director of marketing programmes. We need to assist what we currently do with technology." Susan has got a plan of assessing the LTV of customers. Exhibit-3 shows the relevant calculation.

The relevant calculation for 5 years shows that the value ratio for the first year was negative, and then became positive for each of the subsequent years. Without the baseline data, projections about the future profitability are difficult. Besides, it is rather impossible to answer the question, "Should we be selling to these customers?" Even with the projection, however, which are only as good as the judgment of the marketer, the spreadsheet is a helpful tool that provides the opportunity to do some "what if" analyses. The changes in one or more parameters in the CLV scenario as demonstrated in Exhibit-3 can produce some dramatic results. For example, a 5 per cent increase in the retention rate in the second year results in a 13.54 per cent increase in the CLV by 2007. The increasing retention rates in 2005-2006 improves the 2007 CLV by more than 20 per cent. Similarly, shifting the spending rate in 2005 from $4,000 per customer to 6,000 per customer boosts the five-year CLV of the sample by 12 per cent. Not as dramatic as increasing the retention rate, but arguably easier to achieve. What happens when the retention and spending rates and the SG&A fixed and variables rates are all improved? Over a five year period from 2003 to 2007, the CLV increases by almost 55 per cent.

THE CASE

As part of its relationship building technologies and packages of investigation, the Southwest is studying the ways of gathering data about its customers and utilising that data to offer better service. For instance, it wants to identify which passengers are paying the full price for tickets and travelling business. "Their needs are so different that the leisure traveller and the occasional travellers, and if you can respond to them you keep them longer," Conover says. Southwest also wants its future relationship building technologies and packages to help it share information between the touch points, so that a service counter worker knows that a passenger just called in with an issue to the call center.

Source: Jeff Cannon, CRM network and www.crmguru.com : adopted the case concept with permission

EXHIBIT 2

CALCULATION OF CLV-PROJECTING CLV*						
Revenue	**2003**	**2004**	**2005**	**2006**	**2007**	
Retention Rate		40%	50%	75%	90%	AVE LT
Customer Sample	1,000	400	200	150	135	**1.95**
Spending on travel	**$4,000**	**$4,500**	**$6,000**	**$9,000**	**$16,000**	
Gross Revenues	$4,000,000	$1,800,000	$1,200,000	$1,350,000	2,160,000	
Costs	**2003**	**2004**	**2005**	**2006**	**2007**	**PCT**
Acquisition Costs	$2,000,000					
SG & A Fixed Cots	$1,800,000	$810,000	$540,000	$607,500	$972,000	45%
SG & A Variable Costs	$600,000	**$270,000**	**$180,000**	**$202,500**	**$324,000**	15%
Retention Costs	$0	$90,000	$60,000	$67,500	$108,000	5%
Total Costs	**$4,400,000**	**$1,080,000**	**$720,000**	**$810,000**	**$1,296,000**	

Profit	2003	2004	2005	2006	2007
Gross Profit ($1,000)	($400,000)	$720,000	$480,000	$540,000	$864,000
Discount Rate	0.89.29%	79.72%	71.18%	63.55%	56.74%
Profit NPV	($357,160)	$473,984	$341,664	$343,170	$490,234
CLV=Sum of Profit NPV	($357,160)	$216,824	$558,488	$901,658	$1,391,892
CLV/ Customer	($357.16)	$154.87	$349.06	$515.23	$738.40

	2003	2004	2005	2006	2007
Value Ratio	-0.08	0.04	0.09	0.13	0.17

Source: J Nicholas De Boris, Eric Balinski and Phil Allen (2003), Value-bared marketing for bottomness success New York, American Marketing Association and McGraw-Hill

QUESTIONS:

1. Could you suggest a relationship programme that interlaces both technology, people and programmes for the SW Airlines? Besides, compare the feasibility in the Indian environment by taking the initiatives of Jet Airways.

FUNDAMENTAL CONCEPTS IN RELATIONSHIP MARKETING

2

"We don't ask consumers what they want. They don't know. Instead we apply our brain power to what they need, and will want, and make sure we're there, ready."

Akio Morita, Chairman-Sony Corporation

Learning Objectives

After reading this chapter you should understand:

- How corporate relationship is built, keeping in mind the interest of the consumer
- How relation marketing is conducted in the era of competition
- The strategic importance of Intra-organizational collaborates and external marketing
- The strategies behind the building of brand equity and brand building
- How to treat customer as an asset and the concept of customer value
- The various relationship marketing programmes
- How the nuances of customer behaviour are analyzed by a firm with tools such as the RFM model and web analytical software

INTRODUCTION

Any meaningful relationship between a customer and a business enterprise begins with the expectation of mutual benefits. Through such a relationship the customers expect to (a) realise the cost savings, (b) improve the efficiency of their decision making, (c) reduce their risk by dealing with trustworthy companies, services and products, (d) acquire a solution that is tailored for their particular needs and budgets, or (e) realise the social and other value-added benefits such as simplifying their choice process.

The motives of a business enterprise in such a meaningful relationship are more transparent. These motives include: (a) gaining an advantage that cannot be easily be copied by the competitors; (b) reducing the high costs of acquiring new customers, (c) improving the predictability and efficiency of their operations, and (d) reducing their risk exposure. Hence winning the confidence and loyalty of customers are the focal points of any business enterprise and hence our discussion will start from the basis of building such a relationship.

2.1 BASIS OF BUILDING RELATIONSHIP

The defining beneficial features of a corporate relationship building are based on the assumptions of (a) mutual benefits (the rationale for entering into a relationship), (b) mutual commitments, (c) trust and (d) the connective links. These facets of a relationship work together to form a connective tissue, which can either be a flimsy and short-loved one or one that is stronger and enduring. Central to every market relationship is an exchange process where the value is given and received. Even in the most tenuous and short-lived "relationship", each side of the dyad gives something in return for a benefit or payoff of greater value. These exchange line up along a continuum with a *single transactional exchange* on the one end and a long-run *two-way collaboration* on the other.

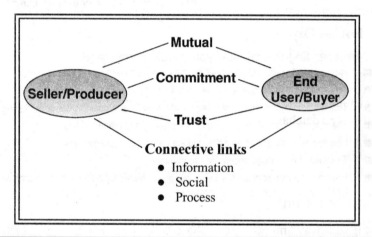

Fig. 2.1 Forming a Relationship

Source: Jagdish N. Sheth and Atul Parvatiyar (Editors), *Handbook of Relationship Marketing,* Response Book, 2002 with permission.

The transactional exchanges include (a) the kind of anonymous encounters (similar to what a visitor to a city has while hiring a taxi or bus service for his movement within the city), as well as (b) the series of ongoing transactions in a business-to-business (B2B) market, where the customer and supplier focus only on the timely exchange as a zero-sum game where one prices.

Between these two extremes are the value-adding exchanges, where the focus of the selling firm shifts from 'acquiring' the customers to 'retention' of customers. The firm pursues this objective by developing a deeper understanding of the customer needs and changing requirements, and then tailoring its offering according to these needs as closely as possible. In the process, the firm continues to provide incentives for the customers to concentrate most of their purchases with them.

The market-driven organisations excel at retaining their most valuable customers. Their strategies emphasise addition of customer value through (a) service enhancements, (b) incentive and (c) tailored interactions that reflect the differences in the prospective lifetime value of each customer. The main intention of such a strategy is to offer compelling mutual benefits and tighten the connections with their customers, so that they could arrest the process of defection to a larger extend.

Among the peculiar features that could be commonly identified among the firms that are best at combating these forces include:

a. Treating Customers Differently

There is a willingness to serve the customers differently, with the best customers given the best treatment. The airline industry has created multilevel frequent flier programmes with dedicated reservation lines, priority upgrades, rapid check-in privileges and so on to recognise the best customers.

b. Information-based Decisions

The decisions of these firms are based on fine-grained information about their customers. The databases extract key data from the internal operating systems (such as an Internet-based transaction system), and merge it with the descriptive information from external sources. This enables the database marketing and micromarketing campaigns.

c. Customer Centric

A "has it your way" mindset prevails among the organisatons. This mindset can range from tailoring the messages to microsegments like the custom binding of parents magazine according to the age of the children, to Nordstrom's ability to enable its clerks to range through the entire store to put together clothing ensembles for their customers.

d. Flexibility

The core processes are flexible and they facilitate multiple modes of producing and delivering the product or service. Measures and incentives are aligned to retention as a priority. Most of the firms cannot measure up to these requirements because they are unable to overcome the conquest mentality that is a part of the traditional emphasis on customer acquisition.

2.2 DEFINING RELATIONSHIP MARKETING CONCEPTS

The concept of relationship marketing has emerged within the fields of service marketing and industrial marketing. Grönroos defines relationship marketing as: "**Marketing is to establish, maintain, and enhance relationships with customers and other partners, at a profit, so that the objectives of the parties involved are met. This is achieved by a mutual exchange and fulfillment of promises**". Such relationships are usually but not necessarily always long-term. Establishing a relationship, for example with a customer, can be divided into two parts: (**a**) to *attract* the customer and (**b**) to *build* the relationship with that customer so that the economic goals of that relationship are achieved.

The 'Promise' Concept

An integral element of the relationship marketing approach is the promise concept which has been strongly emphasised by Henrik Calonius. According to him the responsibilities of marketing do, or predominantly, include giving promises and thus persuading the customers as passive counterparts on the marketplace to act in a given way. A firm that is preoccupied with offering promises may attract new customers and initially build the relationships. However, if the promises are not kept, the evolving relationship cannot be maintained or enhanced. Fulfilling promises is as important as means of achieving customer satisfaction, retention of the customer base, and long-term profitability. Calonius also stresses the fact that promises are mutually given and fulfilled accordingly.

Relevance of Trust

The resources of the seller or the service provider (say, personnel, technology and systems) have to be utilised in such a manner that the customer's trust in the resources involved and, thus, in the firm itself is maintained and strengthened. In a study of relationships on the market for one industrial service, Moorman defines trust as "...**a willingness to rely on an exchange partner in whom one has confidence**".

This definition implies, first of all, that there should be a belief in the other partner's trustworthiness that results from the expertise, reliability or intentionality of that partner. Secondly, it views trust as a behavioral intention or a behaviour that reflects the reliance on the other partner and involves uncertainty and vulnerability on the part of the trustor. If there is no vulnerability and uncertainty, trust is unnecessary, because the trustor can control the other partner's actions. Besides, the relationships are often more complex than mere exchange relationships.

The 'House of Knowledge' in Relationship Marketing

The relationship marketing is still in its infancy as a mainstream marketing concept, although it has established itself as an underlying paradigm in modern industrial marketing and services marketing. Philip Kotler has observed that "the companies should move from a short-term transaction-oriented goal to a long-term relationship building goal". Figure 2.2 shows the House of Knowledge in relationship marketing and its connectivity with the basic elements such as trust, commitment, interaction and dialogue.

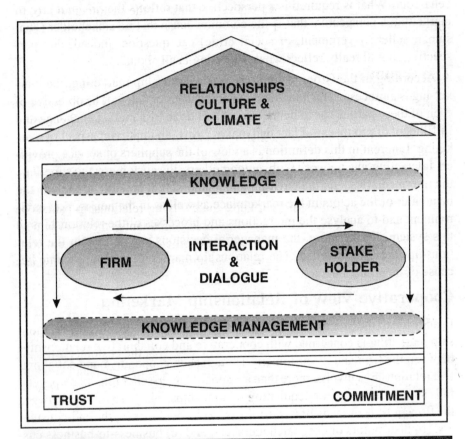

Fig. 2.2 The House of Knowledge in Relationship Marketing

Source: Jagdish N. Sheth and Atul Parvatiyar (Editors), *Handbook of Relationship Marketing,* Response Book, 2002 with permission

Process View of Relationship Marketing

As shown in Fig. 2.2 the relationship marketing is a systems-oriented approach; yet it includes the managerial aspects also. A systems approach is well suited as a basis for a general theory of marketing, because it makes it possible to include all relevant actors, the environmental influence, and even the process nature of marketing. The managerial facets facilitate the actionable and normative elements that are required in such a theory.

Furthermore, Sheth (*et. al.*) express the following views about the scope of marketing and the dominant perspective in marketing: "We need to expand our understanding of marketing to incorporate the basic tenets of marketing, namely, (a) the market behaviour, (b) the market transactions as the unit of analysis, (c) the marketing as a dynamic process of relationships between buyers and sellers, and (d) the exogenous variables that influence the market behaviour. What is required is a perspective that reflects the *raison d'etre* of marketing, a perspective that is the common cause that no stakeholder (consumer, seller, government, or social critic) can question. Indeed, that perspective should really reflect what marketing is all about".

According to the Grönroos definition of relationship marketing, the market-ing is a process, which includes several parties or actors. The objective of each of these parties has to be met and this is done by a mutual exchange and fulfillment of promises—a fact that makes 'trust' an important aspect of marketing. Inherent in this definition is a view of the suppliers or service providers interacting in a network with, among others, the customers, the suppliers, the intermediaries, and the environmental actors. It is possible to include the behaviour of the actors in the marketplace as well as in the non-market environment and to analyse the interactions and processes of the relationships in this system. Furthermore, the managerial decisions and actions in the relationships are also included. The relationship marketing is also dynamic because of its process nature.

Cooperative View of Relationship Marketing

In addition to the process view, there is a general acceptance that the relationship marketing is concerned with cooperative and collaborative relationships between the firm and its customers. Though such cooperative and collaborative relationships involve more than a standard buyer-seller relationship, yet it falls short of a merger or acquisition relationships. They are formed between the firm and one or many of its customers, which includes (a) the end-consumers, (b) distributors or channeled members, and (c) business-to-business customers. Besides, a prevailing axiom of relationship marketing is that the cooperative and collaborative relationships with customers would lead to greater market value creation and that such value would benefit both parties engaged in the relationship. The creation and enhancement of mutual economic value are thus the purposes of relationship marketing. Hence the relationship marketing could be defined as *the ongoing process of engaging in cooperative and collaborative activities, and programmes with immediate and end-user customers in order to create or enhance mutual economic value at reduced cost.*

Role of Market Orientation

Though many studies have shown that market orientation is an important aspect for the firms as it could create a positive impact on their performance, several studies have proven it otherwise (that the relation between a firm's market orientation and its success is weak in some occasions). Therefore, the moderating variables should be considered at least under certain circumstances. As such, the overall message from the market orientation studies is still not defined in a clear manner. The usefulness of the market orientation concept should also be questioned when looking at the realities of business markets. In most cases, the firms' 'surroundings' should be seen as a network of inter-organisational relationships rather than an anonymous market. Therefore, it could be concluded that the relationships are important for any business firm, and that the overall market orientation of the firm should be translated to a relationship level in order to be more effective. It should also be stressed that the market orientation on a relationship level could be interpreted in terms of the firm's employed resources and executed activities dedicated to the relational exchange process

2.3 SERVICE COMPETITION

The more a firm moves to the right on the marketing strategy continuum (away from a transaction-type situation), the more the market offer expands beyond the core product. Service activities (like installation of goods, technical service, advice about the ways of using a physical good or service, the just-in-time logistics, the customer-adapted invoicing, the technical know-how, the information, social contacts and a host of other elements of bigger or smaller magnitude) are added to the relationship, so that it becomes more attractive and profitable for the customer (and other parties as well) to engage in an ongoing relationship with a given partner on the marketplace. The more the firm adopts a relationship marketing strategy, the more it has to understand how to manage these service elements of its market offer.

Further, every firm, irrespective of whether it is a service firm, by the modern definition, or a manufacturer of goods, should learn the ways of coping with the new competition of service economy. Many authors have coined the term 'service competition' for this new competitive situation. In short, the relationship marketing demands a deeper understanding on the ways of managing the service competition, than what is required of pursuing a transaction-type strategy.

Relationship Makes Customer Less Price Sensitive

Interactive marketing has become the dominant aspect of marketing function in relationship marketing. Here, the elements of the marketing mix is not that important as they serve only a supporting function to the interactive marketing function.

The price sensitivity of the customer is often high in a transaction marketing context. Here it is the core product (and sometimes the image of the firm or its brands), that keeps the customer attached to the seller. When a competitor introduces a similar product in the market, the advertising and image of the firm helps in retaining the customers, at least for some time. However, the 'price' factor usually becomes an issue in this context. A firm that offers a lower price or better terms is a dangerous competitor in the transaction marketing process as the price sensitivity of customers is often high in this context.

A firm pursuing a relationship marketing strategy, on the other hand, has created more 'value' for its customers than that which is provided by the core product alone. Such a firm, over time, develops a deeper and intense bondage with its customers. Such ties may, for example, be (a) technological, (b) knowledge- or information-related, or (c) social in nature. If these factors are handled in a proper manner, they could provide customers with added 'value'-a fact that could not be provided by the core product alone. However, this does not mean that price is a totally unimportant factor in the relationship marketing process, but rather the degree of its importance is comparatively low in this context. In other words, it could be said that the relationship marketing makes customers less price sensitive.

Monitoring Customer Satisfaction

A study of market share and undertaking of *ad hoc* customer satisfaction surveys are usually employed as methods of monitoring the customer satisfaction. A stable or rising market share is generally considered a measure of success and, thus indirectly, also of customer satisfaction. However, it should be kept in mind that the market share is a reliable measurement of customer satisfaction only when the customer base remains stable. Very often, it is difficult to understand whether the customer base is actually in a stable position, or whether the firm is losing a fair share of its customers, who are replaced by new customers by means of aggressive marketing and sales. In such situations, the market share statistics would give only a false impression of success, though in reality the number of unsatisfied customers and ex-customers might be growing with a consequent deterioration in the image of the firm.

For a consumer packaged-goods marketing firm (which typically would apply a transaction marketing strategy), monitoring the market share is the best way of measuring its market success. On the other hand, service firms and many industrial marketers, who could pursue a relationship marketing strategy, have at least some kind of interactions with almost every single customer, even if they serve the mass markets. This enables them to monitor the customer satisfaction in a more direct manner.

A firm that applies a relationship-type strategy could monitor the customer satisfaction by directly managing its customer base. Managing the customer base implies that the firm has at least some kind of direct knowledge of how satisfied its customers are. Instead of thinking in anonymous numbers or market share, the management thinks in terms of people with personal reactions and opinions. This requires a medium and method of gathering various types of data through customer feedback, constantly updated by a large number of employees in large numbers of customer contacts.

In combination with the market share statistics, such an intelligence system focusing on customer satisfaction and customer needs and desires could form a valuable source of information for decision making. Consequently, in a relationship marketing situation the firm could build an online and real-time information system. This system would provide the management with (a) a continuously updated database of its customers, and (b) continuous information about the degree of satisfaction and dissatisfaction among the customers. This process could serve as a powerful management instrument. In a transaction marketing situation it is impossible, or at least very difficult and expensive, to build such a database.

The customer ratings could also be used in evaluating the competitive product offerings on each attribute grouping, so that a map of consumer preferences could be drawn up. The designers would then define the opportunities for improving products, given the company's skills and capabilities, in ways that will be important to the customer's perceptions of value, and thereby provide a source of competitive advantage.

The house of quality provides a visual tool in the form of a matrix with the customer perception of product attributes on one dimension and the engineering characteristics on the other. Specific target objectives for the design work emerge while comparing the possible options (given the engineering capabilities), with what is actually desired by the customer. The technique could be potentially applied to any of the company process involved in defining, developing, and delivering superior value to the customers.

Customer Perceived Quality

The quality that the customers perceive will typically differ, depending on the type of strategy adopted by a business firm.

Technical and Functional Quality According to the *model of total perceived quality* developed within the Nordic School of Services the customer perceived quality is basically a function of the customer perception of two dimensions: (a) the impact of the outcome or the technical solution (*what the customer receives*), and (b) an additional impact based on the customer's perception of the various interactions with the firm (how the so-called "moments of truth" are perceived). The former quality dimension is called the **technical quality** of the outcome (or solution), whereas the latter dimension is called the **functional quality** of the interaction process.

A transaction marketing approach includes no or rather minimal customer contacts outside the product and other marketing mix variables. The benefits sought by the customers are embedded in the technical solution provided by the product. The customer could not expect much else that would provide him with added value, except for the corporate or the brand image as in some cases. Hence the technical quality of the product, or what the customer gets as an outcome, is the dominating quality-creating source in transaction marketing.

In relationship marketing the situation is different. The customer interface is broader and the firm has opportunities to provide its customers with added value of various types (technological, information, knowledge, social, etc.). Hence, the second quality dimension, how the interaction process is perceived (functional quality), grows in importance. When several firms could provide similar technical quality, managing the interaction processes becomes imperative from a quality perception perspective also. Thus, in relationship marketing the functional quality dimension grows in importance and often becomes the dominating one. However, this does not mean that the technical quality could be neglected, but rather it is no longer the only quality dimension to be considered as one of strategic importance.

The 'quality function deployment' and the 'house of quality' are useful tools for visualising the relationship between the customer requirements and engineering capabilities. They could be modified and creatively expanded to meet the needs of any design team. Though, they do not offer a panacea for developing successful products, they offer a flexible approach for making a commitment to customer orientation operational.

Customer Feedback   Generally, the consultant breaks the process of customer feedback into five principles or phases:

1. Understanding why the firms are measuring the customer satisfaction and how the results could be utilised in improving the performance of the firm;

2. Letting customers define what to measure:

3. Monitoring continuously the performance *vis-a-vis* the competitors of the firm;

4. Tracking the internal processes that are tied to the result (both the customers' value as well as the end results themselves); and

5. Communicating the results throughout the organisation to everyone involved in the value-delivery process.

The business firm should learn to evaluate itself as well as its management on the basis of specific measures of customer satisfaction. The feedback from the customers must be meaningful to people within the organisation in terms of how they evaluate their own performance.

Advantages of a Direct Complaint

1. The unhappy customers are likely to complain to someone and it might as well be the company. The direct complaint would minimise the negative impact on the potential customers, besides providing an opportunity to the firm to correct the problem.

2. The customers keep changing (or rather increasing) their expectations and the complaint is an opportunity to understand the evolving customer expectations.

3. It is the best opportunity to learn when there is really something wrong, that might not come to the management's attention for weeks or months in the normal channels.(A burned-out light bulb in a hotel room is a good example)

4. The cost of satisfying an unhappy customer is usually much less than the cost of acquiring a new customer.

Customer Complaint Tracking

The customers who are 'less than completely satisfied' are a fact of business life that cannot and should not be avoided. It is not part of the psychological makeup of every customer to be completely satisfied. The customer expectations keep changing in the competitive market place, making the historical (previous) levels of satisfaction obsolete.

The customer complaint can be a window on the changing world even when the product has performed properly.. However, if there is a problem with the product itself, then it is doubly important that it should be identified and corrected. In this context, the companies must learn to listen to the customer, not only through the traditional means of market research, but also through an efficient customer complaint tracking (CCT) system.

The CCT is a process wider in scope than the usual survey of customer satisfaction. It requires following up with at least a sample if not be the total population of recent customers. The CCT system involves identifying the specific problems of the customers which may not surface in the routine questioning about the levels of satisfaction. Here, instead of the standard questions (How satisfied are you? or How would you rank our service?) which often have pre-assigned answers, the customer should be asked open-ended questions (like, Why have you assigned such a ranking for the company?), and given specific opportunities to disclose the real and the perceived problems. Such questions should be analysed one at a time using seasoned judgement.

The *focus-group interview* with the actual customer, though expensive, is one such method for studying the customer complaints in an effective manner. Many business firms provide a toll-free telephone number on their packages or product information brochures, so that the customers know where to call with the questions and complaints.

The feedback in the form of customer complaints provides an opportunity (a) to hear the voice of the changing customer, (b) to gain information to be shared with all employees who are involved in delivering value to the customers, and (c) to identify those opportunities to innovate and solve problems. The feedback also helps to develop the firm's distinctive competence in directions important to the customer.

2.4 STRATEGIC IMPORTANCE OF INTRAORGANISATIONAL COLLABORATION

The level of interdependence between the departmental functions in an organisation depends on whether the firm has chosen a transaction-type strategy or a relationship-type strategy.

In transaction marketing, most or all of the firm's customer contacts are related to the product itself and to the traditional marketing mix activities. Here the marketing and sales specialists are responsible for the total marketing function. Therefore, the internal interface between the departmental functions has very limited strategic importance to the firm.

In relationship marketing the situation is different. The customer interface is much broader in scope involving a large number of part-time marketers in several functions. A successful interactive marketing performance requires that all parts of the firm that are involved in 'taking care of' customers should collaborate and support each other in order to provide the customers with a total perceived quality. Therefore, for a firm pursuing a relationship marketing strategy, the internal interface between marketing, operations, personnel and other functions is of greater strategic importance to success.

2.5 INTERNAL MARKETING AS A PREREQUISITE FOR EXTERNAL MARKETING

The internal marketing concept states that "the internal market of employees is best motivated for the service mindedness and customer-oriented performance by an active, marketing-like approach, where a variety of activities are used internally in an active, marketing like and coordinated way".

The internal marketing is a necessary factor to ensure the support of traditional non-marketing people. The internal marketers should be (a) committed, (b) prepared and informed, and (c) motivated to perform as part-time marketers. As Jan Carlzon of SAS noticed, "only committed and informed people perform". These attributes are expected not only of front-line or back office employees, but also of supervisor, middle-level and top-level managers.

The internal marketing as a process has to be integrated with the total marketing function. The external marketing, both the traditional parts of it and the interactive marketing performance, starts from within the organisation. As compared to the transaction marketing situations, a thorough and ongoing internal marketing process is required to make the relationship marketing successful. If the internal marketing is neglected, external marketing would suffer or rather fail. This concept is discussed in an extensive manner in Chapter 10.

2.6 BUYING DECISION

The nature of the 'buying decision' made by prospective customers under the relationship perspective could be classified using the 'buy grid' concept.

Classification Under the Buy-Grid Concept

The 'buy grid' concept has distinguished the 'buying-classes' as:

(a) **New task:** The customer has no experience of the product or the service type. In this case, the customer would require a lot of information, and may ask friends or colleagues about it.

(b) **Straight rebuy:** A routine reorder without any modification, often handled routinely; and

(c) **Modified rebuy:** Here the customer seeks to change the supplier or some other aspect of the purchase, but wants the same general kind of product or service. The modified rebuys often provide the greatest test of the quality of relationship marketing.

Relationship Marketing vis-à-vis High and Low Involvement Products

The purchase motivation in a typical industrial marketing situation fully understood, while in other marketing situations, there is little that requires to be understood. This is particularly true of routine purchases (e.g. basic products and services) as they are purchased for functional reasons and carry little or no symbolic meaning. The risk that a manager should bear if he makes a wrong choice of supplier or product is comparatively low in this case. This is true for all types of low involvement products as the economic, psychological and social commitment involved is comparatively low.

Most often, the customers feel that there is a high psychological and social risk of making the wrong choice, particularly when the choice is 'worn' or the experience is shared with others. The 'worn' products include not only clothes, but also cigarettes, alcohol, cars, books, home furnishings, and the like. Since these are the high involvement products and services, they are particularly important from a relationship marketing point of view.

Good relationship marketing in high involvement situations greatly reinforc-es the customer loyalty, while poor relationship marketing in such situations could lead to customer disloyalty and a strong word of mouth condemnation. If a decision is important to the customer, then considerable thought should be devoted to the purchase.

Stages of Buying Decision

Usually, the customers go through the following stages while making the buying decision:

(i) **Existence of the need:** The need comes into existence. The firm's customer may not be aware of it, but it is there.

(ii) **Identification or realisation of need:** The need comes to the 'front of mind' (In other words the need is identified and the aspect of realising the need gains prominence).

(iii) **Problem recognition:** The need exists for a reason, typically a problem that needs to be solved (e.g. meeting a want). The firm's customer recognises that the problem exists.

(iv) **Search for information:** The firm's customer seeks information about the products and service to solve the problem. This is triggered by the need for problem resolution.

(v) **Evaluation:** All the relevant accessible information required to make the choice, which will resolve the problem is gathered and analysed. The prospective customers of the firm may or may not have established the choice criteria at this stage. Even if the criteria are already established, it might change at the evaluation stage. The patterns of deliberation are also important. Some customers rely more on personal advice than on information provided by the suppliers. So the outcome of the evaluation depends on various factors, which varies from personality and past experience to the way different companies provide the information. A firm should understand the criteria that their customers are likely to apply while evaluating different products and services. This understanding creates the vital link between relationship marketing and financial success of the firm. For, if the relationship determines the choice between products and services, then it would not be difficult to produce the commercial justification required for investing in the creation and management of such a relationship.

(vi) **Choice:** Some choices are impulsive, or at least would seem impulsive to others. But most of the choices are deliberate and rational, based upon the systematic processing of information. Such processing leads to the formation of an intention to purchase, which would be determined by the formulation of beliefs about the product and its likely performance.

(vii) **Post-purchase review:** After the buying decision, the customer re-evaluates the decision in the light of any new information (e.g. information about product performance).

Cognitive dissonance In some post-purchase situations, the customers might experience the *cognitive dissonance*, i.e. they might feel unhappy about what they happen to know after the purchase. They may experience doubt, and even anxiety, if the product did not come up to their expectation.

The cognitive dissonance could be resolved in several ways:

(a) The customers may look for information, which supports their decision (e.g., others who made the same decision);

(b) The customers might focus on the 'good deal' that they have got in an attempt to convince that they have made the right decision;

(c) They may even ignore, avoid or distort the incoming information, which is inconsistent with what they want to believe.

(d) The relationship marketing after the sale could help the firm's customers in justifying the decision they have made, even if there are problems after the sale.

Value Segmentation

Several organisations has segmented its customers and has given them the option to choose the level of technology sophistication that fits their needs and priorities. Each customer is assigned a different set of value factors, the factors that they employ as a basis of reaching a buying decision. The Dell Computers is a classic case in point in this regard. As revealed through their website, the Dell Computers has managed both its customer segments and changing technology innovations in the marketplace in a highly successful manner.

The discovery and understanding of the purchasing behaviours and value drivers of the individual customers is the first step in value segmentation.

This provides a meaningful basis for targeting those customers who are most likely to 'value' the company offering.

The segmentation process also enables the firm to calculate whether they could serve those customers in a profitable manner. The customer preferences should be analysed in terms of these *trade-offs* which would further shape the company's customer value commitment.

Trade-off Analysis   The trade-off analysis is a widely used customer research technique that helps in determining:

1   The relative importance of each of the desired benefits and the relative costs of a given offering;
2   The desirability of each benefit and cost option; and
3   The optimum combination of benefit and cost options that results in the maximum value.

Conjoint Analysis

The conjoint analysis (CA) is a commonly used method of trade-off analysis. The CA helps a firm in understanding the combination of the benefit and cost values to which the customers will respond. The CA is effective in many situations. It helps in determining (a) the relative importance of each desired benefit or the relative cost, (b) the importance of every option within each combination of benefits and costs, and (c) the value expected from each possible combination.

The term "conjoint" means factors presented together. The conjoint analysis involves the measurement and analysis of customer preferences for benefits and costs. The preferences are driven by the utility functions that influence the customer preferences. The utility functions might differ among the markets or the customer value segments. The conjoint analysis provides an estimate of the value or utility placed on each level of 'value drivers' or preferences for the combinations of benefits and costs. Combining the utility score of various value drivers, a firm could identify the product preferences for optimal benefit-cost combinations.

By quantifying the customer preferences for benefit-cost combinations and the trade-offs, the conjoint analysis could also provide valuable information for (a) new product developments and forecasting, (b) pricing decisions, and (c) market segmentations.

The customer value segments could be defined according to the ways they are differentiated by their preference for the specific offerings. Each customer value segment buys according to a unique set of needs and uses the value ratio to make a purchasing decision. For the innovator customer value segment, the primary value drivers include: (a) the need to maintain a leading-edge, the competitive advantage in the customer's market and (b) to be perceived of as an innovator in its industry by creating value with leading edge products, technology, markets and processes.

The *subjective expected value* from a relational behaviour depends on the customer's assessment of the behaviour's long-run future value, weighted by the customer's trust in the organisation.

Bhattacharya (1995) postulates that the customer would assess the *long-run future value* arising from a relational market behaviour (e.g., purchasing from an organisation), where the alternatives with greater benefits (including customisation of economic, psychological, and social exchange elements) or lower costs (including mental processing costs, search costs, and opportunity losses) are more likely to get considered. In this conceptualisation, the building or maintaining of an existing relationship is the more likely possibility, if the future value of a particular relational market behavior is high [that is, there are high perceived benefits/utility (due to customisation, personalisation, product bundling, and so on) or low costs (due to reduced mental processing, search costs, and the like) in the long run].

Again, it is a fact that the customer loyalty and branding are closely connected. The highly visible and positive branding cannot exist without customer loyalty and customer loyalty depends on relationship in the long run.

2.7 BUILDING BRAND EQUITY

The brand equity is based on the customer's knowledge of, and feelings for, the brand. This include the customer's ability to (a) recognise the brand, (b) recall having seen it before, (c) associate the brand with various messages, attributes, benefits, and experiences, and (d) use this knowledge as the basis for decision making. In theoretical terms, there is a strong cognitive component to the concept of brand equity as well as a strong behavioral predisposition. These positive associations and predispositions in the mind of the consumer result in a more favourable response to the firm's marketing efforts for the brand, giving it a better position on its marketing investments.

A 'strong brand' stands very close to the concept of *distinctive competence*, though these two concepts are not the same thing. The **distinctive competence** implies the underlying knowledge and skills on which the firm develops its brand equity. These competencies might include the underlying technical knowledge.

The brand name becomes part of the definition of quality perceived by the customers as it creates a set of expectations for the product performance.

A strong brand creates high expectations. The consumers develop amazingly strong imagery around a brand name.

It could be argued that the branding is the most powerful form of product differentiation from a competitive standpoint because of the virtual impossibility of a competitor duplicating it. The values inherent in a strong brand image are often based on the communication strategy surrounding the brand as much as on the physical characteristics that have been built into the product.

Steps Involved in Building the Customer-based Brand Equity

According to Kevin Lane Keller (1998), there are four steps involved in building the customer-based brand equity.

1. **Creating brand identity**: How should the firm be known to its target customers?
2. **Developing brand meaning**: What value proposition should the firm expect from the customers to associate with its product?
3. **Defining desired brand response**: What should be required to target the customers to think, feel, and do about the product offering?
4. **Defining the desired brand relationship**: What type of association is desired with the target customers?

Brand Awareness and Brand Salience

In his classic work *Strategic Brand Management,* Keller goes on to explain that the *brand identity* has two components: (a) brand awareness and (b) brand salience. The brand awareness is the customer's ability to recall and recognise. The brand salience relates to how easily the customer would recall the brand under various circumstances. The awareness is obviously the first requirement for band equity. A highly salient brand would have both the depth and breadth of brand awareness so that it could be recalled easily in many different purchase and use situations. The soft drink brands are a good example of highly salient brands.

Brand Meaning

The brand meaning is the embodiment of the value proposition. It is the meaning associated with the brand in the customer's mind. The brand meaning has two dimensions: (a) brand performance and (b) brand image The brand performance concerns how well the product works and provides problem solution and satisfaction. The brand image relates to the less tangible and more abstract psychological and social meanings associated with the brand.

Keller details five aspects of brand performance.

1. Primary characteristics and supplementary features;
2. Product reliability, durability and serviceability;
3. Service quality: the effectiveness, efficiency and the empathy;
4. Style and design; and
5. Price.

The four dimensions of brand imagery include:

1. The profile of the typical user;
2. Purchase and usage situations;
3. Personality and values associated with the brand, such as sincerity, excitement, competence and ruggedness; and
4. History, heritage, and experience.

Brand Responses

Specifying the brand responses desired is a key part of implementing the business model by tying the brand's value proposition and positioning back to the firm's strategic objectives. The desired responses include both the knowledge and feelings. The marketer should convey the meanings associated with (a) quality, (b) credibility and trust, (c) actual evaluation of brand performances, and (d) superior performance, on dimensions important to the target the customer's usage situation. It is also important to be explicit about the ways in which the brand should to be treated both psychologically and socially.

Brand Development

The brand relationships have become increasingly important, as more product and service categories have redefined the market competition around the relationship strategy as against the conventional transactional marketing strategy. The **brand development** requires being explicit about the desired relationship. The dimension of a brand relationship include: (a) purchasing loyalty (The product categories such as beverages and cosmetics engender intense loyalty and repeat purchases.); (b) attitudinal attachment (The strength of attitudinal attachments may vary significantly across the segments within a given product category.); (c) a sense of community; and (d) active engagement with the brand.

The successful brand development will ensure that, over time, the firm derives increased returns from its investments in innovation, business development, and marketing communications. The brand provides leverage on all of the firm's marketing expenditures. The investors are willing to pay premium prices for the shares of companies with strong brands as the brands enhance the future earnings stream of the business. While the brand equity exists fundamentally in the mind of the customer, it can also pay off in an enhanced value for the firm. The customer value translates finally into the shareholder value.

The core or generic product is the starting point for developing a business enterprise. The next step is to understand the expected product, what the customer expects to be offered in terms of product performance, features and services. This is the basis on which the customer will judge the quality of the product offering and be satisfied or dissatisfied. The product features could be distinguished as: (a) physical and (b) services that add to the value of the product offering by enhancing the ease and utility of ordering, taking delivery, storing, using, and disposing of the product.

Product Design and Development

Developing the complete product offering requires a proper understanding of the customers and their needs. Designing the product offering requires decisions about the specific product features that (a) address the specific needs and wants, and (b) offer superior value in terms of how the customer would use the product. The process also requires a proper understanding of the total use and delivery system. The service is usually a critical part of the product offering.

Product Features

The product features are part of the basic product/service offering. They are the tangible and intangible aspects of the product that differentiate the product from its competitive offerings. They also add value for customers in the target market. The product features represent the important 'selling points' in the value propositions.

While continuous innovation and new product features could help sustain the life-cycle of many products, service as part of the product offering is even more important in determining the customer preference and satisfaction. Service as part of the product offering raises a number of important strategic issues, however, not the least of which is the methods of pricing the product.

Bundling

Bundling is the process of incorporating the product features and services as part of the product offering. The bundling makes sense economically and strategically, when there are distinct market segments that require and value the performance provided by the bundled features. Bundling could be the key to product differentiation and augmentation. If the customers start expecting the bundled product, it would create more difficulties for the competitors to enter the market with a lower-price, unbundled product. On the other hand, if the real value is not there or has not been promoted adequately, it may create the opportunity for low-cost niche players to enter the market with one or more components of the total system.

One sophisticated economic model of the bundling decision concluded that the bundling could be more profitable than selling unbundled components under the following conditions:

1. When profit margins could be maintained on the bundled components at levels greater than the individual components;
2. When the firm's components in the bundled systems are clearly superior to those of competitors;
3. When there are not clear market segments that prefer to purchase components and construct their own systems, currently using the competitors components;
4. When the market is not growing significantly (which means that unbundling would merely substitute the lower margin components sales for bundled systems sales instead of attracting new customers;

Value Creation

A strong brand name creates value in four ways:

1   High awareness reflects the familiarity gained from past exposure. It is essential that a brand name should be remembered at the time of purchase because buyers consider surprisingly few brands. The buyers of ink-jet printers consider Hewlett-Packard and only one or two others. If the brand is not in that set, it will have great difficulty in getting a proper distribution.

2   A perception of high quality represents what the customers know about the ability of a product or service to meet their needs. These perceptions of fitness for use are often based on (a) the past experience, and (b) whether the product has delivered the promised benefits.

3   A meaningful brand promise captures all the positive associations that the consumers make with the brand, and any future exchange relationships. The Hallmark's cue is "when you care enough, send the very best"; and Lens master promises "lenses in an hour."

4   Finally, the strong brand loyalty is commanded by string brands because of effective performance during the past relationships. This is why the equity in a brand name is so valuable; there is a

predictable stream of sales at a price premium over the weaker brands. The strong relationship is virtually invulnerable to short-run attacks by the competitor, and the brand could command preferential treatment by the trade. This is one of the most compelling arguments for investing in customer retention.

The brands play different roles in the low-risk consumer product than they do in the high-risk technology products. For instance, since the purchase of a new brand of jeans or a trial of a new cereal is almost risk-free, the brands facilitate and simplify the choice process when there are many alternatives to consider. With a high-risk product like a microprocessor, MRP system, or a communication network, the brand is a symbol of expected performance, quality service and support and gives the buyer the reassurance and confidence. The brand carries with it (a) the history and performance of the company; (b) the technical leadership and (c) past support, and embodies the strength of the relationship.

The value proposition must be communicated to the target market. Just as the product offering is tailored to the needs and requirements of the target market, so must the communication mix be designed to be responsive to the information requirements of the target customers and their characteristic reliance on various means and media of communication.

The **market targeting** defines the audience that should be reached through communication. The **positioning** defines the product concept and the benefits to be presented, explained and developed by the marketing communication programme. The research does support the conclusion that the marketers, who stress the product benefits for the consumer through advertising and personal selling, could build brand equity through product differentiation that reduces its sensitivity to the price competition. This fact is one more piece of evidence in favour of the value-delivery concept of strategy.

2.8 RELATIONSHIP MARKETING AND VALUE CHAIN

The concept of relationship marketing is built around the concept of 'customer value' and the 'value chain'. According to Frederick E. Webster (2002), marketing is the process of (a) defining, (b) developing, and (c) delivering value to customers:

1 *Defining* the value implies identifying, measuring, and analysing the customer needs, and translating these information into requirements for creating the satisfied customers;

2. *Developing the value* incorporates the activities of (a) product development, (b) completing the product offering with services,

and (c) pricing which should be consistent with the customer needs, the competitive conditions and the value inherent in the product bundle.

3.   *Delivering value* includes not only the obvious functions of distribution viz., the transportation, storage, risk-taking, sorting and providing an assortment of goods, but also the process of communicating the product offering through personal selling, advertising, sales promotion, publicity, and display to the intended target market. The customer service functions such as applications, engineering, installation, warranties, and after-sale service could be thought of as an integral part of the process of delivering the value.

The above marketing concept calls for defining the business 'from the outside in' and this definition relates to aspects such as:

1   Finding the customer needs that are not satisfied and customer problems that are not solved;

2   Being "expert" on the class customer problems which implies knowing the customers and their needs and problems better than they know themselves;

3   Creating solutions to the aforesaid problems (mentioned in clause 2) through innovation; and

4   Communicating and delivering those solutions to a carefully defined set of prospective customers whose needs the business enterprise is committed to serving.

The customer relationships are the key strategic assets of the firm. They define the business process. Even if all production is outsourced, the firm would still be defined by the relationships with its own customers. Like all assets, the customer relationships have economic value. Managing the customer relationships as strategic assets is an important development, as it replaces the more traditional sales management views such as the key account strategy.

The purpose of marketing is to create a customer, and not just to make a sale. In other words, the focus should be on profitability and not sales volumes. The profitable sales result from strong, ongoing customer relationships that are designed and managed in the context of a total business model that includes (a) customer selection, (b) the value proposition, (c) the value capture strategy, and (d) strategic alliances with the partners who help deliver the value to those customers. Even with the strategic customers, it often makes sense to have some potential sales go to the competitors.

The actual processes involved in the customer relationship marketing are the traditional domain of sales force and marketing channel (distribution) management. But the concept of customer relationship marketing goes much further into the realm of customer databases, strategic partnering with the customers, and many forms of information and risk-sharing.

2.9 MANAGING THE CUSTOMER AS AN ASSET

The FMCG companies focus generally on the product quality and customer service as a means of building the brand's perceived value. They advertise to position the brand and worry that the promotions will dilute its value. In many brand-oriented companies, the product development focuses on the line extensions meant to leverage the brand name into new arenas. These companies pay substantial attention to how a strong brand could provide power in a battle against the competitors within a multilevel distribution system.

In a customer-driven company, the same elements work much differently. The quality and service act as the customer retention tools. The advertising messages serve to build the affinity between the customer and the company, and promotions function as the strategic events designed to (a) drive the repeat buying, and (b) increase the lifetime relationship value. The new products present opportunities to cross-sell the existing customers as well.

Table 2.1 Illustrative Differences and Norms in Values

Marketing strategy	Brand driven	Customer driven
➢ Product and service Quality	Create strong customer preference	Create high customer retention rates
➢ Advertising	Create brand image and Position	Create customer affinity
➢ Promotions	Deplete brand equity	Create repeat buying and enhance lifetime value
➢ Product development	Use brand name to flankers and related products	Acquire products to sell to the installed customer base
➢ Segmentation	Customer characteristics and benefit segmentation	Behavioral segmentation based on customer database
➢ Channels of distribution	Multistage distribution system	Direct distribution to customer
➢ Customer service	Enhance brand image	Create customer affinity

Source: Frederick E. Webster Jr., *Market Driven Management*, John Wiley & Sons Inc, New Jersy, USA, 2002

Factors Determining the Nature of Relationship

a. Effect of Experience

The customers form requirements and perceptions as a result of several influences. The most important of these is the experience, whether with the business firm, its competitor, or some other 'benchmark' company. All suppliers of products and services are in a sense in competition with each other, and it is particularly so when it comes to relationship marketing. In a competitive environment, the customer who stay in the relationship with the particular suppliers do so because the total package they receive from the supplier—the product, the service, the price, the credit, the relationship marketing and so forth—is right for them. But this does not warrant any room for complacency. The customers of low price suppliers may have 'talked themselves into' accepting the idea that the low relationship standards are worth tolerating because of the low price charged. However, if the competition that emerges is based on low prices rather than high standard of relationship marketing, the customer requirements may change.

b. Word of Mouth

The power of word of mouth is often quoted in terms of how satisfied or dissatisfied the customers communicate their experience to others. The customers who are totally satisfied, or who are dissatisfied and then have their problems resolved by the enterprise, could become powerful advocates for the enterprise. The force of recommendation is as powerful in organisational markets as in the customer markets. The information about the relationship would be communicated first within the buying center—the group of staff who market or influence the buying decision—and later to other buying centres. The *buying centres* are critically important as these centres take the important high-risk decisions, and therefore the member of the buying centre should be highly knowledgeable. Any piece of information about the experience of others is often seized upon and given great weightage.

2.10   STRATEGIC RELATIONSHIP MARKETING

The customers define the business process by the demands they place on the firm. In other words they define this process by asking the firm to do certain things in an effective and efficient manner. The decision to provide solutions to customer problems, to work with the specific customers and to accept their demands, involves a commitment of resources .The choice of markets and customers shapes the business even more than the choice of the products to be offered. Over time, the product offering is adjusted to the changing customer needs. In a stable business, the product is a variable: the served market and the customer are the constants. The customers shape the business, which is why the customer choice is considered the critical strategic decision.

Process of Choosing Customers: Market Segmentation

The process of choosing customers begins with the market segmentation. The market segmentation is both an analytical and creative process, requiring the collection and analysis of data about the potential market and imaginative interpretation of those data by the marketing manager. The essence of market segmentation is to break a large market into smaller pieces, each segment consisting of customers who are similar to one another in ways important to the marketer such as their needs, preferences, buying habits, usage patterns, or media exposures. The customer within a given marketing segment should be similar in their response to the company's product offerings and/or communication.

The customer characteristics chosen as the basis for market segmentation could be *demographic* (age, income, occupation, family status, type or place of residence) or *psychographic* (self concepts-the lifestyle, risk-aversion, the buying decision process). The psychographic segment are often hard to develop as it is difficult to observe and measure such characteristics unless they could be related to more observable attributes such as the age or place of residence. The benefit segmentation is based on the fact that different customers are looking for different sets of benefits from the same product, although this segmentation also requires matching up some characteristics of the customer with these benefit sets.

Market Segmentation versus Product Differentiation

The market segmentation and product differentiation are related but distinct concepts. The marketing segmentation is the strategy of conceptually and statistically identifying the different market segments with different characteristics (These charactesrestics include the needs, wants, preferences, buying habits, usage patterns and communication exposure). The product differentiation involves the strategy and tactics of offering products with distinctive characteristics—based either on the product design and engineering, service features or communication—to these distinct market segments. The selection of target markets is a commitment of resources to deliver superior value to a specific set of customers. No firm has the capability to satisfy all the needs of all potential customers. The recognition of this basic truth is the heart of market targeting. Chapter 3 explains more on segmentation and its suitability in the relationship marketing.

Positioning

Positioning is the development of the value proposition, the statement of how the firm proposes to deliver the superior value to its customers. The positioning involves the communication about the product, not the product itself. The important motives that drive the concept of positioning include:

1. It becomes the selling propositions to potential customers, the reason why they should do business with the company rather than with the competitor.

2. It communicates to the whole organisation a sense of specific purpose and direction, coordinating their efforts towards the common purpose of creating a satisfied customer.

Positioning and the development of value proposition must be based on an assessment of the product offering and the firm's distinctive competencies mainly related to the competitors in terms of quality, technology, service and price. This is inherent in the notion that 'the customer defines value'. The customer defines the value by comparing the company's product offering with those of competitors in the context of his or her own needs, preferences, buying patterns and the use system.

2.11 RELATIONSHIP MARKETING PROGRAMMES

The present millennium has been witnessing vehement changes in the strategies and focus of many promotions and campaigns. A fundamental shift is taking place from *mass marketing* that sends messages about a standard product offering to the anonymous person to *personalised marketing* with messages and offerings tailored to the specific individual. Among the most familiar examples of interactive marketing are the consumer credit cards, which include the banking credit card, frequent flyer cards and frequent traveller programmes. In each instance, the customer is considered as an individual with whom the marketer could communicate directly, sending specific promotional messages and product offerings tailored to that individual. Each transaction (on the telephone, Internet, or mail order, every flight or overnight stay, every log in to the Internet and every piece of information accessed during that session) is entered into the database.

Among the most commonly found techniques for enhancing the customer profitability are the programmes that reward customers for frequent and loyal purchasing behaviour. These take the familiar form of (a) airline frequent flyer awards programmes based on mileage flown, (b) hotel guest awards based on nights stayed, (c) credit card rebates based on the amount charged and so on. The rewards include free travel and other merchandise gifts. Table 2.2 displays the various types of relationship marketing programmes that are prevalent among different types of customers. Obviously, the marketing practitioners in search of new creative ideas develop many variations and combinations of these programmes to build closer and mutually beneficial relationships with their customers.

Table 2.2	Types of Relationship Marketing Programmes

PROGRAMME TYPE	CUSTOMER TYPE		
	Individual Consumers	Distributors/ Resellers	Institutional Buyers (Business to Business
Continuity marketing	Loyalty programmes	Continuous replenishment and ECR programmes	Special supply arrangements (e.g., JIT, MRP)
Individual marketing	Data warehousing and data mining	Customer business development	Key account management
Co-marketing/ partnering	Co-branding	Co-operative marketing	Joint market-ing and co-development

Source: Jagdish N. Sheth and Atul Parvatiyar (Editors), *Handbook of Relationship Marketing,* Response Book, 2002 with permission

2.12 TYPES OF RELATIONSHIP MARKETING PROGRAMMES

Continuity Marketing Programmes

Given the growing concern for retaining customers as well as the emerging knowledge about customer retention economics, many companies have developed continuity marketing programmes that are aimed at both (a) retaining the customers and (b) increasing their loyalty. For consumers in the mass markets, these programmes usually take the shape of membership and loyalty card programmes in which the consumers are often rewarded for their member and loyalty relationships with the marketers. The basic aim of continuity marketing programmes is to retain the customers and increase loyalty through long-term special services that have the potential to increase the mutual value as the partners learn about each other.

Partnering Programmes

This is a major type of relationship marketing programme in the business-to-business (B to B) and business-to-consumer (B to C) segment, and it involves the partnering relationships between the customers and marketers to serve the end-user needs. In the mass markets, two types of partnering programmes are most common: (a) co-branding and (b) affinity partnering.

In **co-branding**, two marketers combine their resources and skills to offer advanced products and services to the mass-market customers. For example, the BPL Mobile and ICICI Bank have co-branded the ICICI BPL Mobile credit card programme providing gains to consumers as well as to the partnering organisations. The affinity partnering programmes are similar to the co-branding programmes except that the marketers do not create new brands, rather they use the endorsement strategies. Usually, the affinity partnering programmes try to take advantage of the customer memberships in one group to cross-sell other products and services.

One-To-One Marketing

The one-to-one or individual marketing approach is grounded in account-based marketing. Such programmes are aimed at meeting and satisfying each customer's needs in a unique and individual manner. Using the online information and databases on individual customer interactions, the marketers aim to fulfill the unique needs of each mass-market customer. The information on individual customers is utilised to develop frequency marketing, interactive marketing, and after marketing programmes in order to develop relationships with the high-yielding customers.

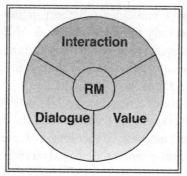

Fig 2.3 The Triplet of Relationship Marketing

Source: Jagdish N. Sheth and Atul Parvatiyar (Editors), *Handbook of Relationship Marketing*, Response Book, 2002 with permission

A key principle of relationship marketing is the need to be in constant dialogue with the customers. This ensures that their needs are being met and that the information on the database is kept fresh. In a dialogue, the information flows both ways. This dialogue lasts as long the customer stays with the enterprise. The dialogue consist of a series of 'conversations', conducted over the telephone followed by mail correspondences, brochures, and other material that confirm or add to what is being said.

Integrated Telephone Marketing

A successful and effective direct response campaign could be achieved mainly through integrated telephone marketing. This is possible when the message that the firm in question communicate with the customer complements with (a) the message delivered by the phone representative and (b) the fulfillment package. The fulfillment package then becomes the first step in converting the inbound caller to an ongoing customer. The integration of an idea, an offer and communication over the media of telephone and a product or service that meets or exceeds the caller expectations has become the formula of success for today's direct marketing companies. The telephone has thus become a key element in customer retention and growth. The inbound call is the first step in developing a customer.

Even though of shorter duration, the first phone call made in response to advertising sets the tone for the relationship that develops between the advertiser and caller. The level of service provided by the inbound call center and the quality of the overall contact, as determined by the readiness and training of the tele-representative (CSP), will directly affect the willingness of a caller to begin a relationship with an advertiser and be receptive to future contact.

2.13 STRIVING FOR INTERACTIVITY

Most customer responsive strategies fall short of this interactive ideal. At best, they could address only the microsegments extracted from huge databases and send personalised messages to the carefully selected individuals. But these are still one-way messages and they compete for attention with other messages flooding the market. A modicum of interactivity is achieved when an advertisement elicits a response such as returning a coupon or making a toll-free call. This response is then stored in the database and replied to with a personalised direct mailing. Higher levels of interactivity are achieved when the incentives and programmes are based on individual behaviour, as in airline frequent flyer programmes.

Role of Internet

The rapid rise of the Internet has changed the rules of interactive marketing. It permits complete addressability and two-way interaction. When a customer visits a web site, many cycles of messages could be exchanged in a short time, and remembered on the next visit. With all this information from the customer, the offering could be prepares a highly personalised manner. The Internet has emerged as a uniquely responsive interactive medium.

The relationship marketing could be delivered through a variety of media, depending on the nature of the contact. The information could be provided face-to-face, on the telephone, via the Internet or other electronic media, on a video screen, on a TV through video on demand, through a loudspeaker, or in print.

The replacement of people-based marketing by automated relationship marketing provides a challenge to the relationship delivery. The relationships are emotional attachments developed over time (in the minority of customers who want one with a company) and high-quality touch points govern them. These touch-points are formulated on the basis of the entire customer experience.

The experience covers all the touchpoints with the customers, from branding, through marketing, sales and service, to the product consumption experience. As Forrester Research pointed out, it is the customer experience that matters, and not the focus on relationships. The dictum is 'deliver a high-quality customer experience and those customers that are relationship-inclined will reward you.' The majority who is not inclined to make a relationship will reward you with their customer too. The studies that have looked at real relationships describe them as emotionally-driven states characterised by high levels of trust, commitment and unique benefits from the relationship.

Some studies conducted in this regard has added a two-way dialogue and the absence of exit barriers too. The trust is considered to be the most important factor in a relationship. The trust is based upon the long-term quality of the customer experience. The relationships exist in a continuum from transactional relationships based upon economic considerations, to real relationships based on belief in the organisation. It should be of no surprise that studies have found that only a minority of customers exist that have anything other than a transactional relationship

The relationship marketing also includes working with operations so that the types of service and interaction experiences that the customers require could be actually delivered, and thereby providing a feedback on the factors that will (and what will not) actually work. This would also provide a continuously improving experience to keep up with the rising customer expectations. The process also includes marketing communications of all kinds, those that support branding, sales, PR, and all dimensions of the customer relationship beyond the effect of experiences themselves.

Interractive Marketing

Peter Drucker has given the best definition of marketing when he referred marketing as "everything the company does, seen from the perspective of the customer". Clearly, the company has to do a lot more than mere "talking". Gronroos has coined a much bigger concept in this regard, 'the interactive marketing'. The concept has an extended scope and covers all the part-time marketers in the customer-facing positions in functions other than what the marketing department generally does. The interactive marketers influence the customers during each customer-facing touchpoint in the customer experience. As Jan Carlzon, the former CEO of SAS airlines puts it, "the SAS is created 50 million times a year, 15 seconds at a time. These 50 million touch points are the moments that ultimately determine whether the SAS will succeed or fail as a company".

The persons involved in interactive marketing include (a) people in the customer service, (b) the field force, and (c) operations or just any other person who could influence the customers sensibility, feelings and thought. An in-depth study to understand (a) the real factors that influence the customer appraisal during every customer experience, and (b) the factors that influence the formation of real relationship, has revealed that the role of marketing department is dwindling in the present day context though much of present day marketing is still product-driven, rather than customer-driven. Perhaps this is why the marketing is currently agonising over its decline in influence in the Boardroom.

The customer service has its origins as the complaint department or a transaction-based function. In both cases, the underlying premise is that the business has a product focus, whether it sells the products or services. The typical customer interaction is a transaction. Until recently, it has generally been assumed that the low numbers of complaints meant that the customers were mostly satisfied with the product. The goal in these departments has been that of efficiency which naturally leads to the view of customer service as an overhead, a cost of doing business that should be controlled.

2.14 LIFE TIME VALUE

The speed or rate of behaviour change is an important factor in the modelling of interactive behaviour, and this aspect is much more important here than in the offline models. Though the small changes over time are to be expected, rapid and accelerating changes are significant signal that demands immediate action from the firm. So once the firm uses scores to identify the customer behaviour, it should also focus on re-profiling their customers at certain intervals and keep track of the scores over time.

The life time value (LTV) of the customer determines the value of a customer to the firm, over the life-cycle of the customer. The application of the concept of LTV has removed the focus on individual transactions with the customers. The LTV is being increasingly used with the development of technology and market research. It is a popular tool adopted by the Internet-based firms. The step by step instruction required for creating the likelihood to respond and future value scores for each customer, and using scores to create the high ROI promotions based on the customer life-cycle is explained in Exhibit 2.1.

EXHIBIT 2.1

LTV CALCULATION MADE SIMPLE

Step 1: **Determining certain figures for business under consideration and make a meaningful projection**

✓ What is the 'average' sale? (Add total sales for a year [in money volumes] and divide that by the total number of sales transactions completed or expect to complete.)

✓ How many times a year does an 'average' customer buy from the firm? (Take total number of sales transactions for a year and divide it by the total number of customers.)

✓ For how many years does an average customer buy from the firm? (Remember, 20 per cent of the population moves every year, so this is typically less than 5 years, depending upon the nature of your business.)

✓ How many people does the firm's average customer tell about the company? (A major factor—the most common average is between 3-12)

✓ What percentage of these people actually become the firm's customers? (Usually between 20 per cent and 70 per cent)

Step 2: **Cold Hard Cash**

Fill in the blanks below (using the numbers calculated in Step 1), to find out precisely what each customer is actually worth to the firm right now.

A. Average sale = _____

B. Number of sales per year per customer = _____

C. Number of years customer buys from the firm = _____

D. Number of referrals from customer = _____

E. Per cent of referrals who become customers = _____

F. Gross sales per year per customer (A x B) = _____

G. Gross sales over life of customer (F x C) = _____

H. Referrals who become customers (D x E) = _____

I. Gross sales from referrals (G x H) = _____

J. **Total value** of satisfied customer (G + I) = _____

Source: www. crmtoday.com with permission

As shown in the Exhibit 2.2, the concept of customer service is being transformed into a customer relationship. The latter term describes something experiential, not merely a transaction. The customer relationship also has the strategic application across the organisation. Many companies in the recent years have tried to deepen their customer relationships by simply offering various services and create more opportunities for the customers even in the impersonal, non-bonding routine contracts and transactions .

2.15 RECENCY

Recency is the most powerful predictor of future behavior. The more recently a customer has done something, the more likely they are to do it again. The recency could predict the likelihood of purchases, visits, game plays, or just about any "action-oriented" customer behavior. The recency explains why the customers receives another catalogue from the same company shortly after they made their first purchase from them.

Consider an e-tailor, say Subhiksha.com calculating their future earnings What good is it to have 10,000 people who have bought or visited at least 5 times, when 80 per cent have not repeated in the past 6 months? The repeaters who have not repeated recently are the former best customers.

Here's an example of why the idea of recency is so important. The lower quality (lower repeat rate) of the new customer behaviour is overwhelmed by the behaviour of older customers, and the firm gets a false reading on the future health and profitability of its business. Everything would appear going smoothly, and new customers would be ramping, but all of a sudden, the sales or visits would go soft. This happens at the point where the new, lower quality customers finally overpower the old, higher quality customers in the database. The future value of the firm's customers has shifted and the company would realise this only at the later stage. The application of recency could serve as an additional filter in the firm's segment tracking as it clears away the past, and provides with a head up view of the future. The 'tracking repeats' (or frequency) by itself is a rear view mirror, because the firm would never know how many of these people are really the current customers without looking at recency. The longer a customer has stopped engaging in a behaviour, the less likely they are to repeat the behaviour and they become defected customers.

The easiest way to fit recency into the tracking of repeaters is to set a cutoff, say 30 days. The firm wants to track the percentage of customers in a segment who are repeaters, where the last repeat action (purchase, visit, page view, download) was in the prior 30 days. It should be observed whether the percentage is rising or falling. These recent repeat customers are the strongest, the most powerful, and the most valuable customers, for the present and the future. They are most likely to repeat whatever behaviour the firm is tracking. If these customers begin to decline in percentage, the company would feel it down the road. A decline in the recent repeaters implies that the company has to readjust its customer acquisition plans, because they may be in the process of defecting from the business.

2.16 RECENCY, FREQUENCY, MONETARY VALUE (RFM) MODEL

The RFM model is applicable in all situations, in virtually every high-activity business specifically in any kind of "action-oriented" behaviour visits, sign-ups, surveys or games. A customer who has visited the company web site recently (R) and frequently (F) and created a lot of monetary value (M) through purchases is much more likely to visit and buy again. A high recency / frequency / monetary value (RFM) customer who stops visiting is the one who has found alternatives to the firm's site. The customers who have not visited or purchased in a while are less interested in the firm's product/service than the customers who have done one of these things recently. By applying the recency, frequency and monetary value together, the company would obtain a pretty good indicator of the interest in their site at the customer level, which is a valuable information that the business firm should possess.

The major assumptions involved in this process include:

➢ Customers who purchased **recently** were more likely to buy again against the customers who had not purchased in a while

➢ Customers who purchased **frequently** were more likely to buy again against the customers who had made just one or two purchases

➢ Customers who had **spent the most money** in total were more likely to buy again. The most valuable customers tended to continue to become even more valuable

➢ The RFM is closely related to the LTV. The LTV is the expected net profit that a customer would contribute to the business over the life-cycle, the period of time a customer remains a customer. Because of the linkage to LTV and the life-cycle, the RFM techniques could be used as a proxy for the future profitability of a business. The high RFM customers represent the future business potential, as the customers are willing and interested in doing business with the company and have high LTV. The low RFM customers represent dwindling business opportunity, low LTV, and signifies a 'flag' and action should be done with those customers to increase their value.

The customers are ranked on the basis of their R, F and M characteristics, and assigned a "score" representing this rank. Assuming that the behaviour being ranked (purchase, visit) using the RFM has an economic value, it could be concluded that the higher the **RFM score**, the more profitable the customer is to the business in the present and in the future. The high RFM customers are most likely to continue to purchase and visit, and they are most likely to respond to marketing promotions. The opposite is true for the low RFM score customers; they are the least likely to (a) purchase or visit again and (b) respond to promotions. Once the firm has scored customers using the RFM, it would be in a position to:

> ➤ Decide on the customers who should be targetted and predict the response rate
> ➤ Optimise the promotional discounting by maximising the response rate, while reducing the overall discount costs
> ➤ Determine which parts of the site or activities attract high value customers and maintain the focus on these aspects to increase the customer loyalty and profitability

The standard approach to the RFM analysis is a "snapshot" method, which measures the customer at a point in time. These new methods make use of the RFM parameters over time in unique ways, and are not dependent on the purchase amount (monetary) as the original RFM model is. The result of using these methods is the very high ROI marketing campaigns and site designs. The customers, through their actions, provide information regarding the most profitable route that should be taken. The most recent customers for any particular activity are always the ones most likely to repeat that activity, and so have a higher potential value. A manager could track the multiple activities for the same customer groups.

EXHIBIT 2.2

DESIGNING LIFETIME VALUE: A REAL TIME APPROACH

Every principle of LTV design ideally recognises and act upon the uniqueness of the customers and employees alike as shown below:

1. **Leverage customer information.** Using the information about customers, the firm should squeeze the most out of every interaction.

2. **Balance the use of people and technology**. Some customers prefer doing business through automated systems. This can save money. Others will prefer to deal with people. Getting the right balance for each customer is crucial. Maintain a tenured, high performance team. Motivated and challenged people will be loyal and work hard to boost service quality.

3. **Sustain management excellence**. Managing successfully requires hybrid skills, and attitudes for which there sometimes are no clear development paths or resource pools.

4. **Build an infrastructure to keep the competitive edge**. Building systems that can assimilate technology changes and re-size to support a volatile marketplace.

5. **The challenge ahead is obvious**. The rewards are high and the technology is now right. It will be the management tools, methods and vision that will transform the potential into results. Those that are successful will find their wallets stuffed with more than just loyalty cards.

Source: www.crmtoday.com with permission

2.17 WEB ANALYTICAL SOFTWARE—DIGITAL SCALE CALCULATOR*

The web analytical software takes the raw data from the web site server logs and turns it into reports. These reports provide information regarding the overall performance of a business firm. The reports so generated should be so organised that:

➢ Intelligent strategies could be developed to help keep the web site visitors on track in the sales process;

➢ The results of those strategies could be accurately measured to assess their effectiveness.

The Future Now Digital Scale Calculator is a webanalytical software designed for the purpose. It takes the data from web site reports and turns it into "actionable" metrics, or statistics, that could be tracked over time, which makes it a valuable tool for any online company irrespective of its size.

All metrics created by the Digital Sales Calculator helps the firm under consideration, in tracking the changes in the visitors' behaviour to their sites and thereby help the firm in taking remedial or supportive actions on the basis of that. One common element that often needs fixing on the e-commerce web sites is the number of clicks it takes a potential customer to make a purchase. A company like Amazon.com has realised that one of the main causes of incomplete purchases and abandoned shopping carts is the long and tedious checkout process that many e-tailers inflict on their potential customers.

One of the key strengths of Future Now's Digital Sales Calculator is that it shows precisely where a potential customer left the company web site before completing a purchase. If a lot of prospects drop out of the sales process at a

Source: www. Jim Novo.com and, Drilling Down project of Jim Novo with permission given point, then it is clear that something is wrong on that particular page. It might be that the company does not make it clear what the potential customer should do next. Or there might be a shortcoming with the design of a page (the lay-out) and various navigations buttons, for instance, could be causing confusion.

Whatever proves to be the case, the important thing is that action could be taken on the basis of information provided by the Digital Sales Calculator. But without solid, informative statistics, a webmaster is foraging around in the dark, hoping that this or that strategy will work, but never being able to prove its efficacy. It is generally agreed that the e-commerce is a numbers game and the trick is to focus on the right numbers so that the firm could make accurate decisions on improving their web site and, ultimately, their CCR (customer conversion rate). The web analytic software takes raw data and turns it into structured information in the form of reports. Once a firm understand the inter-relationships of the data , the benefits of relationship marketing could be shown through accounting techniques, which reveal:

➢   costs of acquiring customers;

➢   changes in the number of customers the firm have; and

➢   change in what each customer is buying from the firm.

The relationship marketing is the use of a wide range of marketing, sales, communicant and customer care techniques and processes to. Because the new field of e-metrics, injects the kind of statistical precision into the Internet that is generally enjoyed by bricks-and-mortar businesses, it looks set to become something of a milestone in the world of e-commerce. With the digital scale one could move from the trial and error to trial, measure, and improve. (Please tune to Appendix-1 for illustration of this software.)

CONCLUSION

Defining and mapping the market is gaining importance what the market looks like in terms of behavior, needs and expectations, channel player and solution providers to discover customer value segments. In its simplest form, it involves altering the mass market to a segmented one composed of clusters with homogeneous behaviour and needs. It is changing from an aggregation of target buyers chosen in a random manner to a linear plot from those most likely to respond to the firm's value commitment to those who will never respond. Everyone is working to improve operations in the fundamental way: cutting costs, improving productivity, restructuring to be faster, simplifying processes, and getting better at satisfying customers while operations and short-term profitability may improve. By understanding the possibilities of relationship building and marketing one could take the firm into new heights.

SUMMARY

- ✓ Corporate relationship building are mutually beneficial, for the company as well as the customer.
- ✓ There are two parts of relationship marketing—Service Marketing and Industrial Marketing.
- ✓ Trust is a very important component of the confidence building measure undertaken by a company.
- ✓ Relationship marketing is system-oriented, it includes managerial aspects, such as monitoring customer satisfaction.
- ✓ Customer Perceived Quality (CPQ) is important because it helps a company to provide its customers with added value of various types.
- ✓ A company must learn to evaluate itself and its management based on specific measures of customer satisfaction.
- ✓ Internal marketing is a pre-requisite for external marketing.
- ✓ In CRM, an internal interface between marketing, operations, personnel etc., are of strategic importance to success.
- ✓ The Buy Grid concept differentiates different buying classes, which a company must know about .
- ✓ Strategic Brand Management has two component-brand awareness and brand salience. There are also the factors of brand responses and brand relationships which play a crucial role.
- ✓ Relationship marketing is built around the concept of customer value and the Value Chain.
- ✓ Market segmentation helps the company to chose its customers and him to retain them. It is a creative, analytical process requiring the collection and analysis of data about the potentials market. It is different from product differentiation.
- ✓ Relationship marketing programmes include continuity marketing programmes, partnering programmes, one to one marketing and integrated telephone marketing.
- ✓ Behavior change is increasingly being recognized as crucial to interactive behavior. It includes the concept of Life Time Value (LTV), Recency etc.
- ✓ Recency predicts the likelihood of purchases or any action-oriented customer behavior. It can be analyzed with the help of the Recency Frequency Monetary value (RFM) Model and Web Analytical Software.

CHAPTER REVIEW QUESTIONS

1. Explain RFM model
2. Illustatate the concept of Recency and Life Time Value for a online firm like fabmart.com
3. State the siginificance of attaining interactivity for a firm with its customers for building relationship in Indian environment
4. Comment on the "touch points and feed back "analysis used in relationship marketing
5. Explain service competition.
6. How do you measure the customer satisfaction of a banker like ICICI Bank?

CASE STUDY
SHOPPERS STOP-STOCKING UP ON EMOTIONS

Less than a decade and half into its existence, the Shoppers' Stop has almost conquered the mind of customers. This brand has gripped the Indian shopping psyche by adopting the latest relationship oriented marketing practices.

Advertising and Marketing Marketing Magezine

BACKGROUND

Until 1990, there were just three international style shopping malls in India—the Spencer in Chennai, the Crossroads in Mumbai and the Ansals in New Delhi. The number had gone to 20, by 2001. The year 2003 witnessed a feverish pitch in the retail activities in India. Large department stores, spacious malls, and brand stores in metropolitan and even smaller cities are becoming part of the Indian scenario. Currently, 96% of all organised retail emanates from the top ten cities in India, with the top six accounting for 86%. By 2005, the top ten cities are expected to account for 84% of the retail business activity, with some spurts of retailing activity spread across the next five towns.

Introduction

It is estimated that the organised retailing business would reach Rs 2,50,000 crore by 2005.

According to a study conducted by the KSA Technopak, nearly 70 lakh square feet of area will be occupied by these shopping malls in the major cities of India. *The KSA study on consumer outlook also suggested that over 80 of consumers preferred a wide range of product at the hand hill shopping.

Though the consumer buying capacity in India was not as good as in the developed markets in the past decade, the trend is clearly reversing. According to KSA Technopak, from the current level of 0.6 % (of the 6,25,000-core retail market), the organised retail market will account for 6% of the core retail market by 2005. Even then it would be miles behind the US benchmark, where almost 90% of retail sales are in the organised sector. The mall developers still complain of limited options in assembling a suitable tenant mix. The same names—Shopper's Stop, Benton, Nike, Reebok, MusicWorld, Color Plus—are coming up again and again.

EXHIBIT 1

TOP PLAYERS IN THE RETAIL BUSINESS IN INDIA

Apparel retaining	Fast-food retailing	Books, Music & related product	Life-style retailing	Food products and grocery
Benetton	Pizzeria	Crossword	West Side	Food world
Weekender	Nirula's	Planet M	Cross Roads	Mother Dairy
Arrow	Domino's	Groove	Hopp	Safal
Lee	Wimpy's	Archies	Ebony	Subhiksha
Van Heusen	McDonald's	Vintage's Hallmark Gallery	Akbar Ally	Nanz
Louis Phillippe	US Pizza	Landmark	Shopper's Stop	Sahkari Bhandar
Raymond's	Pizza Hut	Walden	Health 'n' Glow	Super Bazaar
ITC's Will Sports	Marrybrown	Music World	Lifestyle	Apna Bazaar
Pantaloon			Globus	Nilgiri's
West Side				Globus
Cross Roads				Vitan

The Indian consumer market has been found divided into so many layers and the biggest challenge lies in penetrating into each layer through appropriate retail strategies. The 'super-rich class' which consists of about 400 thousand families with a household income of more than Rs 50 lakh (five million), are the main clientele for the premium product categories. They are also the patrons of the designer boutiques. The next layer of 'sheer-rich' people, of about 0.14 million household, with an income of Rs 20 to 50 lakh (two to five million), consists mainly of a group of early adopters and are frequent customers at the solo shops and boutiques. The 'clear-rich class' of about 0.44 million households is an important consumer group for several product categories in the department stores and even in the specialty chains. The 'near-rich class' of about 1.5 lakh households with an income of Rs 5 to 10 lakh (half a million to one million) is a very huge market and it is the prime target of many readymade brands in the multibrand stores. They are also the aspirational customers who place great important or brand value.

EXHIBIT 2

INDIA'S LARGEST RETAILERS

Retailer	Existing Operations	Future plans
RPG	Space: 200,000 sq.ft. Total sales: Rs. 156 crore 27 Food world, 2 Music World 4 Spencer's outlets	50 Foodworld, 8 Music world, 18 Health & Glow outlets for total turnover of Rs. 23. 75 Crore/Month.
Shoppers' Stop	Space: 100,000 sq.ft. Total sales: Rs. 160 crore 2 outlets in Mumbai, one each in Hyderabad, B'lore. Jaipur and Chennai.	15-17 store in next few years
Vivek & Co.	Space: 100,000 sq.ft. Total sales: Rs. 90 crore 8 stores in Chennai, 3 in B'lore and 1 in Salem.	10 stores in Chennai and B'lore each, 7 in Hyderabad, Vijayawada and Vizag.
Nilgiri's	Space: 80,000 sq.ft. Total sales Rs. 75 crore 17 supermarkets and 14 cakeshops.	30% growth over next few years 289 stores by 2007.
Pantaloon	Space: 90,000 sq.ft Total sales: Rs. 60 crore 12 stores and 40 Pantaloon shops.	11 garments, household and leisure products superstore. Hike retail area to 300,000 sq.ft.

Akbarallys	Space:35,000 sq.ft. total sales: 50 crore 2 furniture store and 3 departmental stores	Company says it's looking at more places across the country for departmental stores.
Nanz	Space: 70,000 sq.ft. Total sales: Rs. 40 crore 15 supermarkets.	Nanz, which has New Delhi's largest retail stores, says it has major expansion plans.
Vitan	Space : 50,000 sq.ft. Total sales: Rs. 25 crore 11 departmental stores.	25 outlets and Rs. 100 crore turnover by the end of next year.
Crossword	Space: 27,000 sq.ft. Total sales: Rs.16 crore Bookstores in 7 locations.	Aims to reach 25 stores in next few years with a mega size store in Mumbai.
Landmark	Space:18,000 sq.ft. One outlet in Chennai and Coimbatore	Opening with Emami, a 15,000 sq.ft in Kolkata, an anchor mall.
Charagh Din	Space: 10,000 sq.ft. One store in Mumbai.	Will remain single location 'destination' store, in the strength of its well-established garment brand.
Kemp Chain of Stores	Space: 1,25,000 sq.ft. 2 stores in Bangalore-Big Kids Kemp and Kemp Fort.	Kemp city retailing-cum-entertainment development over 200 acres.

THE CORPORATE STORY

Back in 1991, when the Shopper's Stop first desided to set up a retailing unit there came the question of 'what to retail'. Should it be a supermarket or a departmental store? Even an electronics store was considered in this context. Finally, the all-male team zeroed in on retail men's wear. They knew the male psyche and felt that they had discerning taste in men's clothing. The concept would be that of a lifestyle store in a luxurious space, which would make the shopping an experience. The first Shoppers' Stop store took shape in Andheri, Mumbai, in October 1991, with an investment of nearly Rs 20 lakh. The second store in Bangalore came in 1995 and the third one in Hyderabad (1998), with the largest area of 60,000 sq ft. The New Delhi and Jaipur stores were inaugurated in 1999. In a span of nine years the annual turnover has reached Rs 160 crore.

Everything went fine right from the beginning, except for one strange happening. More than 60 per cent of the customers who walked into Shoppers' Stop in Mumbai were women, which gave rise to new ideas. Soon, the store set up its women's section and followed by the children's wear household accessories sections. The product range kept increasing to suit customer needs.

The Shoppers' Stop laid the ground rules, which the competition followed. It has leveraged expertise for critical components like technology from all over the world, going as far as hiring expatriates from the Little Woods and using the state-of-the-art ERP (enterprise resources planning) modules. The Shoppers' Stop even went a step further by integrating its financial system with the ERP model. The expertise was imported wherever it was felt that the expertise available in-house was inadequate.

One of the serious problem faced by Shopper's Stop in the course of its development was the availability of trained professionals. Since Indian acadmic scenario did not have the professional retail management course in the early years, people were hired from different walks of life and and an internal training programme was conducted to develop their skills. By 1994, the senior executives at the Shoppers' Stop were taking lectures at management institutions in Mumbai. The Narsee Monjee Institute of Management Studies (NMIMS) even restructured its course to include the retail management as a subject.

The company has also received an exclusive membership to the IGDS (Intercontinental Group of Department Stores) which gave the access to the latest global retail trends and exchange of information with the business greats. The IGDS allows membership by invitation to only one company from a country and Shoppers' Stop rubs shoulders with 29 of the hottest names in global retailing — the Selfridges from the UK, the C.K. Tang (Singapore) and the Lamcy Plaza (Dubai).

UNDERSTANDING THE CUSTOMER

With the logistics in place, the accent moved to the customer. The Shoppers' Stop conducted surveys with the ORG-MARG and the IMRB (Indian Market Research Bureau) and undertook in-house wardrobe audits. The studies confirmed its already held belief that the Indian customer is still evolving and is very different from, say, a European customer, who knows exactly what to purchase, walks up to a shelf, picks up the merchandise, pays and walks out. In India, however, the customers would like to touch and feel the merchandise, and scout for the options. Besides, the Indian shopper still prefers to pay in cash. Therefore, the transactions should be in money as against the plastic cards used the world over.

Additionally, the Indian custom likes being served, whether it is food or otherwise. Accordingly, the company prepared a customer profile which included: (a) the people who want the same salesperson each time they came to the store to walk them through the shop floors and assist in the purchase (b) those who came with families, kids and maids in tow and expected to be suitably attended to and (c) those who wanted someone to carry the bags. The shops, therefore, have self-help counters, with an assistant at hand for the queries or help. The company takes particular care not only in explaining the features of each item in the store, but also the relevance of each item to its customer.

The end result is that the Shopper's Stop has emerged as a premier Indian retail company that has come to be known as a specialty chain of apparel and accessories. With 52 product categories under one roof, Shoppers' Stop has a line-up of 350 brands. Set up and headed by former Carona employee, B.S. Nagesh, Shoppers' Stop is India's answer to Selfridges and Printemps. As it proudly announces, 'We don't sell, we help you buy'.

FIRST CITIZEN CLUB

Wal-mart's success hinges the way in uses its advanced customer shopping information. In tune with the global trend Shoppers'Stopn launched its first programme-First citizen club-FCC in 1994. It is based on 3-tier system with classic card at the entry level, followed by the silver and gold cards. A customer can sign on for the classic card either by spending Rs 2500 in any Shoppers' Stop outlet on a single day or by paying a membership fee of Rs 150. Members who accounted annual spend at least Rs 10,000 will be upgraded to silver card and when they crossed Rs 40,000 in their purchase will entitled for gold card membership. Silver and gold card members will get free subscription of First Update – the news magazine, which covers the latest arrival of goods in the shop. The Gold card members are invited for all exclusive events and get together organized by Shoppers' Stop.

With120,000-members, FCC customers account for 10 percent of entries and 34 per cent of the turnover. It was the sheer experience that kept pulling Shoppers' Stop customers back. Not one to let such an opportunity pass by, the company ran a successful ad campaign in print, for more than eight years. The theme is a TV spot, which likened the shopping experience to the slowing down of one's internal clock and its beauty, was aired. More recently, ads that spell out the store's benefits (in a highly oblique manner) are being aired. The campaign is based on entries made in the visitors' book. None of the ads has a visual - or text reference to the store or the merchandise. They show shoppers having the time of their lives in calm and serene locales, or elements that make shopping at the store a pleasure quite the perfect getaway for a cosmopolitan shopper aged between 25 and 45. The brief to the agency, Contract, ensured that brand recall came in terms of the shopping experience, not the product. And it has worked wonders.

Finally 5 % of 1.2 lakh members of FCC are gold card members followed by 35% with silver cards. Further 5 % of the customers of Shoppers' Stop in any outlet is from FCC, which accounted nearly 40-60% of the turn over. Over wheleming the success, Shoppers' Stop integrated JD Armstrong ERP package which integrates merchandise data with customer data

COST EFFECTIVENESS OF MAKING OFFERS

Trying to increase the size of the market through a one-time investment versus on going marketing costs requires repositioning the Shoppers' Stop's product lines to fit new markets. This generally requires some product modifications, not simply a sophisticated advertising campaign. Sophisticated statistical methods allow Shoppers' Stop to drive down the costs of making offers by matching customers with the appropriate products. This then increases the number of offers that can be made for the same cost, hence increasing the maximum add-on selling rates.

EXHIBIT 3

SHOPPERS' STOP IMPERATIVES FOR RELATIONSHIP MANAGEMENT

1. Know more about potential and in-store customers
2. Measure the asset value of each present and potential customer
3. Manage acquisition
4. Manage retention
5. Manage add on selling
6. Balance acquisition, retention, and add-on selling
7. Manage customer portfolios and
8. Tailor the marketing mix

MICRO-PROFILING OF INSTORE CUSTOMERS

Synergy communications conducted a study on the micro-profiling of Shoppers Stop customers in Chennai and to find out where the shoppers Stop stand amidst the competitors. The synergy charted out a programme for them. The research approach followed in the study was survey method. Stratified sampling method was resorted to for data collection from the population under study. The factors considered for the stratification of catchment areas were (i) the disposable income, socio-economic status in terms of their possession of vehicles, white goods, luxury products, and (iii) lifestyle, a mixed lot of 600 household and 300 in-store customers constituted the unit for data collection. The Statistical judgement sampling was resorted to for the study. Statistical analysis like Likert score and Analysis of variance were carried data analysis and interpretation.

MARKET STUDY FINDINGS

Based on the VALS concept, consultants categorise the various sections of customer buyer behaviour as follows:

i. The 'Evolved Housewives' and Industrialist / Businessmen with a monthly household income of Rs 30,000 and above are found to be more of 'Actualisers' and Achievers, the traditional housewives fall under the 'Strivers' and 'Makers' category. Students are found to be 'Experiencers'. The salaried junior executive falls under 'Believers'. Self-employed / Professionals are found to be 'Fulfillers'. There are transitions in the category with change in the demographic and psychographic factors.

ii. Consultants also observed several instances of customers shopping at a random fashion in the malls and also the their frequencies of shopping are more than once a week. This clearly shows drastic change take place in the life style of the people.

iii. Spencer Plaza and Pondy Bazaar dominate the list of the most shopped place for garments / accessories. The most preferred place of shopping among the retail super stores is lifestyle, followed by Globus and Shoppers' Stop respectively. The average spend by 32% of the respondents at their Favourite shopping place is Rs 501-100 while 22% of the respondents said their average spend at Shoppers' Stop is Rs 501-1000. So the average amount the customers spends does not vary. This gives an idea on the disposable income of the respondents.

iv. In general, respondents ranked Spencers' s First, Pondy Bazaar as second, lifestyle as third, Shoppers' Stop as fourth and Globus as fifth. Considering the new entrant malls, lifestyle leads the lot, followed by Shoppers' Stop and Globus respectively.

MICRO-PROFILING OF MALL CUSTOMERS:

i. It is observed from the findings of the study that 49% of the respondents owned a Credit card, and the other half did not have a Credit card. Fifty percent of the respondents possess air conditioners in their homes and car followed by 46% who had Personal Computers. Again 30% of the respondents were found to be fin the age group 21-25 yr. followed by 19% in 26-30 yr. And 12% in the age group of 31-35 yr.

ii. Regarding their occupation, 22% of respondents were self-employed / professionals followed by 21% of housewives were both traditional and evolved and 19% of salaried/clerks/Jr. executives. They contribute a major share of the target customers. The monthly household Income of 21.8% of the households were Rs 15001-20000, followed by 20.3% with Rs 10001-15000, a criterion that is useful to predict the purchasing power and disposable income of households.

Customer Entry Pattern

i. It is observed that 65% of the respondents were found to shop in random fashion, without specific occasions for Shopping. This depicts the purchase behaviour of respondents. On the overall scene, the instore respondents ranked Shopper's Stop as First. Spencer's Plaza as second, lifestyle as third, Globus as fourth and Pondy Bazaar as fifth. Considering the new entrant malls, Shoppers' Stop leads the lot, followed by lifestyle and Globus respectively. This portrays the brand loyalty among the instore customers of Shoppers' Stop.

ii. The Monthly Household Income of 33.3% of the households were Rs 30,000 and above, followed by 16.7% and 16% with Rs 20001-25000 and 15001-20000 respectively. This clearly portrays the high profile of the customers visiting Shopping malls, in terms of their household income. Again, 36.3% of the respondents were found to be in the age group 21-25 yr. followed by 19.3% in 26-30 yr. 12% of respondents were found to be in the age group of 31-35 yr. Clearly, the age group of customers entering Shopping mall is 21-35 years.

STATISTICAL ANALYSIS

While carrying out one way analysis, it was revealed that a significant relationship exists between the average amount spent/visit by the customer and their monthly household income (Table .1(a)). Again, ambience ranked high among the ideal characteristics of a shopping mall with a Likert score of 1.24 followed by quality of services provided with 1.20. However all malls have to improve their choices offered to the customers in terms of products category and price (Table 1(b)). Further a significant relationship was observed between occupation and frequency of visit among a in-store respondents.

Table 1 A	Relationship Between Average Amount Spend per Visit and Monthly Household income of the Household Respondents in the Catchment Area

Average spend per visit / Monthly Household Income (Rs.)	Upto Rs.500	Rs. 501 1000	Rs. 1001 -2000	Rs. 2001 -3000	Rs. 3001 -4000	Rs. 4001 -5000	Rs. 5001 above	Total
Upto 35 1000	15	10	22	8	9	6	105	
10001-2000	9	84	61	56	21	16	6	253
20001-25000	6	48	10	8	11	5	5	93
25001-30000	10	45	68	190	6	6	4	149
Total	60	192	149	96	46	36	21	600

Table 1 B	One-Way Analysis of Variance

Sources of Variation	Sum of Squares	Degree of Freedom	Mean Square
Between Samples	6076.36	$7 - 1 = 6$	1012.70
Within Samples	7620.50	$28 - 1 = 27$	282.24

Calculated Value of F = 3.58
Table Value of F = 2.46 (for d. f. 6, 27)

| Table 2 | Weighted Average method for Ranking of Shopping Places by the In-store Respondents | | | | | | | |

Shopping Place	1	2	3	4	5	Aggregate Score	Weighted Average	Rank
Spencers	88	50	43	58	25	910	3.03	II
Lifestyle	46	59	57	38	32	745	2.48	III
Pondy Bazar	24	27	27	37	47	430	1.43	V
Alsa Mall	5	9	13	21	48	190	0.63	VI
Rahat Plaza	6	4	8	5	49	129	0.43	IX
Shopper's Stop	96	100	60	41	9	1151	3.83	I
Globus	17	39	63	68	30	596	1.98	IV
Fountain	4	4	16	18	44	164	0.55	VIII
Others	14	8	13	14	16	185	0.61	VII

Note : The weightage assigned to the rank is as follows : 5 for 1st, 4 for 2nd, 3 for 3rd, 2 for 4th and 1 for 5th ranks)

| Table 3 | Showing Likert's rating scale for ideal characteristics of shopping malls in Chennai | | | | | | |

Character-istics/Rating	Excellent	Good	Fair	Poor	Very Poor	Aggr-egate Score	Likert's Score
Ambience	114	151	28	7	0	372	1.24
Quality	87	159	43	7	4	361	1.20
Variety	54	136	77	23	10	201	0.67
Price Range	23	127	101	28	21	103	0.34
Customer Service	76	159	38	11	16	268	0.89

Note : The weightage assigned to the characteristics is as follows : Excellent = 2, Good = 1, Fair = 0, Poor = –1 and Very poor = – 2.

THE CASE

Shoppers' Stop is in the process of establishing tie-ups with Planet M and its store in Chennai will be the first to have a whole floor dedicated to books and music. Big plans are being chalked out and the growth curve is expected to peak in the next 2-3 years. A credit line from 1CICI Bank and internal accruals will fund expansion plans. The study conducted in Chennai for shoppers stop by synergy marketing displays the changing cultural trends and the life style of the people of Chennai. It is generally observe that shopping has taken the form of an entertainment in to-day's' scenario. Shopping malls have the ability to attract customers and make them stay longer than they planned to, and spend more than they had planned to. In this context prepare a promotion e-strategy and divisibility campaign for Shoppers stop.

CUSTOMER ACQUISITION STRATEGIES

3

"You have to live with your product, you have to know it through and through, you have to look at it, understand it, love it then, and only then, you can crystallise in one clear thought, one single theme, what must be conveyed about the product to the consumer."

Bill Bernbach

Learning Objectives

After reading this chapter you should understand:
- The meaning of Customer acquisition strategy
- The relevance of value claim and accounting standards
- Customer Life Cycles-its various stages
- How behaviour marketing is carried out
- The ACTMAN model

INTRODUCTION

The customer relationship marketing strategies are built around three core concepts: **(a)** acquisition, **(b)** retention and **(c)** add-on selling. From the moment a company decides to target the prospective customers to the time these customers make their final purchase, these strategies provide a framework for all marketing decisions. If a relationship marketing manager attempts to learn what is unique about a particular customer, he should go beyond the transaction-based view of understanding the customer. Instead, he should have a picture of the customer as a whole. This picture should be a composite make up of several tangible and intangible factors, including **(1)** the transaction history, **(2)** the socioeconomic characteristics, **(3)** the behavioural traits, **(4)** the long-term potential for additional services, and **(5)** the identification of customer uniqueness. Three key points should be kept in mind in this regard:

First, each firm should be aware of its focus on each stage of its customer relationship and ways of strengthening it.

Second, the strongest customer relationships are built on recognising and acting on the customer's uniqueness, a goal that could be accomplished in various ways.

Finally, the firm should be aware of the key business statistic involved in this process, the customer value which gives a benchmark estimate of the potential involved in this strategy.

The marketing mix of any product or service varies significantly depending on its stage in the customer life-cycle. The prospect marketing is generally focused on awareness generation and trial promotions, whereas the core customer marketing is focused on retention vehicles, pricing, and reinforcing (attitudinal) communication strategies. During the course of time, the firm would develop unique marketing mix strategies by analysing the responses of the life-cycle segment.

The firm should have the ability to balance the number of customers being acquired with the number defecting and this requires the determination of the number of customers in each stage of the customer life-cycle and an anticipation of their migration paths.

We begin our discussion with the concept of customer life-cycle.

3.1 CUSTOMER LIFE-CYCLE

If the firm has too aggressive an acquisition programme, and many early repeat buyers who defect, the company would face a significant cash flow problem. The firms should track the number of customers in each stage of the life-cycle to determine the nature of customer purchasing patterns and thereby the cash flow.

Robert C. Blattberg (2001), a Harvard Business School Professor, has identified five stages in a typical customer life-cycle:

> ➤ Prospects
> ➤ First – Time Buyers
> ➤ Early Repeat Buyers
> ➤ Core Customers
> ➤ Core Defectors

Stage 1: Prospects

The prospects are not yet customers, but they represent potential value (The highly qualified prospects are particularly important.). The firms should manage the prospects as they would treat their initial customers. During the prospect stage, the consumer develops an initial set of expectations about a product or service. If these expectations exceed the customer's product, in other words the quality cut off, the customer would make the first purchase. The quality of the products that the customer already uses, along with information about the new product by the firm through its marketing communications, determines his or her product-quality cutoff. The price is also an important element in this transaction; in other words, the product or service must meet a value cutoff as well.

Stage: 2 First - Time Buyers

The customers move into this stage after making one purchase. These newly acquired customers usually have the lowest retention rates within a firm's customer base. Although they have signalled that the firm's products have met their specifications, they are still in the evaluation stage. They should further get convinced whether the products and customer service levels could meet their expectations. If the product meets the expectations and remains above the quality cut off, the customer would continue to purchase and could be retained as long as the product's value is maintained. If the product does not meet the expectations, the customer would stop purchasing and defect. During these early repeat purchases, just one product failure (in which the product falls below the customer's quality cut off) can cause a defection.

Stage 3: Early Repeat Buyers

The customers advance to this stage after making one repeat purchase. These customers are more likely to buy again than the first-time buyers, and the sales per customer increase as they gain confidence with the firm. However, although two to three repeat purchases indicate the satisfaction with the product, these early repeat buyers are still evaluating the relationship. If the firm provides poor service or the product does not meet the expectations, the customer may defect.

Stage 4: Core Customers

The customers enter the core customer stage once they start making the repeat purchases in a regular manner. The firm's product or service meets their required specifications and value. Unless a major problem arises with the purchasing process, these customers rarely re-evaluate the firm's product. The core customer stage has the highest retention rates and the highest sales per customer. These customers are special and should be treated as such.

Stage 5: Core Defectors

At some point, the core customers become willing to switch suppliers or brands. Several factors can cause this and this include **(1)** competing products or services, **(2)** a customer service problem that was not rectified in a proper manner, or **(3)** boredom. The firm can reactivate a defector if the underlying problem is recognised and rectified. Often, the firms fail to identify the defectors and do not act to bring them back into the fold.

3.2   SEGMENTATION

The segmentation is a way of compartmentalising customers on the basis of the characteristics that affect their behaviour in the market (buying, media etc). There are mainly four types of segmentation:

> ➢ Analytical segmentation
> ➢ Response segments
> ➢ Strategic segmentation
> ➢ Delivered loyalty segmentation

a. Analytical Segmentation In analytical segmentation, the firm analyses the customer and market information to identify the different groups of customers with different profiles, needs and so on. The process begins with broad questions such as: What kinds of customer do the company have? What is their behaviour? Which products or channels are the most successful at managing them?

b. Response Segmentation In response segmentation, the firm identifies different groups of customers for targeting the particular 'promotion' drives. A given customer may belong to a whole series of different segments, according to the objectives of individual promotions. The key success criterion for response segmentation is the success of each of the promotions (i.e. whether the response rates meet the expectations, whether final purchase hit the firms targets or not).

c. Strategic Segmentation The strategic segmentation implies the identification of groups of customers (say for a bank like ICICI Prudential), who should be handled in a distinct manner. For example, the mass-market insurance service provider should identify:

> ➢ the customers who are likely to be of higher insurance risks (in which case their premium will be usually accepted at lower policy benefits which covers the basic risk)
> ➢ the customers who are likely to be moderate or low risk (in which case their premium will be accepted at higher interest rate/bonus/ loyalty addition which covers a range of risk).

Conversely, the low risk or high risk customers will be targeted and marketed to in an intensive manner, and particular attention should be given to the quality of the relationship established with them.

d. Delivered Loyalty Segmentation This is a special case of strategic segmentation. Here, particular groups of actual or potential customers whose loyalty is critical to the firm are identified. Normally, the process relates to the volume and profitability of the business coming from these groups of customers, but it can also be related to other variables (like political sensitivity).

Table 3.1   Charecteristics of Segmentation types

	Analytical	Response	Strategic	Loyalty
Technical approach	Can be left to expect systems and data-mining approaches	Expert/data mining approaches may be used	In-depth business understanding required to define issue	In-depth business understanding required to define issue
Senior management involement	Not required, except to ensure that capability exists	Required if the promotions involves a large share of marketing budget	Important in defining areas of strategic focus	Absolutely critical because of subsequent commitment to comprehensive loyalty management approach
Customer contact implications	Depends on conclusion	Customers experience correctly defined and promotions targeted accordingly	Customers may be required to give more information and should find that they are being offered more appropriate products and services	Customers who are loyal or those having the propensity to be so experience more integgrated management, whatever be the contact point and whatever the product or services.

Source: Jagdish N. Sheth and Atul Parvatiyar (Editors), *Handbook of Relationship Marketing,* Response Books, 2002 with permission

A key aspect of the information systems is that most of the firms use the research findings in planning and managing their relationship.

3.3   ACQUISITION TACTICAL MANAGEMENT (ACTMAN)

The ACTMAN model as suggested by Robert C. Blattberg, Gary Getz and

Jacquelyn* has distilled the acquisition process into six critical elements that a firm could manage for more efficient and effective customer acquisition. These elements include:

> ➤ Targetting;
> ➤ Awareness building;
> ➤ Acquisition pricing;
> ➤ Product trial;
> ➤ Product design; and
> ➤ Post-purchase service.

Targetting

The firm should target both sets of customers: **(a)** who recognise that they have a need or desire for the firm's offerings as well as **(b)** those who have not yet identified their needs or desires, but who could benefit from the firm's offerings. The latter group may be more difficult to acquire because the firm will have to aid their need recognition using vehicles such as suggestive advertising or sampling.

Three methods exist for targeting the customers:

> ➤ individual customer targeting (first degree targeting);
> ➤ segmented targeting (second-degree targeting); and
> ➤ self-selection targeting (third-degree targeting), which relies on the customer to identify himself or herself by responding to the firm's offers.

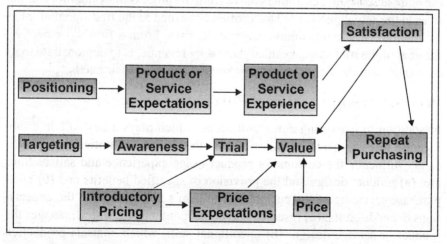

Source: Robert C. Blattberg, Gary Getz, Jacquelyn, Customer equity, Harvard Business School Press, Boston USA 2001

---

*All Harvard Business School professors, and the model was put forward in 2001

Awareness Building

While the customers are in the information-gathering stage of their purchase decision-making process, the firm should have a proper management of the critical steps of awareness building and positioning in order to include the product or service in the customer consideration set. The firms should also be aware of the fact that if the positioning and awareness generation efforts promise too much, then the customers may try the product, but the retention rates will fall short as a result of customer dissatisfaction. Therefore, the firm should carefully balance its initial positioning against the product's ability to deliver the promised benefits, or risk destroying the potential customer equity from retention and add-on selling.

Acquisition Pricing

Acquisition pricing can greatly influence the expectations about retention pricing. The acquisition price acts as a reference price for customers in their assessment of future prices. If the retention price is too high in comparison to the reference price, the customers are less likely to repurchase the product or service. As a result, the pricing strategy should include how a firm will manage the change in price between acquisition and retention. If a very low acquisition price attracts the prospects who would not otherwise try the product, then charging a significantly higher retention price would cost the firm a large number of first-time buyers.

Many firms identify the product trial as a key strategic objective. It marks the point at which the customers move from the process of evaluating alternatives to the actual purchase. This is often construed as the first signal of interest that the customers communicate to the firm. From a firm's perspective, the goal of the trial stage, besides generating revenue, is to demonstrate to its customers that the firm's product or service can meet their needs.

Product Design and Post-Purchase Servicing

In addition to marketing communications, which plays a key role in establishing the customer expectations, two other critical activities that significantly influence the customer's product usage experience and satisfactions are: **(a)** product design and the provision of specified benefits and **(b)** post-purchase servicing of the customer. The firm's ability to meet the expectations depends on its: **(a)** research and development team, which manages the product or service design; **(b)** operational staff, which controls production and delivery; and **(c)** customer services team, which manages the post-purchase servicing.

3.4 COMPUTING ACQUISITION EQUITY

Computing acquisition equity (CAE) sets the stage for using the customer equity data in a company's accounting system. According to Blattberg (2001), the (CAE) is a straight forward process (the only difficulty being in obtaining the data to make the computations), and it consists of six steps which include:

a. Determining the number of prospects contracted over a fixed time period from a completed acquisition campaign;

b. Measuring the marketing and servicing costs associated with contacting and selling to the prospects;

c. Determining the number of prospects who became customers;

d. Computing the sales revenue and gross margin for the new customers' first set of purchases;

e. Computing the acquisition equity of the entire pool of customers by subtracting the costs calculated in step 2 from the revenues calculated in step 4 (Note that this equity number can be negative.); and

f. Dividing the total acquisition equity by the number of customers to determine the average acquisition equity per customer.

Exhibit 3.1

CUSTOMER ACQUISITION ACCOUNTING MEASURES*

Top management is often surprised by the costliness of customer acquisition. Basic knowledge of acquisition costs, initial profit to cost ratios and new customer investment statistics should provide management with a better understanding of their business. As these measures become more widely used, the firms can benchmark other firms in similar industries.

CAC (Cost of Acquiring a Customer) $= \dfrac{Pc_P}{Pa} = \dfrac{C_P}{a} = Ca$

where,

cp = the cost per prospect of acquisition marketing

a = the fraction of prospects acquired (this is firm's customer acquisition rate)

P = the number of prospects targeted

CI (Customer Investment) $= Pc_p$

where,

c_p = cost per prospect of acquisition marketing and

P = total number of prospects targeted

P/C (Initial Profit per Customer Divided by Cost of Acquiring a

$$\textbf{Customer)} = \frac{m}{C_p/a} = \frac{am}{C_p}$$

where:

a = the fraction of prospects acquired

c_p = the cost per prospect of acquisition marketing

m = the incremental gross margin (in value) made on the first year's sales

Source: www.customerequity.com

3.5 PROFILING

Behaviour-based relationship marketing begins with customer profiling. The term customer profiling involves a wide range of marketing and service approaches. Profiling can be as simple as retaining a credit card information at an e-commerce site or as complex as correlating a customer's demographic information with the relevant market segment statistics. The purpose of profiling is to identify potential customers who could generate the maximum profit and determine the best possible ways of marketing to those customers, be it individuals or business enterprises. However, effective utilisation of customer profiling has been a big challenge for every business enterprise.

The simplest way suggested to determine the ways of targetting new customers is to profile the existing ones. While profiling, a firm identifies the characteristics of its best current customers and then targets the non-customers with similar characteristics. These "non-customers" can be first-time purchasers from the firm, or individuals who have purchased from other divisions of the firm.

Difference Between a Profile and a Model

The basic difference between a profile and a model is the element of time involved, making models more powerful predictors of customer behavior. Modelling is a kind of like profiling, but it is action oriented. Models are not about a static state (like a customer profile which records 'the customer is 50 years old); rather they involve action over time (like 'if this customer does not make a purchase in the next 30 days, they are unlikely to come back and make any further purchases with our company). Therefore the marketers who use customer data often talk about customer modelling instead of customer profiling.

Demographic and Behavioural Profiles

Consider the two profiles

Profile: 1 Customer is married, has children, lives in an upscale neighborhood, and reads *Economic Times* newspaper

Profile: 2 Customer visited the site every day for 2 months, but has not visited the site at all in the past 2 weeks

The first profile, involving a set of characteristics is demographic, while the second profile involving the real action of a customer is behaviour-based. Both are important in their own ways. For someone in the advertisement department, or while deciding the content for a website, the first profile is usually important because it defines the market for ad sales and provides clues to editorial direction. *The demographic profile provides vital help in attracting the customer and generating revenue in the early stages of an online project.*

The second profile is more concerned with the customer action and behavior. (Regular questions sought to be answered by observing the behaviour profile include: Will they visit again? Will they buy again?) The customer behaviour is a much prominent predictor of the future relationship with a customer than the demographic information. The data based on customer behaviour provide a better criterion for the business enterprises while forecasting their sales/transactions. Therefore, customer behavior profiling is critical to a company interested in retaining its customers and increasing their value. However, the combination of both the demographic and behavioural characteristics could serve as a powerful database in deciding the future profitability of a customer to a business enterprise

Prior to the computerisation of banking and other retailing operations, organisations used to deal with their customers through a direct human interaction. The local shop manager knew his regular customers personally, as did the clerk at the local bank branch, and they could make sensible judgments on the types of products to be offered on the basis of their observation of the customer behaviour. The introduction of computers has enlarged the scope of organisational activity and provide better services to their customers. The computerisation has also helped in reducing errors and operational costs dramatically.

Best Customer Profiling and Indexing

The best customer profiling technique is a relatively simple form of profiling. The major steps involved in the process include:

➢ Collecting demographic and profitability information about current customers;

➢ Appending this information to each customer record in a profiling database;

> ➤ Adding behavioural (such as sales histories) and other psychographic data to each profile;

> ➤ Determining the variables that distinguishes the best and worst customers, and non-responders; and

> ➤ Application of these variables to identify the 'high-potential' prospects.

Indexing, another form of profiling, compares the general population of a product's customers with the existing customers of the firm for that product. The major steps involved include:

> ➤ Compartmentalising customers in the database using several demographic variables

> ➤ Determining the number of buyers that fall into each partition. The index for each partition reflects the ratio of the number of customers of the firm in that partition to the total number of the buyers in the general population that fit that partition.

However, a note of caution should be maintained while interpreting the profiling indices as: **(a)** Some segments might have a high targeting potential, but not appear frequently in the database; therefore, the profiling is less likely to identify them as attractive targets: **(b)** A firm should assess the potential customer equity of each partition before the application of a profiling technique to target new customers: **(c)** A segment with a low index may actually be a very high asset value segment that the firm's acquisition strategy could underemphasise: and **(d)** Profiling does not include the statistical analyses required to assess the strength of various characteristics as predictors.

3.6   REGRESSION SCORING

Regression scoring is a more difficult, but more accurate technique than profiling. Business enterprises generally employs regression scoring, to target new customers. The process involved in regression scoring include:

1. Drawing a random sample from the overall population of prospective customers;

2. Obtaining data from the sample that profile individual consumer characteristics;

3. Initiating a marketing campaign directed at the random sample and recording the potential individuals who could become customers; and

4. Developing a regression scoring model from the above information—a series of weighted variables that predicts the prospective individuals that are more likely to become customers based on their characteristics.

The preparation of the model estimates should be followed by a series of steps which include:

➢ Calculating the scores for prospects who were not in the random sample by plugging their individual characteristics into the regression equation

➢ Ranking and ordering of prospects from highest to lowest, according to their scores

➢ Targetting the prospects of the firm's marketing campaign with scores above a designated cut off, which is computed on the basis of a combination of financial and marketing factors

Advantages and Disadvantages of RS Models

The primary advantages of using regression scoring models for acquisition are that they could **(a)** measure the relative importance of variables in determining the prospects that should be targetted, and **(b)** provide a scientific method for selecting the cut off values. Thereby the model helps a business enterprise in developing the marketing efficiency of a firm in a significant manner.

The primary disadvantages of regression scoring is its complexity in comparison to profiling.

In spite of its complexity and costs in implementation, the application of regression scoring in the functioning of a business enterprise has been emphatically recommended, even if it involves utlising resources from the outside, owing to the efficiency and effectiveness it could impart in the functioning of an organisation.

3.7 NET PRESENT VALUE (NPV) OF A CUSTOMER

The NPV of a customer is a critical measure that evaluates the future potential of a new customer. It has also been referred to as the **life time value (LTV)** of a new customer. In simple terms, the NPV is the sum of all future purchases (that could be made by a new customer) *minus* the cost of goods sold and the future marketing expenses.

$$\text{NPV of a Customer} = \frac{\text{Future potential of customer}}{\text{Cost of goods sold } plus \text{ Future marketing expenses}}$$

The concept of NPV is elaborated in Exhibit 3.2

Exhibit 3.2

> **CUSTOMER ACQUISITION ACCOUNTING MEASURES**

> ### Steps involved in Computing the New Customer Net Present Value
>
> 1. Compute the **survival rate** (the probability that a customer will survive each year post-acquisition): By multiplying the previous year's survival rate by the current year's retention rate; the first-year survival rate is the same as that year's retention rate.
>
> 2. Compute the **customer profitability per year**: By multiplying customer sales per year times the gross margin per cent.
>
> 3. Compute the **expected profit per year**: By multiplying the customer profit per year by the survival rate for that year.
>
> 4. Compute the **discounted expected profit per year**: By dividing the expected profit for the year by one plus the discount rate raised to the power of the number of years since the customer was acquired.
>
> 5. Compute the **discounted total profit**: By the addition of the discounted expected profits per year across all years (past and present).
>
> 6. Compute the **net present value of customer**: By the addition of discounted total profit with the profit or loss incurred during the first year of the customer-firm relationship
>
> NCNPV (New Customer Net Present Value) =
>
> $$(m_1 - c_a) + \sum_{t-1}^{\infty} \frac{r_t}{(1+d)^t} \, (a_t m_t - c_{r,t})$$
>
> where: c_a = the acquisition cost of the customer; m_t = the gross margin at time t; r_t is the fraction of customers remaining at the start of time t (i.e., the survival rate from time t-1); $c_{r,t}$ = the marketing and customer service costs associated with retaining a customer at the beginning of time t; t = the fraction of customers retained in period t (i.e., the retention rate in period t); and d = the cost of capital for the firm

Source: www.customerequity.com

3.8 ESTIMATING FUTURE VALUE OF ACQUIRED CUSTOMERS

Business enterprises should understand the future value of acquired customers so that they could arrive at a sound judgement on the profitability of investing in new customers. If it is not found profitable, the business firm should change its acquisition approach. The customer-focused data could be employed, among other things, to decide on the following:

> Identifying target customer segments;

> Determining customer acquisition rates;

> Determining customer retention and defection rates;

> Identifying opportunities for add-on selling;

> Understanding and evaluating consumer responsiveness to marketing programmes;

> Tracking and analysing customer buying patterns;

> Measuring the economic value of the customer;

> Forecasting and managing future customer behaviour; and

> Developing more effective customer-focused strategies;

SUMMARY

✓ In relationship marketing one should focus on three things– Strengthening firm–customer relationship, understanding the uniqueness of each customer and analysing customer value

✓ The various stages of customer life-cycle are: prospects, first time buyers, early repeat buyers, core customers and core defectors.

✓ The various aspects of segmentation are: analytical segmentation, response segment, strategic segmentation and delivered loyalty regimentation

✓ ACTMAN distills the acquisition process in a firm. It has six critical elements.

✓ Various degrees of targeting exist as a means to acquire different customers

✓ Acquisition equity sets the stage for using customer equity data in the company's accounting system and this involves 6 steps.

✓ Profiling is key towards behaviour based marketing; it is different from modelling

✓ Profiling can be demographic, behaviour-based and even index-based.

✓ Regression has many advantages in comparison to profiling as it could measure relative importance of variables.

CHAPTER REVIEW QUESTIONS

1. What do you mean by customer acquisition strategy?

2. Explain how relationship building can be represented through value chain and accounting standards.

3. What do you mean by customer life-cycle?

4. Explain the segmentation process for a new generation bank like ICICI.

5. Elucidate the relevance of ACTMAN model.

CASE STUDY
CADILLA.COM –TURNING BROWSERS INTO BUYERS

"We want to integrate the click stream, transactional and demographic data into one comprehensive whole that will allow us to model the customer behavior and to target the campaigns and response rates to figure ROI on our marketing investments"

Aravind CEO, Cadilla.com

BACKGROUND

The consumers across the US, Asia and Europe are familiar with the trusted Cadilla brand name. The pharmaceutical chain had served more than a quarter billion prescription orders in 2003. In a bold move to reach out to their existing customer base and attract new customers, the company launched the Cadilla.com, a web-based customer serving enterprise. Presently, the Cadilla promotes their products and services via both the storefront shops and online, making them a formidable force in the retail pharmacy sector.

MOVING BEYOND CLICKS

The Cadilla.com realised that they should increase their market share rapidly to become an online industry leader. They had an extensive database about the number of customers accessing their site, and how many clicked through the online advertisements. However, the exact reasons for their visit, and the ways of attracting more real buyers, and the nature of advertisements that could actually generate the revenue, rather than just traffic, remained a mystery. The Cadilla.com wanted to identify the behaviour patterns of consumers who made the online purchases, and compare that information with the consumer interaction data from their web logs and demographic data. Specifically, they wanted to compare the behavioural patterns of visitors that made online purchases and modify their marketing strategy accordingly on a daily basis, so that they could target those browsers, who reflected the behaviour pattern of their most profitable buyers, in a better fashion.

Cadilla Strategy

"In relationship marketing, we don't rely on "remembering" the habits of thousands of customers; we measure their behaviour and react on the basis of these measurements" says Nirmita, the relationship manager of Cadilla.com. Generally, the relationship marketing attempts to define the customer behaviour and then looks for the variances in the behaviour. "When we hear people talk about "predictive modelling" or looking for "patterns" using data mining, they are essentially taking a behavioural approach using the latest tools", says Nirmita. " Once the firm know how the "normal" customers behave, they can do two things with their business approach:

> Formally document the normal customer behaviour and internalise it systemically, leveraging what the firm knows to improve the business functionality and profitability

> Set up the early warning systems, or "trip wires" to alert the company to any customer behaviour outside the expected norm. This variance in behaviour generally signals an opportunity to take action with the customer and increase their value—online or offline."

Aravind, CEO of Cadilla.com believes that "What is most important to measure in the relationship marketing is "change". People spend too much time worrying about the "absolute" numbers, like the life-time value. What they should really look at is the change in "relative" numbers over time." Similarly, "It's not nearly as important to know the absolute value of a customer as it is to know whether this value is rising or falling, according to the stages in the customer life-cycle. A comprehensive understanding of the customer life-cycle is the most powerful marketing tool the firm can have."

Generally, the customers in the aggregate tend to follow similar behavioural patterns, and when any single customer deviates from the norm, it could be the forewarning of a problem (or opportunity) ahead. Several factors should be taken into consideration at this point.

> The extend of the customer's behaviour outside the norm

> Whether the variance is a potential problem

> Whether the customer is happily inquiring about adding on more services

> Whether the customer is having any difficulty in understanding the use of the advanced services on the phone

In the last two cases, the company has an opportunity to increase the value of the customer, if the firm has the ability to recognise the opportunity and react to it in a timely manner.

As against the common terminology in estimation, there is no 'average customer', and a business will have many different customer groups, each exhibiting their own kind of 'normal' behaviour. This 'raising of the hand' behaviour by the customers, and the reaction by the marketers, is termed the **feedback loop** which is at the center of relationship or lifecycle-based marketing process. The feedback loop is a repeating 'action-reaction-feedback' cycle.

The customer provides the feedback through action (they cancel the service, or they add service). The marketer reacts to this action, perhaps with a 'win-back campaign', or with a 'thank you' note. The cycle is a constant (and mostly non-verbal) conversation, an ongoing relationship with the customer requiring the interaction to sustain. It is not a relationship in the "buddy-buddy" sense. The general assumption is that the customer does not want to get friendly with a company in an overt manner, but they would like to have the company responsive to their needs, even if they never come out and state the fact to the company in an open manner.

BUILDING LONG-TERM RELATIONSHIP THROUGH LATENCY

The relationship of every customer with the company is assumed to be continuous, till the existence of 'value' in the relationship for both parties. If the customer takes an action and there is no reaction from the marketer, the value begins to slide from the customer's side, giving a chance of defection in the long process. When the value disappears for the marketer (the customer stops taking action / providing feedback), the marketers should stop spending incremental money on the customer. The customers who are in the process of changing their behaviour either by accelerating their relationship with the company products, or terminating their relationship with the product, could be looked upon as the highest potential return customers from a marketing perspective.

However, when the firm can predict the likelihood of an average customer who could be developed into a best customer, and successfully implement a plan process that could encourage this behavioural change process, or when the company can reverse a customer defection before its occurrence, the customer relation strategy of the company could be termed as a positive one. The firm could discover these opportunities through a sagacious knowledge about the customer behaviour and setting up trip wires to alert the company of any deviations from the normal behavior. "Set up the company trip wires and predict the behaviour through these techniques. It's the only way to sense when an average customer is ready to become a best customer. And reacting to a customer defection after the fact is a truly sub-optimal way to "manage" a relationship." says Aravind. The concepts of latency, recency and the RFM analysis can also be utilised to an effective manner while formulating plans for the aforesaid situations.

The concept of trip wires could be introduced in various ways. For example, a win-back programme is triggered when the customer defects. Similarly, the company could also make an effective use of the concept of latency [which refers to the average time relapsed between the customer activity events (for example, making a purchase, calling the help desk, or visiting a web site)] as a trip wire in their anti-defection campaigns.

At the core of a life cycle-based marketing approach is the customer behaviour. The behaviour of customers have a certain degree of uniqueness while dealing with the services and products of a particular company, and if the firm could identify these patterns, they can apply them for a better prediction of the customer behaviour.

New Technology Initiative

When a company relationship manager like Nirmita sees a particular customer's behavior diverge from the average customer behaviour, she gets a trip wire event. Since the calculation of latency is very simple, and the diverging behaviour is easy to spot, she immediately sets in an anti-defection campaign as the divergence could be an ideal candidate for "lights-out" or automated rules-based customer retention campaigns.

Nirmita had identified the product as an ideal one for setting trip wires for Cadilla.com as she was very particular about the option provided by the package. This option provided her with the following features:

➢ a full view of their customer base from multiple data feeds,

➢ exceptional visualisation tools;

➢ quick request process mechanism against the very large Cadilla.com customer databases;

➢ easy integration of IT with other relationship marketing requirements.

"We want to integrate the clickstream, transactional and demographic data into one comprehensive whole that will allow us to model the customer behaviour and to target campaigns and response rates to figure the ROI on our marketing investments. They took a slice of our data-web logs, transactions and demographic data-and put it into their tool. We were able to slice and dice on command—it was absolutely breathtaking." Aravind, CEO, Cadilla.com, said in *PC Week* (January 2003).

This flexibility to drill down and analyse the consumer behaviour, and provide the incentive programmes in an immediate manner is exactly what the Cadilla.com marketing department had been searching for. The customer conversion provided them with an excellent opportunity to closely look at all their customer data (and also made them dealing with the "why..."and "what if..." questions).

THE CASE

In the first place, the Cadilla was able to achieve a considerable ROI through appropriate site changes and implementation of effective problem solving techniques which could respond in a quick fashion (enabling them to correct their mistakes quickly besides helping them in targetting other key audiences). The Cadilla.com could now look at the reaction of consumers to special offers, track the nature of consumers who are accessing their site, and make purchases. Most importantly, this increased awareness provided Cadilla.com with a strategic advantage in formulating their ways to achieve their goals, increase market share and build a loyal customer base.

1. Discuss the relationship tools and strategies which the Cadilla.com could make for establishing its relationship with the customer.

CUSTOMER RETENTION STRATEGIES

4

"There is nothing more difficult to carry out, nor more doubtful of success than to initiate a new order of things. For the reformer has enemies in all those who profit by the old order."

Niccolo Machiavelli, The Prince

Learning Objectives

After reading this chapter you should understand:

- ■ The significance and implementation of customer retention and its various stages.
- ■ How customer retention can be represented through value chain.
- ■ Learn more about retention strategies.

INTRODUCTION

The rising interest in relationship marketing in the early 1990s has served as a catalyst to work on the concept of customer retention, particularly on the impact of customer retention on profitability. In their pioneering work, Reichheld and Sasser have found a high correlation between customer retention and the profitability in a range of industries. Based on a survey of the literature on customer retention, Clark and Payne identified some key concepts for retention improvement. Many researchers have also proposed a three-stage corporate strategy; **(a)** customer retention measurement, **(b)** identification of causes of defection and key service issues, and **(c)** corrective action, to improve retention in the long run. The first stage, the customer retention measurement, is of considerable interest to both academics and managers and we begin our discussion with the need for customer retention.

4.1 SIGNIFICANCE OF CUSTOMER RETENTION

Traditionally, the focus of business enterprises have been on making sales rather than building relationship—the emphasis being laid on pre-selling and selling, rather than on the customer care afterward. Unfortunately, even most of the marketing theories and practices also center on the art of attracting new customers rather than retaining and improving relationship with the existing ones. It would be expedient for a business firm to make a regular assessment of its customer satisfaction, as it is an essential determinant of its customer retention capabilities. The general assumptions in this context are that a highly satisfied customer would **(a)** stay loyal for a longer period of time, **(b)** buy more when the company introduces new products and upgrades its existing products, **(c)** talk favourably about the company and its products, **(d)** pay less attention to the competing brands and is less sensitive to price, **(e)** offer product or service ideas to the company and, above all **(f)** cost less to serve than the new customers because transactions are routine.

Customer Retention Defined

The customer retention could be simply defined as *the capability of the business firm's offer to its customer to purchase or patronage its product or service over a specified time period.* This could be possible mainly by delighting the customer with some surprise services/offers. These services/offers need not be considered as a costly affair as it could turn beneficial for the business enterprise in the long run. However, not all products (especially high valued, low–frequency–of–purchase products) are frequently purchased to make this definition universally applicable [For example, in the financial service industry, a customer who does not buy a tax-saving bond from the Reserve Bank of India (RBI) /the Industrial Development Bank of India (IDBI) / the Industrial Credit Investment Corporation of India (ICICI) within a fixed time period (e.g., a quarter or year) may nonetheless intend to buy, when his tax burden is within limits]. This leads to an alternative definition of customer retention:

➢ *for products with short purchase cycles:* The customer continues to purchase the product or service over a specified time period.

➢ *for products with long purchase cycles :* The customer indicates the intention to purchase the product or service at the next purchase occasion.

The customer loyalty is not merely created by the costs-selling strategies or the customer cloud. The loyalty is a physical and emotional commitment given by a customer in exchange for their needs being met. Therefore, an effective retention strategy should reflect a thorough understanding of the customer behaviour and needs. Some companies think that they are getting a sense of customer satisfaction by tallying the customer complaints, though research findings have revealed that nearly 96 per cent of the dissatisfied customers do not complain: most of them just stop buying. Therefore, a business enterprise should devise simpler and easier mechanisms and procedures by which the customer could address his/her complaints in an easy manner. Suggestion forms, toll-free numbers and e-mail addresses could serve as effective tools for this purpose. For instance, the 3M Company, which specialises in stationary products, has made over two-third of its product improvement ideas come from listening to customer complaints.

4.2   MAJOR CUSTOMER RETENTION STAGES

The concept of customer retention could be differntiated into various stages, with increasing loyalty commitment from the customer matched by increasing service levels and bonus. Following are the major customer retention stages observed by a relationship oriented firm:

1. Welcome Cycle

This is an opportunity to welcome and reassure the customers, build loyalty and gain additional customer information. The stage also serves an opportunity for the firm to serve the customer with the initial offers. The appropriateness of the welcome cycle is directly related to the length of life-cycle of the customers.

2. Upselling

Given a positive reaction to the product / service, the next natural step would be to promote the higher-value product/service. In the case of a bank credit card, say from HDFC, it could be a privileged customer gold card, or in the case of a music product it could be a package of albums that could appeal a buyer of a single CD/cassette album. The appropriate timing of the offer could be determined by the previous customer histories. Most often, this could be achieved by testing and applying the test results using the regression analysis to the customer database to give each record an individual score. (The IT-enabled marketing techniques are discussed in Chapters 8 and 9)

3. Cross-selling

This is a conscious strategy to switch your customers across the product categories. For a HDFC VISA credit card, it could be promoting a home shopping service or a travel club. For a book, it could be a collection of music albums. In both up and cross-selling, some incentive should be provided to retain the loyalty of loyal customers. This concept is discussed in detail in Chapter 5.

4. Renewal

The length of the renewal cycle should be tested to achieve the optimum results for the minimum expenditure. Inducements to reward the loyal customers for their continued patronage are the cost effective tactics. Often a renewal cycle would represent a number of timed, relevant, and personal communications before the date of renewal, on the date of renewal, and after the date of renewal. Once the customer has passed the final renewal cycle date, the customer becomes lapsed.

5. Lapsed Customers

Reawakening the lapsed customer is a more cost-effective process than the recruiting of a totally new customer, unless they have lapsed because of a fundamental problem in the relationship (e.g. product quality) or because they have passed out of the target market (e.g. ageing). There may also be problems with the quality of the information about the lapsed customers. However, when the data on lapsed customers is available, its value could be tested, and therefore the profitability on promotions to lapsed customers does not have to be guessed.

6. Inactive Customers

The cost-effectiveness is a critical issue in this aspect also. The inactive customers are people who have not bought any product or responded to a promotion for a longer period than the lapsed customers. Here also it is advisable to test and compare the results to the acquisition programme in terms of cost justification.

EXHIBIT 4.1

> ### REPEAT RATE AND FUTURE VALUE OF ONLINE CUSTOMERS: IMPORTANT GUIDELINES
>
> Certain variables affect the future value of a customer. Prominent among them include:
>
> ✓ Repeat rate by **media source of the customer-search engines** *versus* **banner ads**, or comparing the repeat rate of customers generated by different banner ads. Usually, there will be a huge difference and this metric can help the firm to improve the long term ROI of ad-campaigns.
>
> ✓ Repeat rate by **category** or **item of customer's first purchase**, and **category of ongoing product preference** is another major differentiation of customer behaviour. This will enable the business firm to understand the type of products which can be more profitable in a long-term perspective or formulate the plans to promote the product among new and current customers alike.
>
> ✓ Repeat rate by the **price of first purchase** is an idea

similar to the one above. This will enable a business firm to under-stand the profitable price range that could be featured to new customers, because customers buying in this range tend to repeat.

✓ Repeat rate by **the content area favoured by the customer during the first visit**, and repeat rate by **ongoing preference to a content area**: This enables the customer to understand the areas of the firm's site that create the most loyal (highest repeat) customers.

✓ Repeat rate by **demographics** or other self-reported data: Grouping by non-behavioral data can be effective, and it will be dependant on the accuracy of the data available.

Source : www.crmguru.com with permission

4.3 AN ALTERNATIVE MODEL OF CUSTOMER RETENTION

Business firms often seek to manage the customer retention by maintaining the customer satisfaction level. In fact some business enterprises strive to maintain a certain level of satisfaction among all its customers. Although this has some merit, these firms can also get easily victimised in a customer satisfaction trap as they might fail to reap any of the benefits—such as increased sales, profitability, or customer loyalty–supposedly associated with the higher customer satisfaction levels. Hence it becomes imperative to look at the customer retention from another angle, viz., the loyalty/repeated purchase point of view of the customer.

4.4 LOYALTY/ PURCHASE VIEW OF THE CUSTOMER

Generally, the customer retention process begins during the stage of acquisition, which creates the customer expectations, including the perceptions of product value and uniqueness. The initial product usage determines whether these expectations are met or not. This will be followed by other factors such as the ease of exit, ease of purchase and the customer service. Together, these factors affect the long-term customer behaviour and determine the relationship between the seller and the buyer. The types of relationships that are predictable in this context include:

➤ The highly loyal and committed customer
➤ The customer who is willing to continue purchasing the product or service, but who is vulnerable to competitive offers and
➤ The defector, who abandons the product

A critical factor in determining the retention is the difference between the customer's expectations and the delivered quality of the product or service. Raising the expectation levels generates trial, but overly high expectations can contribute to low retention. A business firm, therefore, should strike an optimal balance between the expectations and delivered quality. The firm could provide greater value either by offering the higher quality and matching the competition on price, or by offering the same quality at a lower price. It has been commonly observed that the more different (or less substitutable) a product is, the greater will be its retention rate. The loyalty mechanisms could generate high retention rates for a firm or its product, even if the competing products or services available in the market are almost identical in their features. The ease of purchase should be a matter of consideration not only for the retail companies but also for the manufacturers of specialty industrial goods.

The customer service of a business firm has several components and different parts of the organisation contribute to it. For instance, the accounting department solves the customer's billing problems, logistics handles customer service problems (problems related to delivery of product in time), while the engineering department tries to create an awareness about the proper utilisation of the equipment or seeks ways of increasing the production line speed through a minor product modification. The customer service opportunities are mostly pervasive in any organisation.

Exit Barriers   The exit barriers offer one strategy for increasing retention. Examples of these barriers include: **(a)** programmes that reward continued use based on historical usage; **(b)** product-design characteristics that make it difficult to change suppliers; and **(c)** product-learning curves that make it costly to switch to competing products. (The learning curve is explained in more detail in Chapter 10.) Products with high switching costs tend to promote retention, as to experimental products, because it is difficult to evaluate a service prior to its first use and costly to change it afterward.

In short, the attrition (defection) occurs when the customer has decided not to use the product or service any longer, and has communicated to the firm that he or she is no longer a customer. However, most customers do not communicate to the firm their intention to defect. **Silent attrition** occurs when the customer has decided to no longer purchase the product or service, but has not indicated to the firm that he or she is no longer a customer. In most of the business settings, the silent attrition poses serious problems because managers cannot identify 'when a customer is no longer a customer'. This makes it very difficult to determine whether the customer should be retained.

4.5   CHANGING RETENTION RATES

The retention rates can be altered by increasing the spending on retention programmes or by improving the effectiveness of the current retention programme. Both approaches are useful and commonly applied. Improving the retention programme has the advantage of being a one-time investment, but a firm could face trouble in identifying the necessary changes. Increased spending could help a firm to attain its optimal retention-spending rate, but it carries the risk of inefficient overspending. For a successful alignment of acquisition, retention and add-on selling strategies, and for identifying the appropriate time to settle for sub-optimal profits, managers should develop an in-depth understanding of customer behaviour, characteristics and the likely customer responses to the firm's tactics. In this regard, the managers, in addition to recency, frequency, and monetary value data on past purchases, should also address the following points:

> ➢ The change in buying patterns over a time period;
> ➢ The number of customers that could be compartmentalised in a particular product category;
> ➢ The nature of customer purchase in complementary categories;
> ➢ The response of customers to various promotion drives; and
> ➢ The level of customer's disposable income.

This information would provide a more holistic view of the relationship between the customer and a firm than the simple data on purchase levels, and could serve as a better predictor of customer behaviour. The firm would require a sophisticated customer database of warehouse to develop this type of customer profile. (Chapter 8 describes the use of customer database and its application in retention in detail.)

Profit Impact of a Retained Customer

In general, the best customers of a business firm **(a)** are less price sensitive because of their greater preference for the product, **(b)** have become "locked in" over time to use the product, or **(c)** do not search for alternatives. On the other hand, the new customers often get discounts for trying a product, which makes their prices lower than the current list price. A firm rarely lowers the price for the existing customers, who thus end up paying more than their newest customers do. Ironically, this is an excellent pricing strategy in most situations.

The profit impact method is a satisfactory method to obtain a 'quick feel' for the retention value of a customer. It involves four basic steps:

1. Determining the average retention rate of the cohort of customers.
2. Computing the average expected relationship duration of a customer with this retention rate.
3. Determining the average per period margin and the costs that are associated with retaining this customers, and

4. Multiplying the period net profits by the number of periods the relationship lasts.

Calculating Retention Equity with Survival Analysis

Blattberg (2001), has identified twelve steps in the computation of retention equity using the survival analysis. These steps include:

Step 1: Identifying a cohort of customers to be analysed. Generally, all customers in the cohort should have been acquired within the same time period.

Step 2: Obtaining data regarding each customer's retention rate per period. The retention rate for a given period is the probability that the customer will repurchase in that particular period given the current product offering.

Step 3: Obtaining data for sales, gross margin and marketing, and customer service costs.

Step 4: Determining the number of periods that will be computed into the future retention equity

Step 5: Projecting the future retention rates for the customer using extrapolation.

Step 6: Projecting the future sales, gross margin, and marketing and customer services costs.

Step 7: Obtaining from financial sources the discount rate to be used in the analysis.

Step 8: Employing historical and projected retention rates to estimate the number of customers who survive each period.

Step 9 : Computing the profits for each period using the projected number of customers and the relevant sales and cost data.

Step 10: Discounting all future profits using the discount rate arrived at in Step 7.

Step 11: Addition of all discounted profits for the past and projected periods. This is the retention equity for the entire cohort.

Step 12: Dividing the sum in Step 11 by the number of customers who began in the cohort to find the retention equity of each customer.

4.6   MEASURING CUSTOMER RETENTION

The accurate determination of the retention rate is not a simple task. The typical defection and retention rates are average rates, influenced equally by the retention rate of newer customers and the retention rate of customers who have had longer relationships with the firm. However, as discussed in the section on customer life-cycle in Chapter 3, the retention rates can vary among the different stages of the customer-firm relationship. For example, a first time repeat buyer would have a lower likelihood of buying again than a customer who has repeat purchased several times. Therefore it would be better to rely on the duration-adjusted retention and defection rates. The duration adjusted rates account for differences in the customer "stickiness" at different stages of the customer-firm relationship. If retention rates do not change over time, a duration adjustment is not necessary.

Exhibit 4.2

RETENTION ANALYSIS: COMPUTATION AND MEASURE

Firstly, the current and future profit of the new customer would be analysed to set a bench mark for the retention analysis by using the following equations:

New-Customer Current Profit $= N_p a S_a m_a - N_p c_p$

where:

N_p = the number of prospects

a = the acquisition rate,

S_a = average sales generated by a new customers;

m_a = margin percent for a new customers,

c_p = the cost of marketing to each prospect

New Customer Future Profit at time $t = \sum_{t-1}^{\infty} \dfrac{N_p \left(r_{t-1} \, a_1 \, m_{r,t} - r_{t-1} \, c_{r\,2} \right)}{(1+d)^t}$

where:

N_p = the number of prospects

r_{t-1} = the fraction of customers remaining at the end of time t–1 (i.e., the survival rate at time t–1)

r_t = the retention rate (i.e., repeat purchase probability) at time t,

$m_{r,t}$ = the per customer retention margin at time t

$c_{r,t}$ = the marketing and customer service costs associated with retaining a customer at time t

d = the cost of capital for the firm.

The future customer equity™ for new customers equals the sum of discounted future profits for all periods after the initial period

Gains (Losses) From Retained Customers, Current Period

This metric shows the incremental profits (or losses) in the current period that the firm gained by keeping a portion of the prior periods' customers in the current period. If the customer margin decreases compared to the prior period, then losses occur. The reverse is true if the margins increase. Retention rates and margins are the two most important variables affecting gains (or losses) from retained customers in the current period. Instead of taking an infinite sum, some firms would add the expected profits over a fixed number of periods (for example 10 periods). The number of periods that is reasonable will vary from business to business

Gains (Losses) from Retained Customers, Current Period

$$= \sum_{i-1}^{\infty} N_{T-i} r_{T-ii} \left(m_{T,i} - m_{T-1,i} \right)$$

where:

T = the current period

N_{T-i} = the number of customers who were acquired i periods ago

r_{T-i} = the proportion of customers who were acquired i periods ago that still remain at the end of time T (i.e., the current survival rate for cohort of customers acquired i periods ago)

$m_{T,i}$ = the margin after marketing costs in the current period for customers acquired i periods ago

$M_{T-1,i}$ = the margin after marketing costs in the prior period for customers acquired i periods ago

Gains (Losses) From Retained Customers, Future Periods

Like the previous measure, this metric is valuable for demonstrating the incremental payout of retaining customers from one period to the next. However, this metric projects the payout into the future.

Expected Gains (Losses) From Retained Customers, Future Periods

$$\text{where: } = \sum_{i-1}^{\infty} N_{T-i} \sum_{k-1}^{\infty} [\frac{r_{T+k,i} \left(m_{T+k,i} - m_{T+k-1,i} \right)}{(1+d)^k}]$$

T = the current period

N_{T-i} = the number of customers acquired i periods ago

$r_{T+k,i}$ = the proportion of customers acquired i periods ago that still remain at the end of T + k (i.e., the survival rate at time T + k for the cohort of customers acquired i periods ago)

m_{T-i} = the margin after marketing costs in the current period for customers acquired i periods ago

$MT-1_i$ = the margin after marketing costs in period T–1 for customers acquired i periods ago

d = the discount rate

Expected Lost Profit from Defecting Customers, Current Period

This computation is similar to the ones mentioned above, except that it determines the number of lost customers rather than retained customers. With this number, firms can compute the amount of lost customer value

Expected Lost Profit from Attriting Customers, Current

$$\text{Period} = \sum_{i-1}^{\infty} N_{T-i}\, r_{T-1-i,i}\, (1 - a_{r,i}) \cdot (m_{Ti} - c_{T,i})$$

where:

T = the current period

N_{T-i} = the number of customers acquired i periods ago

$r_{T-1-i,\,i}$ = the proportion of customers acquired i periods ago that still remain at the end of T –1

$1 - r_{T,\,i}$ = the attrition rate for the current period for customers acquired i periods ago

$m_{T,\,i}$ = the margin in the current period for customers acquired i periods ago

$c_{T,\,i}$ = the marketing cost in period T for customers acquired i periods ago

d = the discount rate

Expected Lost Customer Equity from Defected Customers, Future Periods

This computation determines the loss in future equity represented by customers lost in the current period. If this loss differs significantly from the loss during other periods because of changes in retention rates, then this can adversely affect the current period's **Customer Equity**.

Expected Lost Customer Equity from Defected Customers, Future Periods

$$= \sum_{i-1}^{\infty} N_{T-i} r_{T-1-ij} \sum_{k-1}^{\infty} \left[\frac{\left(1 - p_{T+k,i}\right) \cdot \left(m_{T+kj} - C_{T+k,i}\right)}{\left(1+d\right)^{k}} \right]$$

where:

T = the current period

N_{T-i} = the number of customers acquired i periods ago

$r_{T-1-i,\,i}$ = the proportion of customers acquired i periods ago that still remain at the end of T−1

$1 - r_{T,\,i}$ = the attrition rate for the current period for customers acquired i periods ago

$m_{T+k,\,i}$ = the margin for period k for customers acquired i periods ago

$c_{T+k,\,i}$ = the marketing and customer service costs for period T+k for customers acquired i periods ago

d = the discount rate

Profit from Retained Customers, Current Year

This measure calculates the current–year's profits for all retained customers in all cohorts.

Profit from Retained Customers, Current Year (year t) =

$$= \sum_{i-1}^{\infty} N_{t-i} \left(r_{t-1-ii}\, p_{t,i}\, m_{t,i} - r_{t-1-i,i}\, c_{rij} \right)$$

where:

N_i = the number of prospects targeted t−i periods ago,

r_{t-1-i} = the fraction of customers acquired i periods ago that remain at the end of time t −1 (i.e., the survival rate at time t −1−i)

$r_{t,i}$ = the retention rate at time t for customers acquired i periods ago;

$m_{t,i}$ = the per–customer margin at time t for customers acquired i periods ago;

$c_{r,t,i}$ = the marketing and customer service costs associated with retaining a customer, acquired i periods ago, during the current period t.

Based on this mathematical formula it is assumed that the revenues are not received until the end of the period but all of the customers active at the beginning of the period contribute to the costs

Profit from Retained Customers in Future Years

This measure calculates the discounted future profits represented by retained customers from all customer cohorts

Profit from Retained Customers, Future Years

$$= \sum_{i-1}^{\infty} \frac{\sum_{i-1}^{\infty} N_{t-i} \left(r_{t-1-i} \, p_{t,i} \, m_{t,i} - r_{t-1-i,j} \, c_{rij} \right)}{(1+d)}$$

where:

N_{t-i} = the number of prospects targeted $t - i$ periods ago

r_{t-1-i} = the survival rate of customers remaining at the end of time $t - 1$ who were acquired i periods ago

$r_{t,i}$ = the retention rate for customers in period t who were acquired i periods ago

$c_{r,t,i}$ = the marketing and customer service costs associated with retaining a customer, acquired i periods ago, during period t

d = the discount rate

$m_{t,i}$ = the margin at time t for customers acquired i periods ago

Source: www.customerequity.com

CONCLUSION

The goal of customer retention management is not to strive for zero defections; instead, a firm should manage its retention rate and choose retention strategies and tactics that best support its main focus—optimising customer equity. Customer retention does not occur without incurring some costs. Companies can maximise customer equity by matching those costs to the retention values of individual customers rather than by acting on the myopic view that "retention is free".

SUMMARY

✓ Customer retention is defined as the ability of a firm's offer for a customer to purchase or patronage its product over a specific time period.

✓ The major customer retention stages are: welcome cycle upselling, cross selling, renewal, lapsed customers and inactive customers.

✓ Managing customer satisfaction is the key to customer retention.

✓ A critical point in determining retention is the difference between a customers expectation and the product quality delivered.

✓ The changing retention rates helps the company to analyse its faults over a period of time, however it may lead to over spending in the short-term which should be minimised.

✓ The profit impact of a retained customer is great as much so that the firm does not have to introduce heavy discounts to lure them as it does with newer customers.

✓ The goal of customer retention management is not to strive for zero defection, instead a firm should focus on optimising customer equity.

CHAPTER REVIEW QUESTIONS

1. What do you mean by customer retention strategy?

2. Explain how customer retention could be represented through value chain and accounting standards.

3. What do you mean by 'stages' in the customer retention cycle?

4. Explain the changing retention rates for a new generation service provider like Airtel and Reliance Infocomm.

CASE STUDY
DIGITAL SOLUTIONS OPENS VISTAS FOR
INSURANCE COMPANIES

WE are able to manage our customer information and use it to make effective, profitable business decisions for our company, as well as move our customers smoothly after 9/11.

Mary Tucker, MIS manager, Royal & Sun Alliance

BACKGROUND

Royal & SunAlliance was formed in the early 2000 upon the merger of two industry stalwarts in the UK. Royal had been writing insurance policies since the mid-1800s, SunAlliance since the 1700s. The combined company is the sixth largest insurance business in the world, with customers in 130 countries and a premium value of $17.6 billion. Royal & SunAlliance has relied on SAS, the leading MIS service provider for 20 years to meet a wide range of business and technical needs in property, commercial, casualty and personal insurance.

BUSINESS SITUATION

America's economic crisis after the 9/11 disaster wreaked havoc on some business, causing an estimated 12 out of 30 top corporations in insurance sector to downsize their operations by 20 to 50 per cent. During times of catastrophe, the insurance company's help could have provided peace of mind and financial stability to property owners. "With SAS, Royal & SunAlliance turns volumes of disparate data into useful information. Information leads to knowledge, and knowledge leads to value", says Mary Tucker, MIS manager at Royal & SunAlliance's U.S. operations center in North Carolina. SAS enabled the company to automate the existing processes, put reports online and clean the data sources within existing applications.

During early 2003, the longer-established insurance providers suffer from a low brand image in a mature market, new entrants with considerable branding experience are successfully entering the financial service arena. Some industry experts believe that the advent of Digital TV will be the catalyst to bring the World Wide to the masses, though more complex products, including pensions and investments, will most likely continue to be sold through traditional channels, where face-to-face meetings with highly trained staff play an important role.

FACE THE TEST

In various business situations, relationship equity measures the customer's tendency to stick with the brand, above and beyond objective and subjective assessments of its worth. Sub drivers of relationship equity include loyalty programmes, special recognition and treatment programmes, community building programmes, and knowledge building programmes which helps the company to drive away its competitors. New initiatives like Database marketing thrust up on an interactive approach to marketing, which uses individually addressable marketing media and channels (such as mail, telephone, and the sales force)

Tucker and her co-workers saw improves access to data, a revival in creativity and innovation and new opportunities for studying data. "Have you ever heard the phrase 'data-rich and information-poor?" Tucker says. "The traditional approach has been to reduce the size of data by summarizing detailed transactions, taking a subset or only looking at certain attributes. Data mining, on the other hand, is searching for trends and anomalies and answering questions."

It is a fact that Customers are expensive to acquire and not easy to keep. If companies neglect the acquisitions and retention of customers, they will incur high marketing costs relative to any competitors that take more trouble. The marketing information system must therefore give an accurate and up-to-date picture of acquisition and retention. The relevant management report is the customer inventory. It is hard to calculate, but an approximate answer worked out quickly based on the following:

➢ Customer inventory and recruitment, retention and attribution rates.

➢ How much customers in various segment invested with the company;

➢ How much it costs to acquire customers of various types

➢ How much it has cost the company to manage the relationship and

(Cost of marketing, sales, service and sometimes distribution

DATA, DATA EVERYWHERE

While digging for more detail in the company's data, Tucker discovered that Royal & SunAlliance was using several different database platforms. With some SAS consulting, tucker re-engineered the mainframe processes onto the client-server environment, reducing to two days a process that previously had taken as long as four months. "That's a huge benefit," Tucker says. "I need to pull information form a lot of different places and put it all together. Now I have a resource for location-level data, and it's all done through SAS data warehousing."

Meanwhile, SAS' Web-enabled data warehousing solution is revolutionising the ease with which Tucker deals with her clients. "As people call me to request a report, I just walk them through the Internet application over the phone," Tucker explains. "Not only do they receive an immediate answer, but they also are enabled and encouraged to make suggestions on how the applications could be improved. They give a request and immediately they see changes in the very next release." "Before, we didn't have a way to deploy our information over the Web," Tucker says. "We were sending paper copies and e-mails with attachments that would turn into paper copies, so we needed a better way. With SAS, we can now start looking to the future and deciding how we really want to serve our clients." SAS provided welcome access to consultants, Tucker says. "I've worked with SAS data warehousing consultants, contract consultants and developers. In some instance, the end result is new application developments, but I also find value in using SAS consultants as a sounding board to make sure I am on the right track. They've been very helpful, and I'm looking forward to doing more work with them."

A true relationship-marketing database can be great value of all marketing and sales staff. Sales staff will use it for contract management and journey planning, marketing staff for marketing planning and analysis. For example, a list could be produced of customers in a particular market sector with a particular product who have not responded to the last mail short on the subject. These could either be followed up more forcefully (e.g., by telephone), or (if there were other priorities) be omitted from a telephone prospecting campaign, because lack of response (perhaps after a second mailing) demonstrated lack of interest.

Besides speeding up processes and making work easier for clients, Tucker expects SAS, the leading service provider to generate operational saving at Royal & SunAlliance.

"If we don't have to run the processing five times, that's going to save money", she explains. "If our clients only have to enter data once, that's going to save money. And if they don't have to work so hard at data entry, the quality of the data will improve, and then there will be tremendous savings. "SAS helps make all that possible," Tucker adds. "With SAS, we always have the right tools for any job."

QUESTIONS

1. Comment on the company strategy of extracting customer information for their continued success by way of customer retention, customer acquisition and add on selling.

2. Critically analyse the merit of using database marketing as a tool for gaining competitive advantage for insurance operations in India.

(Adapted from www.crmtoday.com with copyright permission)

THE ADD-ON SELLING STRATEGIES

"...in the factory we make cosmetics, in the store we sell hope."

Charles Revlon

Learning Objectives

After reading this chapter you should understand:
- How Add–on selling strategy is formulated in an organisation.
- The meaning of customer af finity.
- The various analytical methods to measure Add–on selling.
- Cross–buying strategy.
- The impact of marketing mix on customer value analysis.

INTRODUCTION

The real worth of any business or relationship marketing concept emanates from the business firm's ability to **(a)** foster better decisions, **(b)** generate higher profits, and **(c)** increase shareholder wealth. However, many firms, during the course of their business operations perform, as though the strategic elements of the customer equity acquisition, retention and add-on selling are functioning in an independent manner. For instance, most often the business firms analyse the data about the existing customers without considering the response and interaction data about the non-acquired prospects from becoming customers.

The failure to link the customer acquisition process to the retention process could also lead to other errors, including inaccurate forecasts about **(a)** the period that a customer is likely to stay, **(b)** the profitability of customers, and **(c)** the impact of marketing efforts. A successful strategy, therefore, should first aim at acquiring a new customer and then induce the customer to stay on with the company offerings. During this process, the company will naturally look for new ways of serving the customer, with up-selling and cross-selling of the company products. For example, the ICICI Bank, first acquires a customer for personal banking, and then induces him for using the Internet and telephone banking services, followed by offers with credit cards, home loans, personal loans, tax saving bonds, mutual funds, share trading, insurance policy and so on.

5.1 ADD-ON SELLING STRATEGIES

The **acquisition transaction perspective** says that the customer acquisition ends with the first purchase made by a customer. The acquisition process perspective, however, extends the process and states that the acquisition includes the first purchase as well as other non-purchase encounters that precede and follow the purchase, up until the time the customer makes a repeat purchase. The retention phase of the relationship begins once the customer decides to make the first repeat purchase.

The **selective customer acquisition approach** assumes that not every potential customer is worth the customer acquisition investment. Further, if the profiles of the acquired customers are more likely to match the firm's ideal target market, the retention rates and the add-on buying rates are likely to be higher. Hence, a firm should identify the type of products offered under add-on-selling on relation to the customer needs and wants.

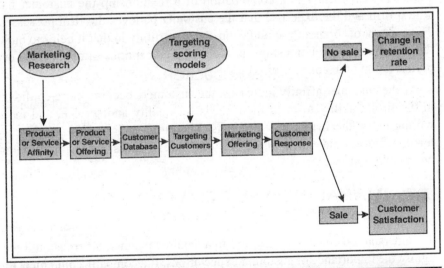

Fig. 5.1 Determining the Value of Add-on Selling Strategy

Source: Robert C. Blattberg, Gary Getz and Jacquelyn S. Thomas (2001), *Customer Equity*, Boston, Harvard Business School Press

The value of a firm's add-on selling efforts depends on many factors: the number of add-on offers a firm can economically provide per period, the response rate to these product offers, sales quantity per offer, how much it costs the company to make the offers, the size of the customer universe to which the firm can add-on sell, and the margins on the offered products.

Five primary factors determine the response rate, as shown in Fig. 5.1.

1. The value of the product or service: The higher the perceived value, the higher the response rate.
2. How the product fits in with the firm's other products: The greater the fit with other products of the firm, the more likely it is that the consumer will attribute expertise to the firm in that product area. The result is a higher response rate.
3. The affinity the customer has with the firm: The higher the affinity, the higher the response rate.
4. The total expenditure for the offered product: Generally, the higher the total expenditure, the lower the response rate.
5. Specific marketing communications aimed at the customer: The better targeted and positioned the messages, the higher the response rate. Customer service and general image advertising also affect the response rate.

Customer Affinity

The customer affinity is a combination of a relationship the customer has with a firm and the expertise that the customer believes the firm possesses. The concept of 'branding' could contribute to affinity in that it helps to build the customer-firm relationships and to create perceptions of quality and expertise among the consumers.

As the customer affinity increases, the customers become more confident in the firm's ability to meet their needs for quality and service, and more willing to try the firm's new products. Therefore, a firm with greater customer affinity could expect higher response rates besides increasing the number and type of its offers.

5.2   MANAGING AND DELIVERING ON CUSTOMER EXPECTATIONS

To understand the customer affinity in a detailed manner, a firm should recognise the importance of customer expectations. If a company could meet the expectations, it could build strong relationships with its customers. The firm does not have to provide the maximum customer service or the highest-quality product; it does have to deliver on the specific expectations it has nurtured among its customers.

Analyses Determining Add-on-Selling Strategies

Several types of analyses could be conducted to target the customer and products for add-on selling. Table 5.1 summarises the application of analytical tools to add-on selling.

| Table 5.1 | Application of Analytical Methods to Add-on Selling |

Analytical Method	Purpose	How it Improves Add-on Selling
Cross-purchase analyses log-linear models; hence which product to add sell on	Effectiveness	Determines which products are purchased together
Collaborative filtering: which products to add-on sell	Effectiveness	Identifies similar customers buying behaviour and hence
Logit/regression; nets	Efficiency	Determines which customers neutral to target

Source: Robert C. Blattberg, Gary Getz and Jacquelyn S. Thomas (2001), *Customer Equity*, Boston, Harvard Business School press

Cross-Buying Analysis The cross-buying analysis focuses on determining the products that have a high propensity to be purchased jointly. It measures the likelihood of cross-buying between two products or services. It results in a measure that reflects the overall purchasing levels of the products analysed. It is simple to compute and takes into account the two products' overall purchasing levels.

Collabroative Filtering The collaborative filtering is one of the most interesting techniques in the advanced date analysis. The method compares and put together the customers having similar purchasing profiles in order to identify the appropriate products for add-on selling to the specific customer types. It recognises that if two customers purchase one set of similar products, then are likely to buy other products in common as well. The collaborative filtering is based on the assumption that similar purchasing implies similar tastes and interests.

Response Modelling The response modelling identifies those current customers most likely to respond to an offer. Its typical methods are (a) regression analysis and (b) logit models. Theses methods predict the response to an add-on offer using a set of explanatory variables, such as (A) (a) recency, (b) frequency, and monetary measures; (B) marketing tactics implemented; and (C) demographic and geographic data, if available. The three basic premises that should guide the collection of data to develop and adaptive the marketing system include:

1. Individual customer purchase behaviour which is essential in managing all aspects of customer equity to their potential.
2. Many customer-firm interactions do not relate directly to marketing, which means that a firm has to collect additional data beyond the customer purchase data (e.g., customer service data) in order to manage customer equity.
3. Tracking marketing activities by the customer which significantly improves the efficiency and effectiveness of marketing programmes. This, in turn, enhances the customer equity.

The first premise implies that the traditional marketing research information, which contributes to a general understanding of the customer, does not provide the specificity required for customer equity management. A firm needs to understand the specific customer behaviour, which it can track for the lifetime value modelling and link to the specific customer responses.

The second premise addresses the problem that many important customer interactions do not get measured. The inaccurate invoices and poor product delivery are examples of such interactions. The firms should realise that all interactions, not just marketing communications and encounters, could affect their customer's attitudes.

Finally, the third premise recognises that causal data, with which firms could relate specific marketing actions to responses, are extremely valuable. With these data, the firms can improve their acquisition, retention, and add-on selling strategies and implement tactics that are significantly more customer-focused.

Table 5.2	Impact of Marketing Mix on Customer Value Analysis

Element of the Marketing Mix	Acquisition	Retention	Add-on Selling
Advertising copy	Awareness	Direct customer communication	Affinity with the firm; targeted communications regarding offers
Media selection cost–effective	Mass media	Database marketing	Database marketing
Customer service	Affects word-of mouth communications	A primary vehicle for creating high retention levels	Increases response rates for add-on offers

Product quality	Affects word-of mouth communications	Product reliability creates high retention levels	Increases response rates for add-on offers
Product positioning	Affects the size of the target market; creates customer expectations	High retention rates occur when positioning and delivery of product benefits match	Creates affinity with customer base, which increase add on seling response
Promotions	Generates trial among potential customers	Can increase retention	Increases response rates to add-on selling offers
Channels of distribution	Third-party channels can increase customer acquisition	Third party channels decrease because the channel owns the customer	Direct channel makes it easier to target third party customers

Source: Robert C. Blattberg, Gary Getz and Jacquelyn S. Thomas (2001), *Customer Equity,* Boston, Harvard Business School Press

Table 5.3	Marketing Mix by Stage in the Customer Life Cycle

	Prospects	First time Buyers	Early Buyers	Core Customers	Defectors
Advertising Sales force	Awareness	Reinforcement	Reinforcement	Personal	Apology
Pricing	Low	Moderate	Increasing	Higher	Higher
Promotions	Trial	Similar to	Limited	Reward	Apology
Product offerings	Lead	Second Lead	Add-on	Add-on	Broad
Customer service	Limited	Problem focused	Problem focused	Problem focused	Problem focused

Source: Robert C. Blattberg, Gary Getz and Jacquelyn S. Thomas (2001), *Customer Equity,* Boston, Harvard Business School Press.

EXHIBIT 5.1

ADD-ON SELLING MEASUREMENT

Using Average Response Rates, Margin, and Cost Data to Compute Add-On Selling Equity

This approach builds on the similar approach outlined in the retention equity computation. There are four basic steps:

1. Use the average retention rate to determine the expected relationship duration. This process was done in steps 1 and 2 of the retention equity computation mentioned in the chapter-4

2. Determine the average per period margin and costs that are associated with add-on purchases.

3. Determine the average likelihood that a consumer will make an add-on purchase.

4. Multiply the net profits by the likelihood of purchase and the expected relationship duration

Using a Survival Model to Compute Add-On Selling Equity

Computing add-on selling equity using this approach could be done within the same framework and using the same data that were used to compute retention equity using a survival model as mentioned in the Chapters 3 and 4. The only additional information required is the number of add-on sales offers made each period (n_{a-1}), the probability of response to each offer (r_{ao}), and the sales per offer (s_{a-o}). These figures will allow you to compute the expected add-on selling sales in each period. Specifically, the expected add-on sales profits equals the number of offers times the probability of response to each offer times the sales per offer (i.e., $n_{a-o} * r_{a-o} * s_{a-o}$ = expected add-on sales).

Add-on Selling Accounting Measures:Duration-Adjusted Average Sales and Profits per Retained Customer

This is for assessing the effectiveness of add-on selling efforts to retained customers, taking into account differences among customer cohorts.

DAASRC (Duration-Adjusted Average Sales Per Retained Customer, for period t) $= \sum_{i=1}^{t=1} f_i \, PF_{it}$

where:

$PF_{i,t}$ = the observed average profits per customer in period t for cohort I

$\overline{f_i}$ = the percentage of the total number of repeat purchasers represented by cohort I

Change in Sales and Profits for Retained Customers

This indicates whether the firm is growing sales effectively within its customer base or observing sales changes because of customer acquisition. Shows whether the firm is increasing (decreasing) sales and profits from retained customers in current periods. If sales and/or profits are decreasing from retained customers, firms need to have significant growth in new customers. It also shows whether the firm's marketing programs are failing to generate growth through existing customers. This metric is particularly useful when compared to the changes in sales and profits from the firm's entire base of customers

Source: www.customerequity.com

All these methods are important in one way or the other. While the first helps to determine the market communication strategies, the second to target potential customers with the right products, the third helps in targetting the customers in general.

CHAPTER REVIEW QUESTIONS

1. Explain the add-on selling strategy
2. Explain the ways of determining the value of add-on selling for an insurance service provider?
3. Describe customer affinity.
4. How do you manage and deliver on customer expectations of the Pizza Hut?
5. Describe the various application of analytical methods to add-on selling
6. Explain cross-buying analysis.
7. Narrate response modelling with suitable example.
8. Analyse the impact of marketing mix on customer value analysis.
9. Narrate the influence of marketing mix by stages in the customer life-cycle.

CASE STUDY
E-BANKING SYSTEM*

ICIC Bank, a new generation MNC bank with its registered office in Channai occupies the top position in the ASIAN financial markets. The bank has a world-leading Internet banking and e-commerce operation with 12.8 million customers and the largest customer base of any financial services group in the Asian region. Bank serves a total of 10.6m Internet users, most of whom use its pioneering Solo service. From the beginning, Solo allocated its users a continuous list of passwords, each to be used only once. To boost security, the fixed password system has to be confirmed by a programme on the user's computer, confining the user to a single computer. The success of DoCoMo's I-mode in Japanese market revolutionised the mobile phone market especially by addressing the need for accessing internet through mobile phone.

PIONEERING E-BANKING IDEAS

Solo has always been accessible from home, the office or abroad. Today, Solo services are equally accessible from a normal telephone, a mobile phone, a WAP phone, a PC or a television. Transactions and balances can be checked without a password from a GSM phone, and the service can also be reached via invoice payment ATMs. The range of Solo services are available anywhere, offering equity, mutual funds, bond and file insurance investments, and foreign payments, among other services.

Customers can also sign agreements using their Solo ID as a signature. Solo customers are an ideal target group, with modern attitudes and purchasing power, who are familiar with online operations. By accepting Solo payments, a company can eliminate invoicing and credit risks, and thus achieve significant savings. A personal digital phone is a very suitable medium for managing and monitoring payments and financial matters.

With this in mind, in May 2003, ICIC together with Nokia and VISA International, announced a pilot project, involving the use of wireless application technology and mobile phones, to make payments over the Net, an open network, or at a merchant point of sale-Electronic Mobile Payment Service (EMPS). Using a Nokia WAP GSM phone, WAP technology, authenticated card payment, EMV and the VISA Open Platform, customers will be able to make secure remote payments, or pay at a merchant point of sale.

---

*Adopted the case concept from www.crmtoday.com and Banking Technology Inc.USA with copyright permission: July 2003.

MOBEY THINK FORUM

In September 2003, major financial institutions, together with leading mobile phone manufacturers, announced the creation of a global forum to encourage the use of mobile technology in financial services, and to promote the adoption of open standards in the financial services field. This new forum is called the Mobey think Forum, and its founding members include Nordea, ABN AMRO Bank, Hispano, HDFC, Deutsche Bank, HSBC Holdings, UBS, VISA International, Ericsson, Nokia and Siemens.

Mobey Think Forum's activities are promoting a sustainable business environment for mobile financial services, such as the open provision of services in a mass market, the use of mobile phones, open standards and non-proprietary security concepts like client identification, dual chip (EMPS), and mobile PKI.

MASS ADOPTION OF NEW TECHNOLOGY

Achieving a critical mass is a key factor in electronic banking. Satisfied users will, themselves, market the service. As the number of users rises, there is increasing demand for specialist services from a fast-growing number of modern-minded customers who are prepared to use e-commerce and invoicing. Wired banking is becoming more wireless. This is due to the fact that mobile phones are perfectly suited to banking and making payments.

QUESTIONS

1. Comment on the company strategy of extracting customer information for their continued success by way of floating Mobey think Forum and specialized e-banking system, Solo

2. Critically analyses the merit of inter-linking technology and Communication devices as a strategic tool for gaining competitive advantage for banking operations in India.

CUSTOMER LOYALTY

"On an average, the US corporations lose half their customers within five years, half their employees in four years, and half their investors in less than one year. We seem to face a future in which the only business relationship will have opportunistic transactions between virtual strangers".

Frederick F. Reichheld

Learning Objectives

After reading this chapter you should understand:
- The significance of customer loyalty to a particular firm
- How customer loyalty can be maintained and serviced.
- How to devise loyalty based relationship building strategy
- The meaning of loyalty economies

INTRODUCTION

The loyalty master, Frederick F. Reichheld's* experience has revealed that the disloyalty at current rates would stunt the corporate performance by 25 to 50 per cent, and sometimes even more. By contrast, the business enterprises that concentrate on finding and retaining good customers, productive employees and supportive investors still continue to generate superior results. The loyalty factor remains one of the key elements in the success of a business enterprise. In fact, the principles of loyalty and business strategy (what has been commonly called the 'loyalty-based management') are alive and well at the heart of every company with an enduring record of high productivity, solid profits, and steady expansion.

The founders of the great industrial companies has underlined the relevance of delivering 'value' to their customers and employees as well as to their investors in enhancing the prosperity of their enterprise. To quote Henry Ford, "Business must be run at a profit...else it will die. But, when anyone tries to run a business solely for profit.....then also the business must die, for it no longer

---

*Frederick F. Reichheld (1996), The Loyalty effect, Boston Bani and company, Harvard Business School Press.

has a reason for its existence." It is a fact that firms always look for more profits, defend competition or offer unique products/services. The bottom line of all such is the spread of their customer database. Generally, successful firms will grow only with customer bare which, in turn would generate incremental profit and monopolies the service/product of the firm direction. For example, the good old solid and dependable advantages of the market share, cost position, and the service quality no longer guarantee success. The General Motors, instead of reaping the spoils of market share leadership, are struggling to pull itself out of a downward spiral. However, a low-cost manufacturer like Caterpillar suddenly finds itself at a cost disadvantage in the key markets. A service-quality blue chip like Delta Airlines is downgraded to junk the bond status. None of our received business wisdom seems as constant at it once did. The companies like Wang and IMB are profiled as the case studies of excellence one day and as management turnarounds in the following year. The discussion in this chapter begins by analysing the impact of loyalty in business.

6.1 LOYALTY EFFECT

In simple terms, loyalty is best defined as a state of mind, a set of attitude, beliefs, and desires. Most of the companies benefit from the customer's loyal behaviour, which is an end-result of the positive state of mind shown by the business enterprises in serving their customers. The *relationship marketing ladder of loyalty* is a useful tool for enhancing awareness about the customer segmentation opportunities; for example, the emphasis on different elements of the marketing mix may vary for customers on different steps of the ladder. In addition, there is also a general recognition that not all customers are suited to the higher rungs of the ladder: customers with low profit potential are not considered worthy enough for the investment that might be required in taking them to the level of advocates or partners.

Research Findings on Loyalty Effect

Palmer and Bejou Palmer and Bejou extended the concept of the relationship ladder and present evidence of a buyer-seller relationship life-cycle. In their examination of investment services organisations, they identified how the elements binding the buyer and a seller fluctuate as a relationship progress. They also identified the sales orientation/selling pressure, ethics, and empathy as different constructs that have varying importance at various stages of the relationship life-cycle. The finding of this research implied that a *firm should seek to move customers rapidly through the stages of relationship development*, as *too much selling pressure may deter adoption of mutual understanding*. Palmer and Bejou acknowledge that since the relative importance of various constructs differ across the customer segments, sellers must tailor their sales messages according to the needs of the different segments, which are related to the duration of the buyer-seller relationship.

Knox and Denison: Understanding the factors affecting customer loyalty in the retail sector is the focus of interest for a number of researchers. Knox and Dennison undertook an empirical study of consumer loyalty in five retail sectors, examining the extent to which the store loyalty is associated with the level of consumer spending. They investigated the effect of loyalty in a broad range of retail sectors, including gasoline, groceries, "do it yourself" mixed retail, and the department stores. They used a composite index, the Enis-Paul measure, to measure loyalty.

The **Enis-Paul** measure considers the (**a**) mean of consumer store patronage, (**b**) propensity to switch over, and (**c**) total budget allocated to the first-choice stores. Knox and Dennison compared their results with those of similar studies conducted in the US in the 1960s (e.g., Enis & Paul, 1970) and found that the UK consumers are relatively less loyal to their first-choice stores, suggesting that the recent trends in retailing such as higher mobility levels and more impersonal sales systems, have contributed to lower customer loyalty. The results also indicated that the different retail sectors typically demonstrate differing levels of customer loyalty, with do-it-yourself and department stores scoring the lowest.

Reichheld and Sesser*:   A study of one hundred companies in two dozen industries by Reichheld and Sasser found that the firms, with each 5 per cent increase in the customer retention, could improve their average profitability per customer between 25 and 85 per cent. This is under the assumption that the increased loyalty leads to greater profitability in two ways. First, it helps in widening the customer base as the rate of defection slows down; if the rate of new customer acquisitions stays steady, but more customers are retained, the net effect is growth in the total number of customers. Secondly, the loyal customers are more profitable. This second profit lever is due to the relationship of loyalty and the profit per customer.

Profitability of Loyal Customers

Several reasons could be pointed out to show why the loyal customers (i.e., repurchase a high proportion of their needs from the same source) are much more profitable:

   a.   **Lower costs of service**   The loyal customers are easier and cheaper to service. Since they are familiar with the products and services, they (**a**) would not have as many questions, (**b**) are less likely to make mistakes, and (**c**) would have adjusted their behaviour to simplify their relations with the supplier.

---

*Frederik F. Reichheld (1996), *The Loyalty Effect,* Boston Bain and Company and Harvard Business School Press.

b. **Increased purchases** The loyal customer tend to buy more as the time progresses, either because they learn about part of the product line or they give a higher proportion of their spending to the favored source.

c. **Less price sensitivity** They tend to become less price sensitive and may pay a premium. As the relationship strengthens over time, they are less susceptible to the competitors' appeal, and since they are satisfied by what they are receiving from the enterprise, they are prepared to pay more.

d. **Favourable word of mouth** Finally, the loyal buyers are more likely to pass on favorable recommendations to others who also tend to be higher quality prospects. This helps in reducing the high costs of new customer acquisition.

e. **Sustainable Advantages** Another reason for the rising interest in the market relationship is the 'durability factor' involved in a committed relationship. In fact the proper chemistry of positive relationship is hard to understand, copy or displace. This is a persuasive argument, in cases where the product-based advantages are short-lived and new competitors are posing challenges on all sides. Furthermore, with network technologies that could enable the addressability, interactivity and demand chain coordination, business firms are currently better equipped with both the motive and means for moving closer to their customers.

6.2 SIGNIFICANCE OF LOYALTY

Business loyalty has three dimensions: (a) customer loyalty, (b) employee loyalty, and (c) investor loyalty. They are far more powerful, far reaching, and interdependent. The retention is the central gauge that integrates all dimensions of a business and it measures the success of the firm in providing 'value' to its customers. The consistently high retention can create tremendous competitive advantage, boost the employee morale, produce unexpected bonuses in productivity and growth, and even reduce the cost of capital. Conversely, persistent defection signifies that the former customers viz., people convinced by the inferior value of company offerings, would eventually outnumber the company's loyal advocates and dominate the collective voice of the market place.

The general assumption followed here is that creating value for the customer builds loyalty, and loyalty in turn builds the growth, profit and more value. Even though the profit has always occupied the center stage in conventional thinking about business systems, it is not the primary one. The loyalty leaders choose the human assets carefully and then seek ways to extend their productive lifetime and increase their value. Indeed, the loyalty leaders engineer all their business systems to make their human inventories permanent.

They view the asset defection as unacceptable value-destroying failures, and they work constantly to eradicate them.

By decreasing the defection rates in all the three groups-customers, employees, and investors—the enterprises have achieved prodigious growth both in profits and cash generation. They have discovered that the human capital, which unlike most other assets, does not depreciate overtime. The zero-defection approach to human-inventory management implies and altered theory of business. The current approach might be called the *profit theory,* where all business skills and competencies stand or fall within their capacity to contribute to profits. The new theory envisions the value creation as the fundamental mission of a business rather than the profit.

The loyalty leaders naturally prefer long-term partnerships and seek out customers, employees and investors with the same predilection. Since they expect their team to work together for a long period, they are so particular in the choice of their partners. They try to maximise the character and integrity among their pool of partner candidates, while setting a reasonable threshold for raw talent, which is very different from the more common practice of maximising the rate talent and setting a reasonable threshold for the character. In the abstract sense, the loyalty-based management is more about "people", and concerned with types of humanistic values and principles that people may find devoting to in their lives outside the work and sometimes on the job as well. Yet desired people find the job only as necessary evil, the unavoidable means of achieving a desired standard of living. To manage the customers as an asset, the firm should be capable of evaluating them as an asset, implying that they should be capable of quantifying and predicting the customer duration and the life-cycle cash flow.

In this regard, the analytical process should be made compatible with the financial systems currently employed to allocate resources and run the business enterprise. The process should also seek ways in supporting to financial system to decide on the investments that could improve the long-term profits and customer loyalty.

6.3 BUILDING LOYALTY THROUGH CUSTOMER RETENTION

It is a fact that loyalty will be developed over time, if the parameters for the relationship are planned and implemented by the firm in a proper manner. Imagine the two companies, one with a customer retention rate of 95 per cent, the other with a rate of 90 per cent. The leak in the first firm's customer bucket is 5 per cent per year, and the second firm's leak is twice as large, 10 per cent year. If both the companies acquire new customers at the rate of 10 per cent years, the first will have a 5 per cent net growth in the customer inventory per year, while the other will have none. Over fourteen years, the first firm will double in size, but the second will have no real growth at all. Other things being equal, the five percentage-point advantage in the customer retention translates into a growth advantage equivalent to double to customer inventory every fourteen years. An advantage of ten percentage points accelerates the doubling to seven years.

As the time period of the relationship between a customer and business firm increases, the profit accruing from such a customer towards the company also makes a corresponding increase. The life-cycle profit pattern looks alike in several representative industries. The economic consequences of losing mature customers and replacing them with new ones are not the neutral processes. In businesses like auto insurance or credit cards, the firms actually lose money on the first-year customers. No number of new prospectus could fill the void left by a seasoned customer also defects. In several other industries, new customers contribute to the profits right away, but it still takes several new comers to compensate for the loss of one veteran.

In addition, the consequences of customer retention compound over time, and in ways that are sometimes surprising and 'non-nutritive'. Though a change in the defection rates may have little effect on a particular year's profits, even a tiny change in the customer retention could cascade through the whole business system and multiply over time. The resulting effect on the long-term profit and growth could be enormous. Once the relationship is established on a solid foundation built on the superior value and trustworthiness, it is time to strengthen the relation between the firm and its customer. The objective is to make it more attractive for the customer to remain loyal and more difficult to defect. Brands also help tighten these connections. The brands have great value to the firms that own them, because they represent the history of past relationship. Because of the deeply-embedded quality of these relationships, the firms have long recognised that their brand names could be their most valuable asset.

6.4 DEGREE OF LOYALTY

The degree of customer loyalty varies among three levels—(a) hard core loyal, (b) loyal and (c) soft loyal. The loyalty is therefore developed by the approach of a business firm towards its customer, which develops a positive state of mind and the associated behaviours. The primary objective is to improve the loyalty base of those customers that are most likely to respond. Some customers are more likely to respond to the incentive, some to be differentiated service provided only to loyal customers, while some may respond only to a combination of the two. The exchange of information is one of the keys to customer loyalty, and provides a critical bridge between the state of mind and the behaviour. The loyal customers are more likely to give information (because they trust the company and expect the firm to use it with discretion and to their benefit). They also expect to access that information during the transactions with them. The **privileged communication** is an essential element of the loyalty programme as the loyal customers also expect more information from the company.

The loyal customers often believe that they would get better service from the enterprise because they are loyal. They feel that they should be rewarded for their loyalty. This process has two major implications: Firstly, the loyalty approaches should seek to differentiate the relationship and service package provided to the loyal customers and secondly, the ways of giving 'special recognition' at the point of customer contact should be employed. Further managing the loyalty implies not only managing the behaviour alone but also a state of mind. It implies influencing the customer's attitude to do business with the supplier over the long-term, not merely until the next visit or the next purchase.

6.5 DEVISING A LOYALTY-BASED RELATIONSHIP BUILDING STRATEGY

A relationship advantage is reinforced by a virtuous cycle of loyalty. The company should deliver superior customer value, and thereby provide increasing customer satisfaction. Only when the customers are fully satisfied with the company's performance that they initiate efforts to tighten their connections with the company. These closer connections lead to stronger feelings of loyalty, and the relationship created by this loyalty allows the company to develop the customer-specific information, and capabilities that are hard to match. When there is not virtuous cycle, the advantages are usually short-lived. This applies to many programmes launched under the guise of relationship building, that involve "micromarketing" by tailoring communications to narrow segments, or product line extensions that aim of offer greater variety to the fragmented markets.

A strategy that successfully activates the virtuous cycle of loyalty to gain a relationship advantage meets the following conditions:

> ➤ Delivery of superior customer value by personalising the interaction
> ➤ Demonstrating the trustworthiness and
> ➤ Tightening the connections with customer

The relationships that add value for the customers require some form of personalised interaction. They are built on the recognition that every relationship is different, that it is based on two-way-communications, and that it should continue to build and change over time. The frank and frequent personalised communications are effective means of demonstrating the trustworthiness. This is especially important with high involvement, long-term service commitments like auto or life insurance.

Major Steps in Devising a Corporate Strategy

Following are the major steps envisaged in devising a corporate strategy for converting the 'customers' to 'loyal customers'.

a. Defining objectives The need to develop a loyalty approach over and above existing marketing, sales and service approaches should be identified as part of an overall audit of the customer relationship management. Such an audit should reveal, for example.

> ➢ Competitive attempts to target precisely the firm's best customers
> ➢ Falling repurchase rate among the firm's best customers
> ➢ Falling levels of the 'state-of-the-mind' loyalty
> ➢ Increasing rate of customers switching away from the firm's products and service

The company objective for the loyalty approach should be set in quantified terms. These objectives should always contain some financial component. The segmented lifetime value analyses would indicate that smaller, but regular buyers contribute a greater profit margin and life-time value than the single large purchasers do. The company customer base is the greatest potential market-research tool that a firm should possess. The tool could provide market researchers with an excellent sampling frame, which is why the formal research process should be built into marketing contracts, involving where possible the use of questionnaires and the structured telephone interviews. If executed properly, the research would reinforce the brand and values that the firm intends to transmit to its customers.

b. Development This involves the activities such as identification of the desired aspects of the marketing and service mix which could be deployed most effectively to reinforce and build loyalty. The elements of the product/service mix which have the highest perceived value to the customers should be identified, but at relatively low costs of provision. This idea might look like a strange point, but it is the key to most of the schemes that work in the long time. The financial director is not keen on giving away profits. The justification of loyalty schemes is that they should reduce the marketing costs as less the cost incurred in acquiring a new customer is more than what the company has to spend on retaining the existing customer as the firm already know them and have access to them. The loyalty scheme could also reduce the service costs, partly because the existing customers have learnt the ways of working with the firm. But these financial benefits would take some time to emerge. Meanwhile, the costs of the loyalty approach would continue to accumulate.

c. Defining the qualification levels, segments, implement the capabilities, and measure
This is a detailed analysis of the profile of the firm's best customers. It is better to start with a broad definition of the best, rather than just say at the top 20 per cent because the next 40 to 50 per cent may offer huge potential. A thorough profiling and tracking of their purchase histories, transactional values, promotional responses, and source is vital here. Besides, it helps in identifying the potential market size of similar customers for the acquisition programme. This is sometimes referred to as a **relationship marketing audit.**

Many financial institutions, when they have undertaken this activity, have been surprised to understand the number of customers and families who have made the multiple purchase of the products. The firm should work out the groups of customers to which the they should provide the benefits of loyalty approach, and the divisions between these groups of customers. Then the company has to implement the strategy and analyse the response or success of the programme. Many credit card and debit card companies offer loyalty points while purchasing/shopping through their cards. This will guarantee the use of cards. For example, the Amex card offers a loyalty point for every addition of Rs 40 to their bill and the ICICI offers the same at every addition of worth Rs 100 to their card holders. (Please refer Chapter 11 for more details on the relationship marketing strategies.)

6.6 LOYALTY ECONOMICS

The loyalty economics is a rigorous method of measuring the value of a customer in the concrete terms of cash flow, and providing the tools that would enable a company to mange the real drivers of cost, growth, and profit. There are dozens of ways for the companies to undermine their own future health and welfare by embracing some form of adverse selection. For example, the need for growth can cause the companies that have captured the best of their natural customer base to recruit more and more of the less desirable customers who remain. But, as the customer quality declines, so does the firm's ability to deliver the value; which in turn discourages good customers, stifles growth, demotivates employees, weakens the process of value creation, and encourages the sales force to chase customers who are even less likely to be profitable and steady. In short, the entire spiral turns upside down and drills the company into a hole. The commercial banks and the credit card companies are often good examples of self-inflicted adverse selection.

The loyalty-based companies follow the three rules of thumb:
1. Some customers are inherently predictable and loyal, no matter the type of company they are doing business with. They simply prefer the stable long-term relationships.

2. Some customers are more profitable than other. They spend more money, pay their bills more promptly, and require less service.

3. Some customers will find the products ad services more valuable than those of the firm's competitors. No company can provide all good things to all people. The firm's strengths will simply fit better with certain customer needs and opportunities.

During the process of building loyalty or even relationship, every company would incur different type of expenses like the acquisition cost and operations cost, plan base profit and sales growth and would analyse the impact of referrals and price premium on their business success. These elements are explained in the following sections.

Acquisition Cost

Almost every business should invest money up front to bring new customers through the door. Most of these costs are easily identifiable: advertising directed at new customers; commissions on sales to new customers; sales force overhead; and so forth. Take one concrete example, the first big expense in the credit card business, say ICICI Visa, is the cost of direct mail. With a response rate of 2 to 3 per cent, a company has to mail out thirty thousand to fifty thousand solicitations to get just a thousand applications. When the cost of credit evaluation, card issuance, and the cost of putting a new account into the bank's data-processing systems, is also added to this factor, the ICICI would end up with a price tag of Rs 150 to 200 for each new customer. (In fact this concept has already been delay with in an earlier section of the book.)

Operating Costs

As customers get more awareness about a business firm, they learn themselves to behave in an efficient manner. They don't waste time requesting services that the company does not provide. The familiarity with the company's products make them less dependent on its employees for information and advice. In most industries, the cost benefits of loyalty spiral directly from the way the long-term customers and the long-term employees interact and learn from one another. The repeat customer tend to the pleased with the value they receive, and their satisfaction is a source of pride and energy for employees. The motivated employees stay with the company longer and get to know their customers better, which leads to better service, builds greater customer satisfaction, and further improves the relationship and the company's results. This human factor, the personal loyalty, is a powerful element in customer relationship.

Per Customer Revenue Growth

One advantage of holding on to the firm's customers is that in most business relationship, the customer spending tends to accelerate over time. In retailing, for example, the customers become more familiar with the store's full product line. A leading credit card firm the American Express, for example, discovered that it could accelerate its loyal customer life-cycle, and thereby, the profits of loyalty. It used rewards and pricing to encourage the cardholders to consolidate their use of plastic money more quickly, and found that it could bring the customers to mature sales and profit levels just a few years after singing them up. Bankers like the ICICI, HDFC too have found that they could accelerate the growth of customers for checking, savings, investment, and credit card accounts, all bundled together in a single statement.

Price Premium

In most industries, the old customers pay effectively higher prices than the new ones. This is sometimes the result of trial discounts available only to be brand new customers. A retailer like Food World offers a coupon to all its customers, but finds that the mature customers are less likely to use it. The so-called loss leader in retailing works on the high probability that the customers who come in to get the bargain would buy other products with higher margins, but studies show that the loss leaders make up a smaller fraction of on old customer's shopping basket.

Base Profit

All customers that buys some product or service from the customer could not be termed customers. Moreover, with rare exceptions, the prices they pay are higher that the company's costs. This basic profit on basic purchases, unaffected by the time, loyalty, efficiency, or any other consideration, is what we call base profit.

CONCLUSION

It is realised from the discussions, that attention should be closely paid on the value of incoming customers in a marketplace where the best and the loyal are already spoken for the company products and services. In this context, it is better to take a very close look at the net present value of the new customers equipped for replacing the old, one or to strengthen the data base. At the same time, one should be aware of the quantity for its own sake: winning more and more new customers may put the company slowly out of business. Across the business spectrum, companies that expect to achieve sustainable high performance must begin studying the life-cycle profit and tenure patterns, then use their insights to focus their customer investments. Another benefit of the long-term customer loyalty is that the satisfied customers recommend the business to others. It has already been proved in India from the experience of companies like the ICICI Prudential that the firm receives far more new customers from the referrals than from any other source. Hence we could conclude that the loyalty is not dead..... indeed it is the most powerful tool one can have.

CHAPTER REVIEW QUESTIONS

1. Describe the significance of customer loyalty for a supermarket like Food World.
2. Devise a loyalty-based marketing strategy for a 'tour operator'.
3. What do you mean by loyalty economics? Explain.
4. Formulate a loyalty building strategy for the Reliance Infocom.
5. Explain the loyalty effect with some examples from the Indian environment.
6. Describe the degree of loyalty among the cellular customers towards their service provides in India.

CASE STUDY

AIRTEL—WINNING CUSTOMERS THROUGH LOYALTY PROGRAMME

BACKGROUND

A major cellular service provider, AIRTEL hired the service of Synergy Marketing, an agency specialised in devising the loyalty programmes, to prepare an innovative customer loyalty programme. The initiative sought to improve the customer acquisition and retention rates of the cellular phone customers, in a market marked by fierce competition (where the cost of acquiring one new customer was nearly Rs 100).

The programme implementation methods called for an accurate tracking of the customer behaviour using control groups—customers like those in the loyalty programme who were not offered membership in the programme. By comparing the behaviour of the customers in the loyalty programme with those not in the programme, the financial impact of the loyalty programme could be very precisely determined. Since this programme was not advertised, but informed through the mail to specific customers, a perfect "blind test" of loyalty programme effectiveness was created in the cellular market.

COMMUNICATION PLAN

Synergy communication had two objectives before them while creating and managing the value of cellular customers. These included:

1. Hold on to the most valuable customers; and

2. Try to convert the less valuable customers to the more valuable one.

For the purpose, AIRTEL had to provide information to the consultant regarding (a) the value of their customers and their likelihood to respond to a programme, (b) whether the programme is customised on the basis of the services already availed, and (c) whether it utilises the loyalty points, or its customer service and value added services offered.

In other words, AIRTEL should reach out to the customer and communicate the firm's marketing and service programmes. They should answers to three questions:

> ➤ WHO to communicate to,
> ➤ WHEN to communicate to them, and
> ➤ HOW you're going to execute the communication.

In addition, the firm should also care about how much they spend on the marketing and service programmes. Ideally, instead of blasting out expensive stuff to every customer, the firm would like to spend money on the customers most likely to do whatever the firm want them to, and not waste money on those who are not.

Sample selection

The customers who had been active for at least 6 months in 2002 and having an average monthly cellular bill payment of at least Rs 5000 over a 3-month period were eligible for participating in the programme. A random sample of these eligible customers was selected in accordance with the cellular company's budget for the programme. Those customers eligible for the programme, but not selected randomly for inclusion in the programme became the "control group". According to Shashi Menon, Executive Director of Synergy marketing "This selection process ensured that the customers of all types who fit the initial selection screen were evenly represented in both the loyalty programme and the control group".

The customers could not apply for the programme as it was not "advertised"; and those randomly chosen to participate in the programme came to know about it only when they were selected to join and received a membership package in the mail. The AIRTEL supplied the billing records of their post-paid customers to Synergy Marketing each month, regardless of whether the customer was enrolled in the rewards programme or not. "This approach allowed the Synergy to create and track groups of customers just like those in the programme, who had no knowledge of the programme. The behaviour of these "control groups" would

FINANCIAL INDICATORS

The financial success of the programme was measured by comparing the financial performance of customers in the programme to an identical group of customers not in the programme. The customers were ranked by annual sales and divided into five equally-sized groups called quintiles. The quintile five contains the top 20 per cent of customers ranked by their annual spending while quintile 1 contains the lowest 20 per cent of customers ranked by their annual spending. Over the 12 months period from July 2002 to June 2003, the customers in the loyalty programme spent an average of 35 per cent more than the customers who were not in the programme. After calculating the EBITDA margin on this increase and subtracting the cost of the programme, it was found that the loyalty programme generated a return on investment of 252 per cent annually over the 12-month period . The ROI on the top 20 per cent of spenders averaged 365 per cent for each month. Another notable factor in this programme was the increased customer profitability that came from both the churn reduction and increased spending by customers. The programme resulted in significant sales improvement across all customer spending segments, from the highest 20 per cent (quintile 5) to the lowest 20 per cent (quintile 1).

The cost of the programme was offset by the rise in profits per customer for almost every customer spending segment. The lowest value customers did not increase their spending or decrease churn enough to cover costs, but the average change in behaviour across all customers resulted in a significant increase in profits on customers in the loyalty programme, when compared with those not in the programme over the same time period. The programme returned Rs 112.52 in additional profit for every Rs 100 spent after covering all costs. Examples of increased revenue drivers included phones per account increasing by 16 per cent and add-on services "sampled" by customers using loyalty programme points being converted to billable services.

The churn rate decreased an average of 3.1 percentage points across all customer spending segments annually—a 15.6 percent decrease in churn over the 12 months period. It should also be noted that the greatest reduction in churn rate occurred in the critical "middle class" customer group. When combined with the accelerated average spending per customer, the churn reduction really pushed increased profits to the bottom line.

WHAT MADE THE PROGRAMME SUCCESSFUL?

The cellular rewards programme was designed to create a high impact from the very beginning. The members were welcomed with a personalised letter and rich welcome package detailing all the benefits and rewards of membership. More than 100 "standard" reward choices were provided, many chosen specifically for their unique appeal to this market and group of members. The members interested in dining options had their choice of not only the leading restaurant chains, but also more than thirty different local places selected to appeal to this specific members base. The Shopping rewards included all of the well-known retailers, as well as the local favorites. A full range of wireless services including free airtime, paging, and other accessories was also offered as reward options.

A second critical element in the design and success of the programme was the creation of what Synergy called the "special opportunity rewards", offered initially to members through periodic mailings and then later through the programme website. Offering members the opportunity to redeem their points for highly desirable rewards at very low point levels early in the programme encouraged member involvement.

Another unique feature of the programme was the opportunity for members to earn additional points through loyalty programme partners. The cellular members were able to earn points through long-distance services and by using a nationally known travel service. The programme partners paid for these points. The member communications which were able to break through the clutter were a critical feature of the programme. The comprehensive annual membership packages and high impact periodic newsletters promoted the special opportunity rewards. The introduction of the programme website was announced to members via a four-colour oversized postcard. Throughout the programme, Synergy kept the focus on communicating to members in ways that were designed to capture their attention.

The programme was enormously successful from a financial perspective for AIRTEL. Post analysis showed not only a decrease in churn rate, but also a significant increased in the overall spending by customers in the programme when compared with customers not in the programme. The programme generated a 15.6 per cent decrease in customer churn, as well as a substantial increase in the overall spending by customers in the programme when compared with customers not in the programme.

THE CASE

1. Do you agree in the methodology and data analysis followed by Synergy communications in desigining and implementing loyalty programme? Comment

ANALYSING PROFITABILITY OF CUSTOMERS

"We are what we repeatedly do. Excellence, then, is not an act, but a habit."

Aristotle

Learning Objectives

After reading this chapter you should understand:

- The concept of lifetime customer value (LCV)
- The evolution strategy of a value centred thinking
- The hierarchy of customer behaviour
- What is customer-product profitability and how it is analysed
- The value chain analysis
- The value profit chain and its implications
- The reasons why customers defect
- The measurement hierarchy

INTRODUCTION

The relationship marketing practice aims at optimising the combination of business process, people, capabilities, resources and capital that are focused and implemented in various steps so that the firm could understand, commit to, create, and capture value with the customers and sustain its own profit growth. As Day and Reibstein suggest, the basic foundation of any successful business exchange is that the customer obtains value, not products or features. The proper customer relationship is rooted on the ability of the firm to consistently provide superior value to its customer than that of its competitors. We will start our discussion with the concept of lifetime customer value (LCV).

7.1 ELEMENTS OF CUSTOMER-CENTRIC MARKETING STRATEGY—THE LIFETIME CUSTOMER VALUE (LCV)

As it has been explained in the earlier part of the book, the focus of a customer centric-marketing strategy will always be on the **potential value** of the customer which is also called the lifetime value of a customer (LTV). This value will be estimated over a period of time (say 5, 10 or 15 years) and it depends on the interaction level and customer affinity bonding of the business firm. The LCV as a concept is adopted from direct marketing (especially mail order), where the long-term customer behaviour is considered the key to success, and where the difference between costs of acquiring customers and the benefits and costs of retention are taken as the norms. The concept is also widely used in the consumer goods brand management, where the key calculation is on determining the amount to be spent in preventing consumers from brand switching.

The LCV could be calculated using the historical data of customers available with the firm and later extrapolated, making adjustments where necessary. Though market experience has proved the LCV as the most reliable method of forecasting customer behaviour, many business firms are reluctant of applying it, mainly because the LCV uses only the past data in predicting future purchase behaviour.

Moreover, most business enterprises find it very difficult to think in terms of financial consequences of a customer relationship beyond the current deal or perhaps the current budget period. A piece of equipment, a product development or a brand may have long-term value, but the customer relationship exist only in the present. The startling fact is that the loyal customers actually become more valuable over time.

It is a fact that, for many business enterprises, the profits gained from the initial deal or even during the first year may not defray the costs of gaining the customer in the first place. The real value starts developing only when the customer is in a position to purchase a variety of products or services from the company, and savings are gained through aligning processes and preferred relationships.

The lifetime value of a loyal customer could be astronomical. Research studies conducted (in the US context) by the Harvard Business School has estimated that the lifetime revenue stream from a loyal pizza eater can be $8000, a car purchaser $3,32,000 and a purchaser of commercial aircraft literally billions of dollars.

It is presumed that the relationship marketing is the art of attracting and retaining profitable customers. According to American Express, the best customers outspend others by ratios of 16 to 1 in the retailing sector, 13 to 1 in the restaurant business, 12 to 1 in the airline business, and 5 to 1 in the hotel industry. Yet every company loses money on some of its customers.

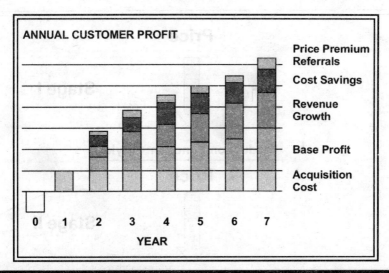

ANNUAL CUSTOMER PROFIT

Price Premium
Referrals

Cost Savings

Revenue
Growth

Base Profit

Acquisition
Cost

0 1 2 3 4 5 6 7
YEAR

Fig. 7.1 Savings in Customer Retention

Source: www.customerequity.com & www.crmtoday.com with permission

The well-known 20-80 rule says that the top 20 per cent of the customers generate as much as 80 percent of the company's profits. Many researchers have modified this to a 20-80-30 rule to reflect the idea that the top 20 per cent of customers generate 80 per cent of the company's profit, half of which are lost serving the bottom 30 per cent of unprofitable customers. The implication is that a company could improve its profits by "fisting out" its worst customers. A **profitable customer** is a person, a household, or a company that over time yields a revenue stream that exceeds by an acceptable amount the company's cost stream of attracting, selling, and servicing that customer. Here the emphasis is on the lifetime stream of revenue and cost, not on the immediate profit from a particular transaction. Although many companies measure customer satisfaction, most of them fail to measure the individual customer profitability.

Value-Centered Thinking

The next step in achieving a value-centered organisation requires not only repositioning but a rethinking of shared values viz, policies, practices, procedures, and processes in a manner that leverages results over the costs for customers, employees and other important constituencies.

According to Earl Sasser Jr of Harvard Business School, the redefined business practices (from products and services to results) recognises that the customer does not simply buy a product or service, but they buy the 'results', applying a greater emphasis on the way they are delivered, togetherly otherwise refered to as the 'process quality'. In essence, it is a repositioning of a business practice in relation to the new or existing customers and competitors through a metamorphosis from price to value.

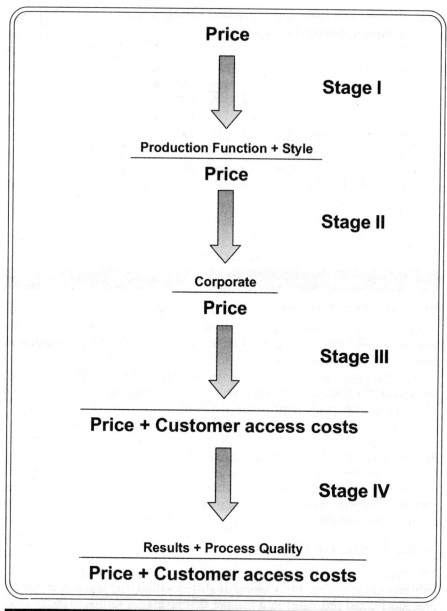

Price

Stage I

Production Function + Style
Price

Stage II

Corporate
Price

Stage III

Price + Customer access costs

Stage IV

Results + Process Quality
Price + Customer access costs

Fig. 7.2 Evolution in Value-Centered Thinking

Source: James L. Heskett, W. Earl Sasser Jr. and Leonard A. Schlesinger (2003), *The Value Profit Chain,* New York, Free Press

The path to sustainable improvements in value is being mapped in Fig. 7.2. Despite this, Hurdles in a value-centric relationship strategy. Despite the increasing concern for value in customer relationship, only a few firms have ventured beyond the widely accepted economic value added (EVA) measures to explore the non-financial concepts for improved value creation. Typically, organisations maintain a bias towards the best practices that they have already been following, and are reluctant of applying an alternative to that. For instance, a designer and manufacturer of computers is inclined to pass the task of servicing to others. It may even outsource the manufacturer of components, assuming that it can add more value to the production process, as it could muster much of its internal resources to concentrate more on the development of new designs and computing processes. Similarly, it has also been found that the organisations do not take that much of responsibility in educating buyers about the use of new products, leaving the task to the amateur instructional "word of mouth" that attends the introduction of many high-tech products, with the resulting high variability in the quality of instruction, learning, and usage.

Secondly, those who have ventured to utilise the value-centered concepts in laying out and implementing strategies have found that the process is time consuming, sometimes even more than what the impatient investors would allow.

Third, although the concepts are straightforward, the actions behind them are complex. The process of change or, just as important, the reaffirmation of the shared value comprising the core of an organisation's culture requires a sensitive ear and close attention. The process is more time consuming if the change is to be engineered without disturbing, or rather preserving the existing strengths of the organisation.

Similarly, the way in which an organisation positions itself in relation to its customers and competitors cannot be changed overnight. The changes in operating strategy should support a repositioning effort besides being extensive, if the internal consistency in the elements of the operating strategy is to be achieved.

Steps Involved in Establishing LCV

A comprehensive knowledge about the hierarchy of relationship between a business firm and the customer, otherwise known as hierarchy of customer behaviour, is essential in understanding the concept of lifetime value. The hierarchal is graphically shown in Fig. 7.3. Here, establishing *customer satisfaction* is only the preliminary stage in a relationship process that gradually develops to *loyalty,* where a customer not only expresses an interest in repurchasing, but also starts devoting a larger share of the total 'wallet' to a given brand. This will be followed by *commitment,* where the customers attempt (either successfully or unsuccessfully) to influence or rather elicit others to purchase. Finally, over time, a sense of ownership is established in which the customer actually endeavour to provide or service improvements, by taking the trouble to complain or provide a continuing stream of suggestions.

In fact the critical factor that influences the customer lifetime value is the likelihood that a customer will voice his/her satisfaction or dissent to others (the customer's "viral behavior") and the level of influence that it could create on others.

Ownership
(Taking responsibility for the continuing success of)

Apostle-like behaviour
(Exhibiting a high degree of loyalty while
telling others of one's satisfaction)

Commitments
(Demonstrating loyalty while telling
others of one's satisfaction)

Loyalty
(Devoting a large "share of
wallet" to repeat purchase)

Satisfaction
(Getting as much as or more
than, what was expected)

Fig. 7.3 Hierarchy of Customer Behaviours

Source: James L. Heskett, W. Earl Sasser Jr. and Leonard A. Schlesinger (2003), *The Value Profit Chain,* New York, Free Press.

Factors Determining the customer's "Referral Value"

1. The value of customers varies widely, ranging from large negative values for *antagonists* (those who are not only dissatisfied with a product or service but also are active—in current terminology, *viral*) who goes on venting about their dissatisfaction, to large

positive values for *viral loyalists*, especially apostle/owners. (Apostles exhibit positive viral behaviour and exerts greater influence over friends, a characteristic which distinguishes them from other viral loyalists.)

2. Together, apostle/owners and viral loyalists are capable of fostering significant revenue growth through referrals of potential customers, typically those who are followers in the adoption of new products or services. They would also play a pivotal role in formulating the marketing strategies.

3. Both apostle/owners and viral loyalists tend to exhibit ownership behaviour, communicating a stream of constructive complaints and suggestions back to their "partners".

4. Between antagonists and apostle/owners is a wide range of intermediate players exhibiting varying behaviors. These include (**a**) hostages—dissatisfied customers, with no where to turn for alternatives, some of whom may also be antagonists; (**b**) mercenaries, those who switch from one product or service to another due to the price factor; and (**c**) loyalists, those who remain loyal to a product or service, but rarely tell others of their loyalty.

Having identified the characteristics influencing the lifetime value, the next step in change-producing process is the development of a profile of the customer portfolio. Most important to this process is the establishment of criteria for defining the groupings of customers. Such criteria are unique to each organisation.

7.2 CUSTOMER–PRODUCT PROFITABILITY ANALYSIS

According to Kotler (2002), the useful type of profitability analysis is in line with the product profitability as shown in Fig. 7.4. Here the customers are arrayed along the columns and products along the rows. Each cell contains a symbol for the profitability of selling the particular product to a particular customer.

➢ Customer **1** is highly profitable; he buys three profit-making products (*P1, P2,* and **P4**).

➢ Customer **2** yields a picture of mixed profitability; he buys one profitable product and one unprofitable product.

➢ Customer **3** is a losing customer because he buys one profitable product and two unprofitable products.

Customers

	C₃	C₂	C₁	
P₄	+	–	–	Highly profitable product
P₃	–	–	–	Profitable product
P₂	–	–	+	Losing product
P₁	+	+	+	Mixed-bag product
	Losing Customer	Mixed-bag Customer	High-profit Customer	

Fig. 7.4   Customer–Product Profitability Analysis

Source: Philip Kotler (2002), *Marketing Management,* Prentice-Hall

Activity-Based Costing

The customer profitability analysis (CPA) is best conducted with the tools of an accounting technique called **activity-based costing** (ABC). The company estimates all revenue coming from the customer, less all costs. The costs should include not only the cost of making and distributing the products and services, but also such costs as taking phone calls from the customer, travel expenses incurred while visiting the customer, entertainment and gifts, and the cost of all company resources that were utilised while serving the customer.

While doing this analysis for each customer, it is possible to classify the customers into different profit tiers:

➢ platinum customers (most profitable),

➢ gold customers (profitable),

➢ iron customers (low profitability but desirable), and

➢ lead customers (unprofitable and undesirable).

The company's job is to move the iron customers into the gold tier and gold customers into the platinum tier, while dropping the lead customers or making them profitable by raising their prices or lowering the cost of serving them. The company's marketing investment ought to be higher in the higher profit tiers (Figure 7.5).

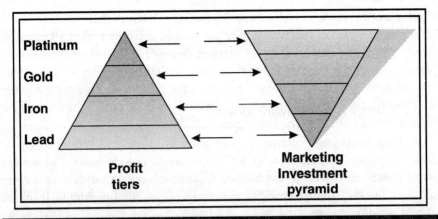

Fig. 7.5 Allocating Marketing Investment

Source: Philip Kotler (2002), *Marketing Management*, Prentice-Hall

Blackshaw, cofounder of P&G interactive, the company's Internet-based marketing organisation, on a special assignment consulting with the P&G's consumer relations department, found that consumers who provided the feedback via the Internet were the most viral (that is, most willing to talk with others about the products). Those who identified themselves through the feedback process as 'satisfied' P&G product users passed on an average of 16 full-sized P&G product sample to friends, when given the chance. Just as important, 85 per cent of consumers offering negative product feedback were found to be prepared to switch the brand allegiance after making a complaint.

However, only 1 in 25 consumers inclined to give the feedback were found to do so, the reasons being lack of time, inconvenience, lack of knowledge about the person to contact, cynicism about the possibility that it would matter, and the passing of the 'feedback moment'

Actions Triggered by the LCV Analysis

The estimation of customer lifetime value could trigger several types of action which include:

➢ communications of the information;
➢ identification and tracking of customer behaviour;
➢ organisation in response to customer behaviour; and
➢ allocation of resources to foster the lifetime value.

The communication of the LCV estimates to the members of an organisation can create a profound impact on the behavior of customer-facing personnel.

For example, in Pizza Hutt, the delivery personnel were encouraged not to argue with the customer about the 39-minutes delivery guarantee (a novel offer placed by Pizza Hut where they guaranteed delivery within 39 minutes, failing which the customer could claim a free gift. Most often the delivery personnel had to encounter fierce altercation with the customer over the exact time of delivery). Instead, they were given the latitude to give the customer the benefit of doubt in the hope that it would produce viral behaviour in the form of stories about Pizza Hut's great service.

Tracking behaviour patterns for consumer products and services may be done for groups of customers as well as on a one-on-one basis. The market share trends may also be established through a number of data collection services, but they really represent symptoms of potential problems, resultant of past actions.

Increasingly, the customer-centric organisations serving consumers are establishing a variety of *listening posts* for tracking the customer behaviour as well as the customer concerns that produces the behavioural changes. Ideally, the listening post include a customer service organisation prepared not only to solve the customer problems, but also to collect ideas for product or service improvements. Increasingly, they have sought the regular involvement of focus groups, Internet chat rooms, and Internet-based feedback devices to provide an early-warning system to address the concerns of the customer in a proactive manner.

The customer relationship management, for which the LCV estimates provide a strong justification, requires a customer-centric organisation. An organisation comprising separate business units marketing to the same set of customers can benefit from (**1**) efforts to communicate the estimates of organisation-wide lifetime value for potential customer, (**2**) policies assigning lead marketing responsibility for a particular relationship to the business unit with the earliest sales opportunity or greatest margin opportunity, and (**3**) measurement and recognition practices that distribute the rewards among business units realising the varying margins from products or services sold to the same customer.

However, a relatively small number of research findings have also suggested that a small proportion of customers exhibiting price-sensitive mercenary behaviour have the mind-set or the economic means to become loyalists. Here the customer psychographics (the mind-set) probably outweighs the demographics (economic means). The negative margin flows associated with the antagonists and the hostages also deserves attention in the allocation of marketing resources. At the very least, efforts should be expended to neutralise such customers. Often, recognition of the situation and the solicitation of feedback from the customer is considered a more successful way of doing so, than any product incentive or service giveaway, particularly in a situation where the customer had already registered his dissatisfaction with the current product or service.

Perhaps the best investment of marketing funds for retention purposes is that devoted to the development of virality among loyalists and eventually the expansion of the pool of apostle/owners. Once they are identified, steps could be taken to involve them as partners in the marketing effort by providing them with additional information useful in fostering the viral process. Product samples should be made available for distribution to potential customers at their suggestions. Through frequent contact, they could be made to feel that they are special emissaries of the company, members of a club or community of like-minded customers.

EXHIBIT 7.1

BASICS TO BE FOLLOWED BY COMPANIES ASPIRING TO FORM STRONG CUSTOMER BONDS
✓ Get cross-departmental participation in planning and managing the customer satisfaction and retention process.
✓ Integrate the voice of the customer in all business decisions.
✓ Create superior products, services, and experiences for the target market.
✓ Organise and make accessible a database of information on individual customer needs, preferences, contacts, purchase frequency, and satisfaction.
✓ Make it easy for customers to reach appropriate company personnel and express their needs, perceptions, and complaints.
✓ Run award programmes that recognises the outstanding employees.

Source: www.crmguru.com with permission

Berry and Parasuraman have gone beyond these basic points and have identified three retention approaches:

➤ Adding financial benefits;
➤ Addition of social benefits; and
➤ Addition of structural ties.

However, Lester Wunderman, one of the most astute observers of contemporary marketing, contends that talk about 'loyalising' customers misses the point. People could be loyal to their country, family, and beliefs, but less so to their toothpaste, soap, or even beer. The marketer's aim should be to increase

the consumer's proclivity to repurchase the company's brand. His suggestions for creating structural ties with the customer are as follows:

- ➢ Create long-term contracts;
- ➢ Charge a lower price to consumers who buy larger supplies; and
- ➢ Develop the product into a long-term service;

Increasing Company Profitability

The companies by following relationship marketing practices could create high absolute value at a sufficiently low cost. The competitive advantage is the company's ability to perform in one or more ways that competitors cannot or will not match. Michael Porter urged companies to build a sustainable competitive advantage. But few competitive advantages are sustainable. At best, they may be leverageable. A **leverageable advantage** is one that a company can use as a springboard to new advantages, much as Microsoft has leveraged its Operating System to Microsoft Office and then to networking applications. In general, a company that hopes to endure must be in the business of continuously inventing new advantages.

Levels of Profitability Analysis*

In the relationship and services marketing, strategies are focused on the "moment of truth" (Normann, 1991) or the "service encounter" revelations (Solomon, Surprenant, Czepiel, & Gutman, 1985). In a relationship context, such encounters could be termed episodes (Strandvik, 1994). The **episodes** are events that represent the complete functions from the customer's point of view. Examples of episodes are a visit to a restaurant, staying overnight at a hotel and so on. In this context the word "relationship" implies that the link between the service provider and the customer lasts longer than one episode. Here, a long-term relationship between a customer and provider involves two aspects: (a) that it involves a string of episodes and (b) that the benefits/value that the customer receives during the relationship is not provided in one episode. Rather, the benefits are delivered in "smaller portions" during the entire relationship.

Episode Configuration Matrix Provided that a topology of possible episodes can be created, relationships can be depicted using an episode configuration matrix such as that shown in Fig. 7.6. The horizontal axis describes the customer relationship and shows the types of episode (not the number of episodes) the provider has had with the customer. The matrix could be analysed from the provider's perspective or from the customer's perspective. From the provider's point of view, the number of

---

*Adopted from Jagdish N. Sheth and Atul Parvatiyar (ed, 2002), *Handbook of Relationship Marketing*, Sage Publication.

episodes needs to be added. The total number of episodes is the sum of the demand of all customers who have chosen the specific type and the variation of discrete episode. The building blocks of a customer base consists of customer relationships, and each customer relationship is configured of a specific pattern of episodes. Each episode is, in turn, built out of a specific set of activities. The profitability can thus be analysed on four levels: (a) the customer-base levels, (b) the relationship level, (c) the episode level, and (d) the activity level. Different aspects of profitability gains importance in the corresponding levels.

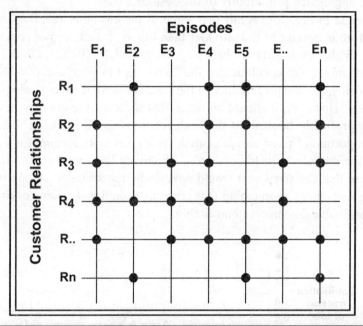

Fig. 7.6 Episode Configuration Matrix

Source: Jagdish N. Sheth and Atul Parvatiyar (Editors), *Handbook of Relationship Marketing*, Response Book, 2002 with permission

Profitability Analysis at Customer–Base Level
On a customer-base level, the key tool for analysis is the distribution of profitability within the customer base. The distribution could be used to measure the sensitivity of the customer base because it indicates how dependent the company is on a few customers and shows the cross-subsidising effect in the customer base. This, in turn, could be used to compare different customer bases as to their potential value and risk-profile. Cooper and Kaplan (1991) suggest that in certain industrial markets, 20% of the customers account for 225% of the total customer-base profitability. Empirical evidence from retail banks has shown that 210% of these banks' customers account for between 130% and 200% of the total profit (Storbacka, 1994).

Stobachoff Curve As the distributions of profitability in customer bases are very skewed, they are best anlaysed as ordered distributions. These distributions could be represented in a Stobachoff Curve (Fig. 7.7). Here the vertical axis shows the cumulative profitability of the customer base as a fraction of the aggregated customer-base profitability. The customers are ranked on the horizontal axis according to their profitability so that the most profitable customer is to the far left of the axis. The profitability of the second customer is added to the profitability of the first customer, and the sum is compared with the aggregated profitability of the customer base.

The logic in Fig. 7.7 reveals that some of the customer relationships are much more important to the provider than others. Infact, 25 per cent of the most profitable customers are basically the provider's lifeline. On the other hand, one might also conclude that the 25 per cent or so of unprofitable customers that erode the profitability to the final level are the most unimportant customers. However, it should be noted that these customers may have become unprofitable because of the high relationship costs. Since there is a large proportion of fixed cost allocated, these customers account for a major part of the provider's fixed-cost mass. Removing these customers would in fact mean that the fixed cost would have to be redistributed among the remaining customers—something that certainly would make some of the currently profitable customers unprofitable.

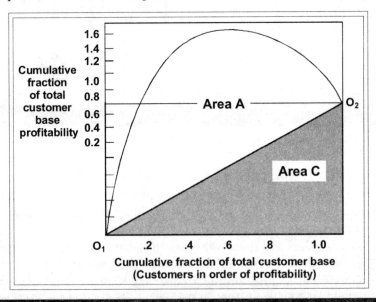

Fig. 7.7 *Profitability Distribution of a Customer Base :*
The Stobachoff Curve

Source: Storbocka (1994)

If every customer were equally profitable (and all customers were profitable), the Stocbachoff curve in Fig. 7.7 would not be a curve but instead a linear function (a straight line between the points O_1 and O_2). The curve's shape correlates with the equality of the distribution and thus with the degree of subsidising between the profitable and unprofitable customers. Based on the above discussion, an index (the Stobachoff index) for the distribution of profitability could be developed. Let the profitability distribution be represented by a vector $(\mathbf{p_1}, \mathbf{p_2},..\mathbf{p_n})$, where $\mathbf{p_1}$ is the profitability to the 1th customers $(i = 1,2,...,n)$. In the curve drawn in Fig. 7.7, the profitability is arranged according to size.

$$P_1 / p_2 /...p_n \tag{7.1}$$

If the total profitability of a customer base is p, the points in the Stobachoff curve correspond to the following co-ordinates.

$$(0,0); \ 1/n, \ p_1/P); \ (2/n, \ (p_1 + p_2)/P);.....; \ (1,1). \tag{7.2}$$

The area of the curve above the O_1, O_2 line (area A) compared to the total area of the curve above the X axis (area A + area C) can then be used as a measure of the distribution. The bigger area A is in comparison with area C, the more unequal the distribution and the more extensive the subsidising effects. The Stobachoff index is thus based on the comparison of these areas. Let the area under the Stobachoff curve (between the curve and the X axis) be T $(T=A+C)$. The area of T could be estimated using the trapezoid rule.

$$T = \frac{1}{2n} \sum_{i=0}^{n-1} p_i + p_{i-1}$$

$$\text{where, } \ P_i = P_{i-1} \ \frac{P_i}{P} + - \ \text{ and } p_0 = O \tag{7.3}$$

The are a A above the O_1-O_2 line can be expressed as follows (by noting that area C = 1/2)

$$A = \frac{1}{2n} \sum_{i=o}^{n-1} (p_i + p_{i-1}) \frac{1}{2} \tag{7.4}$$

The Stobachoff index (S) can thus be calculated as a quota of A and T:

$$S = A/T. \tag{7.5}$$

The Stobachoff index is actually a measure of the studied customer base's deviation from an "ideal" customer base. When the Stobachoff index is zero, the profitability is equally distributed (i.e., all customers are equally profitable) and all customers are profitable. As soon as the index is greater than zero, the profitability is unequally distributed. The theoretical maximum value for the index is 1, and this value is reached only if there is one profitable customer with infinite profitability, a large number of customers with zero profitability, and an unprofitable customer with infinite negative profitability.

The Stobachoff index is a measure of the cross-subsidising between customers in the provider's customers base. Hence the provider can use the Stobachoff index as a management instrument that could facilitate the assessment of different customer bases over a period of time.

In an analysis of the different theoretical shapes that the Stobachoff curve could assume, it becomes obvious that an additional measure is needed in order to show the skewedness of the curve. In an extreme customer base, a hypothetical situation could exist in which there is one extremely profitable customer and the rest of the customers in the customer base and unprofitable (or close to zero). The Stobachoff index for this customer base could be the same as for a customer base with a large proportion of profitable customers. Given the same Stobachoff index, the customer base with the greater proportion of profitable customers would obviously be prefered. The **profitability proportion** is one of the measures applied to deal with such situation.

Let n_u be te number of unprofitable customers in the customer base and n the total number of customers. The profitability proportion (P) could then be expressed as

$$P = (n - n_u) /n. \tag{7.6}$$

The higher the proportion of profitable customers, the better (given the same Stobachoff index).

7.3   CUSTOMER–BASE PORTFOLIO ANALYSIS

The Stobachoff index, combined with the proportion of profitable customers could be utilised in several ways. It could be used to follow the development of a certain customer base over time, besides grading the customer bases within the same company. In companies where, for instance, customers are affiliated administratively to different geographic areas, the index may be used in making comparative studies of the customer bases in each area. The indices will give information of the sensitivity of the profitability of the customer bases and thus on the risk involved in the management of the customer relationship in the particular area.

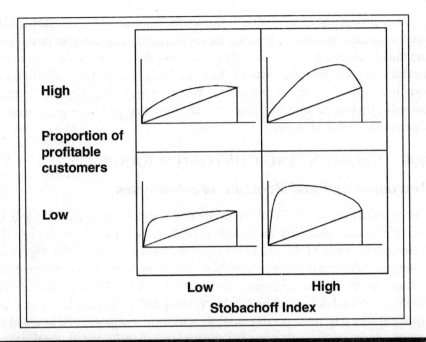

High

Proportion of
profitable
customers

Low

Low   High

Stobachoff Index

**Fig. 7.8   Customer-Base Portfolio Analysis (Verbal and Graphic
Depictions)**

Based on the index, the analysis of the genetic development situations of a customers base coulod also be made by combining the two dimensions. The generic situations are valid when one compares the profitable companies with the same level of aggregated profitability. The combination is depicted in 7.8. The best situation would be that the Stobachoff index is O and the proportion of profitable customers is 1. In this situation, the risks involved in dealing with the customer base are proportionally smaller as the company is not as dependent on a small number of customers. The need to segment the customer base grows smaller as P approaches 1 and S approaches 0. Thus there would be no need to find ways to group the customer base in situation.

Having a high Stobachoff index combined with a high proportion of profitable customers would indicate that there are a small number of very unprofitable customers eroding the aggregated profitability. Thus the unit under investigation may radically improve its profitability by identifying the unprofitable customers and influencing the reasons behind the unwanted economic results. In a situation where the unit total cost is to a large extent variable, it may be an interesting alternative for the company to try to terminate its relationship with the most unprofitable customers and thus radically improve the aggregated profitability of the unit. This would not be the case, however, in most retail banks, where the total cost is to a high degree fixed.

A low proportion of profitable customers combined with a low Stobachoff index indicates that there probably are no extremely unprofitable customers and thus, even though there are only a small number of profitable customers, the risks involved with the customer base are fairly low. As the profitability is equally distributed, there is probably a little need for a differentiated strategy towards different customers. Hence it is unlikely that there is a great need to segment the customer base.

7.4   SEGMENTING CUSTOMER BASES

Retrospective and Prospective Analyses

It is generally observed that there exists two distinct segmentation needs in maintaining and enhancing the customers relationships. First, there is a need to determine the state of the existing customers base in terms of the degree of homogeneity over a number of variables describing both the documented patronage behaviour of the customers and the background data on the customers. This type of analysis could be labeled **retrospective** because it is based on historical data. The retrospective analysis is more of a strategic tool as it makes possible decisions regarding product and price positioning and discrimination. It also allows for systematic evaluation of the state of the customer base in terms of possible risks and possibilities within the customer base.

The second type of analysis could be labelled prospective because it deals with the provider's ability to enhance the existing customer relationship. The **prospective** analysis is operative or tactical in nature, because the key issue involved in the process is to find ways to enhance a particular relationship or a group of relationships. Such analysis is oriented towards creating practical solutions on ways of (a) approaching customers (b) communicating with them, and (c) influencing their behavior. These concepts have already been explained in the earlier part of the book.*

7.5   VALUE CHAIN ANALYSIS

Concept of Value

The strategic value vision targets customers for which the value is to be created, primarily through the vehicle of a "value concept". The value concept is a business definition based on results and the way they are to be attained (process quality), rather than the products or services. According to Nicholas De Bonis *(et.al)*(2003*),* the value concept is achieved with the maximum benefit for customers, employees, partners, and investors through an operating strategy

---

* For detailed information on this topic, refer *Handbook of Relationship Marketing,* Jagdish N Sheth and Atul Parvatiyar, Califorina, Sage Publications.

that seeks to leverage results over cost by means of such factors as organisation, policies, processes, practices, measures, controls, and incentives. All this is supported by a value delivered system comprising elements of an organisation's infrastructure.

In the seminal work done by Lanning, Philips and others in the early 1980s, the customer value (**v**) was defined as the equation:

End-Result Benefit (B) *minus* Price (P)

Or

V = B – P

The value is a quantification of what the customer will get *minus* what the customer has to pay. The benefits are frequently confused with the features, to which anyone who's ever worked in sales could attest. The benefits are the desirable consequences or specific advantages sought from an offering by a customer to satisfy a need. It's always a creative challenge to take a product or service, its features, and the outcomes of those features and derive a benefit (for example, the viscosity of ink—the feature that permits consistent application of a legible product time.) The price in the original value equation was defined as the cost paid for the product or service.

'Benefits' and 'price' are delimiting terms. And since the purchasing decision is a trade-off, it makes more sense to us to treat the value (V) as a ratio of 'desired benefits' (DB) over 'relative costs' (RC) or V=DB/RC. In this context, the 'value' is a quantification of what the customer will get *divided* by what the customer has to give up in the exchange. The terms 'desired benefits' and 'relative costs' are used deliberately as more efficient descriptors in describing the value in an exchange. The 'relative costs' are more than the 'price'. The 'cost' is what the customer has to give up to acquire the 'desired benefits' derived from the products or services, which is more than the price of the product or service. According to Nicholas De Bonis *et .al* (2003*)* the three basic components of relative costs are:

1. **Acquisition costs:** This include the net price, ordering costs; time, energy, and effort in the purchasing process; cost of mistakes in order; prepurchase evaluation costs; risk; and trade-offs

2. **Possession costs;** This include the storage costs; shrinkage and obsolescence; taxes and insurance; materials management and inventory; transportation; and maintenance.

3. **Usage costs:** This include the labour costs: process costs: product shelf-life costs; replacement costs: and disposal costs.

A fourth, component of cost is **opportunity cost**—what is traded off or forfeited by the spender deciding to incur the cost. The trade-off could be forgoing quarterly sourcing and negotiation for a long-term supplier contract. The 'cost' can also include the perceived level of risk: failure to use substitute products; the time, energy, and effort required to make the purchase decision, among other situations.

To increase a value ratio, the firm should either increase the 'desired benefits' and/or decrease the 'relative costs'. In reality, there are three value ratios relevant to the customer the expected value (Ve) ratio, the value proposed (Vp) ratio, and the actual value derived (Va) ratio.

(a) In the pre-purchase stage, a need drives the buying behaviour. Here, the major preposition is the belief that a customer buys value, not the product or the services. The customer's purchase decision is motivated by the belief that it would get more value than expected, that is

$$Ve \leq Vps$$

(b) If the expected value to be derived from the firm's product or service is greater than what the customer is promised, i.e.,

$$Ve \geq Vp,$$

then the likelihood in the occurrence of a transaction is relatively small.

(c) The customers should obtain at delivery a value greater than or equal to what they were promised, i.e.,

$$Vp \leq Va.$$

This leads to the repurchase behaviour.

(d) If the customers fail to obtain the value they expected (as offered in the firm's communications and representations prior to sale), i.e.,

$$Vp \geq Va$$

(there might be problems with payment on the purchase order, expectations for adjustments to the purchase agreement), there is less chance of a repeat business.

(e) The value ratio chain that ultimately leads to a relationship over time is

$$Ve \leq Vp \leq Va.$$

This means that the actual value delivered (Va) by the firm must equal to or exceed the perceived value (Vp) promised to be delivered. In other words, the perceived value promised to be delivered must equal or exceed the expected value (Ve) the customer is seeking in a transaction with a supplier. The evaluation and adjustment of the customers' value expectations will become easier to maintain as trust builds during the lifetime of the customer relationship. The result is the ability to partner with the customers and proactively anticipate what their 'desired benefits' and 'relative costs' are going to be.

According to Nicholas De Bonis *et. al.* (2003), this powerful relationship position creates a long-term sustainable competitive advantage. It's also important to understand that the firm has also got a value ratio, defined as the 'desired benefits' derived from doing business with a customer or the value segment divided by the relative costs of acquiring, maintaining and retaining that customer or

$$V = DB/RC$$

7.6 VALUE PROFIT CHAIN

The value profit chain, as suggested by James L. Heskett (2003) *et.al* is based on "value equations" for the customers, employees, partners, and the investors. The strategic value vision is a framework for strategic planning based on several assumptions which include:

1. People buy results and process quality (the way results are achieved), not products or services, often termed a value concept, and this is very useful in forming a business definition.

2. To understand the type of results and process qualities that are sought; the targeted customers should be carefully delineated, in both demographic (age and income, for example) and psychographics (such as lifestyle, needs and fears) terms. Similarly, efforts should also be made to describe the customers that are not being targeted.

3. The primary goal of an organisation should be to leverage results and process quality over costs. This is achieved through a focused, internally consistent operating strategy comprising policies, procedures, organisational controls, incentives, and an organisational culture designed for the purpose.

4. The operating strategy is supported by the information systems (more popularly known in the present day Internet-based retailing terminology as "clicks"), locations, technology, and the "bricks and mortar" comprising the value delivery system.

5. The value could be attained by maintaining both the market and operating focus, through which both superior results for the customers (often termed "differentiation" by scholars of strategy) and low costs could be achieved at the same time.

Based on the above assumptions, Heskett derived the appropriate value equation for customers as :

$$Value = \frac{Results + Process\ Quality}{Prise + Customer\ Access\ Costs}$$

For employees, it should be read as:

$$Value = \frac{Capability + Work\ Place\ Quality}{1/wages + Job\ Access\ Costs}$$

Further, they also observed that the employee value leads to satisfaction, loyalty, trust, and commitment. The satisfied, loyal, trusting, and committed customers are (a) the primary driver of company growth and profitability, and (b) important determinants of investor value. Finally, the fruits of growth and profitability are reinvested in value for partners (suppliers, communities, and others), employees, customers and investors.

$$\text{Employee Value Eq.} = \frac{\text{Capability to deliver results} + \text{Quality of workplace}}{1/\text{Total Income} + \text{Job 'Access Costs'}}$$

$$\text{Partner Value Equation} = \frac{\text{Revenue} + \text{Quality of Relationship}}{\text{Costs of doing business}}$$

$$\text{Investor Value Equation} = \frac{\text{Returns to investors} + \text{Investments in} \atop \text{R \& D, Employyes, Customers, and Partners}}{\text{Investment Base}}$$

$$\text{Customer Value Equation} = \frac{\text{Results} + \text{Process Quality}}{\text{Cost (Price)} + \text{Customer Access Code}}$$

According to James L. Heskett (2003) *et al* the value profit chain comprises a series of inter-related phenomena organised according to the following principles:

1. Customer loyalty and commitment are the primary drivers of growth and profitability.

2. Customer loyalty and commitment emanate from customer satisfaction compared to competition.

3. Customer satisfaction results from the realisation of high levels of value compared to competitors.

4. Value is created by the satisfied, committed, loyal and productive employees. Its perception by customers (both internal and external to the organisation), suppliers, and other important constituents of an organisation is enhanced most by the satisfaction levels of those employees in direct contact with constituents.

5. Employees satisfaction results from several factors, the most important of which include: (a) the "fairness" of management; (b) the quality of one's peers in the workplace; (c) the opportunity for personal growth on the job; (d) capability, the latitude within limits to deliver results to customers; (e) the levels of customers satisfaction achieved in customer facing jobs (the so-called mirror effect); and (f) monetary compensation. Several studies into the phenomenon have revealed that these factors often occur in the above mentioned order. It is at the heart of efforts to build the organisational capability to deliver both high value and low costs.

6. The relationships between elements of the value profit chain are self-reinforcing. They could work for or against the organisational performance.

7.7 CUSTOMER DEFECTIONS

One of the most illuminating units of failure in business is customer defection, because it sheds light on two critical flows of value. First, a customer defection is the clearest possible sign of deteriorating stream of value from the company to its customers. Secondly, increasing defection rates diminish the cash flow from customers to the company even if the company replaces the lost customers (as a result of reduced customer duration).

Opportunity Costs

The opportunity costs is an inevitable element in the analysis on the profitability of the customers. The opportunity cost involves the cost of serving the defectors. Here the underlying assumption is that one rupee saved in the cost of serving the customer is as equivalent as one rupee gained from them. This concept is adopted from the production management.

Defections are not the only customer measure that requires systematic tracking with an eye towards failure detection and analysis. It is also important to measure the rate at which a company is adding new customers to maintain a healthy level of growth. One valuable statistic for this purpose is the **gain rate**, the number of new customers added during the year as a percentage of the total customers at the beginning of the year. Because of up-front acquisition and start-up costs, the high gain rates usually penalise the current year earnings. However, if the quality of inflow is high, and if the retention of mature customers also remains high, then the future of business could be viewed of as standing on a solid ground.

7.8 REDEFINING BUSINESS PERFORMANCE THROUGH CUSTOMER- CENTRIC MARKETING

Measurement is a business idiom. The choice of what a business measures (a) communicates values, (b) channels employee thinking, and (c) sets management priorities. Moreover, through their inclusion in the feedback loop that underlie all organisational learning, the measures define what a company would eventually become. Deciding what to measure and determining the ways of linking these measures to incentives are among the most important decisions

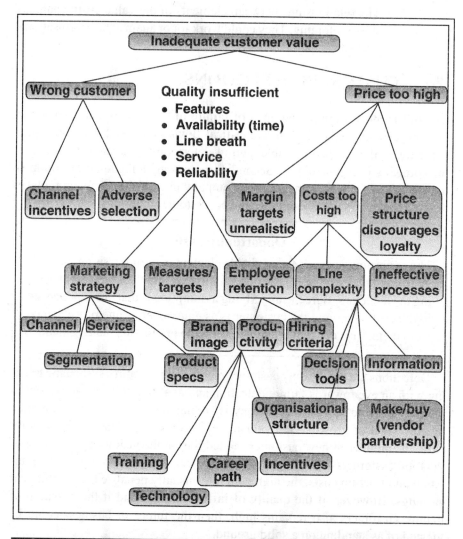

Fig. 7.9 Analysis of Customer Defection

Source: Frederick F. Reichheld (1996), *The Loyalty Effect,* Boston, Bain & Co Inc. and Harvard Business School Press

that a senior manager is expected make. The development of the right kind of measurement system is therefore an important aspect in this regard. Ideally, the new system should be compatible with the familiar profit-based measures on which most firms operate. However, it should also incorporate the critical dimensions of the value creation process that are hidden in the shadows of profit accounting.

The **growth cycle** of a businees enterprise consist of three sectors: customers, employees, and investors. The 'measurement approach' as suggested by Frederick F. Reichheld specify two basic reports for each of the three sectors. They are analogous to the balance sheet covered human capital rather than the financial assets, and in place of the income statement, they had developed a value-flow statement to show what drives the human capital balance sheet.

The second report measured not only the flow of value to the investors ("profit" on the accounting income statement), it also monitored the other five streams of value that drive the human capital balance sheet:

➤ the value flowing from the **company** to the *customers* and *employees*, and

➤ the value flowing from **customers**, **employees**, and **investors** to the *company*.

This new integrated system of measures linked each sector to the other two, permitting the organisation to manage the entire value creation spiral systematically.

Measurement Hierarchy

The measurement hierarchy is given in Fig.7.10. The uppermost line, called the **full value**, is the price above which the customers will defect—the price above which the customers get less value than they have paid for. The difference between the full value and actual price is the **consumer surplus**.

According to Frederick F. Reichheld (1996), a business enterprise should require reports like the customer balance sheet and a customer value flow statement to study and manage its customer base net present value (NPV). On the balance sheet, the customer base is divided into (a) new customers, (b) gainers, (c) decliners, and (d) defectors. The gainers and decliners are the current customers who are doing more or less business with the company than in the previous years. Once the firms have divided their distinctive customer population into well-defined categories, the firm could very well attribute the revenue growth along the same lines. By combining this information with an estimate of the future inflows of new customers the firm could calculate the estimated NPV of their customer base. Tracking these balance sheet items over time will provide the biggest opportunities for a firm for further improvement.

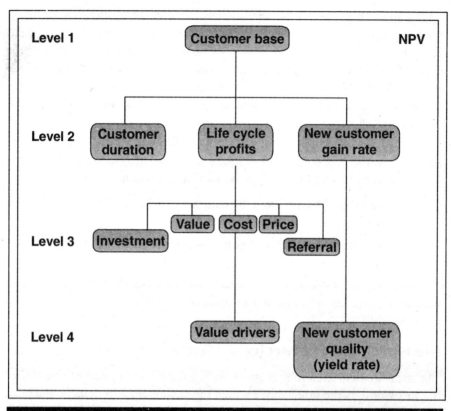

Fig. 7.10 The Measurement Hierarchy

Source: Frederick F. Reichheld (1996), *The Loyalty Effect,* Boston, Bain & Co Inc. and Harvard Business School Press

CUSTOMER BALANCE SHEET				CUSTOMER VALUE FLOW STATEMENT			
Customer category	*Number*	*Percentage of Revenue*	*NPV*	**Value Drivers**			
Beginning balance	—	—	—	• Target customers			
				• Dimensions of value analysis			
+ New customers	—	—	—	• Measures			
				• Source of advantage			
+ Gainers	—	—	—	*Value delivered to customer*			
− Decliners	—	—	—	competitor			
− Defectors	—	—	—	*Company*	X	Y	Z
= Ending Balance	—	—	—	**Price**	—	—	—
				Qlty Drivers	—	—	—

		competitor		
Retention	— — —			
Share of				
Wallet	— — —			
Gain	— — —			
Yield	— — —			
Value received from customer.				

Company	X	Y	Z
New Cust. NPV	—	—	—
Current Cus. NPV	—	—	—
Defector NPV	—	—	—
Avg. profit per Cust.	—	—	—
Average revenue per Customer	—	—	—

Fig. 7.11   The Customer Balance Sheet and Value Flow Chart

Source: Frederick F. Reichheld (1996), *The Loyalty Effect*, Boston, Bain & Co Inc. and Harvard Business School Press

According to Frederick F. Reichheld (1996) an accounting of the flows of value to and from customers, brings us to the *value flow statement*. The stream of value flowing to the customer is probably the single most important element in any business. Creating and delivering superior value to the customer is the center of the value creation cycle and it underpins all business success.

Below the value proposition, the *value flow statement* should list the critical measures employed to monitor the relative value of the firm's offering. One important element to track in this regard is the *pricing factor in relation to competitors*. Another is a set of benchmark *statistics for* the crucial dimensions of *quality*. In some business enterprises, timeliness is the critical dimension; in others, reliability. Still others find that fashion and features drive the value. Sometimes the measures are simple and straightforward (e.g., the number of rings before a phone is answered, or the number of days to settle a claim). Two more statistics appear in the second part of the customer value flow statement. These are the *gain rate* – the ratio of new customers to the current customer base—and the *yield rate* – the percentage of customers solicited who actually sign up. A healthy gain rate is evidence of a superior value proposition, especially if it is accompanied by good retention rates.

The average profit per customer and the average revenue per customer are also practical statistics for monitoring the flow of value to the firm. However, the companies whose inflows of new customers have varied over time must be cautious and should analyse these statistics, one tenure group at a time. One final dimension that could be revealing is the quality of defectors versus the quality of new customers. Ideally, the defectors should be of low value and the new customers should have high expected net present values (NPVs), thought that is rarely the case. Many companies find just the opposite where the defector quality exceeds the quality of new customers.

The company's first step should be to calculate its investment in each new customer. It allocates the cost of the advertising and marketing that brought in each new group of customers, then adds the cost of processing and setting up of each new account. Close attention to product margins and activity levels then allows the company to calculate the yield it requires on these investments to bring each new class of customers to the profitability range. With its investment per customer and its required yield nailed down, the company goes on to track new applications as a percentage of the current customers. It watches the rate at which new applications turn into real accounts (i.e., accounts that the customers actually fund) and the percentage of those that become active enough to contribute to profits. Finally, using the life-cycle profit and attrition patterns for similar older customers, the firm could quite accurately predict the percentage of any new class that will eventually produce a profit and a positive NPV for the company.

CONCLUSION

We can conclude this chapter by looking at the future implications of customer analysis and company profit enhancing capabilities. In this context one has to understand two critical factors. First, we will need to acknowledge the inherent variability of consumers' expectations. Second, we will see greater divergence in organizations' abilities to deliver on their promises. Those who win, will be able to:

➢ Define and focus on core customer groups
➢ Define a relevant, feasible value proposition for that core group
➢ Deliver improved, consistent experience across all points of interaction, resulting in a stable, positive perception of the brand
➢ Streamline business processes and adopt technology solutions to accomplish all this effectively and efficiently.

The discussion provided in the chapter will certainly lead our companies to focus more on customers … not necessarily all … but very few…they can meaningfully participate in the relationship building process with company people, product and services. In short, profitability analysis can provide organisation to focus on core customer groups that make a difference to their business success.

SUMMARY

✓ Lifetime customer value is the potential value of customer which the firm estimate over a period of five to fifteen years depending on the interaction level and customers affinity.

✓ The first step is establishing awareness of the importance of lifetime value is to understand the hierarchy of relationships.

✓ Customer-Product Profitability Analysis (CPA) conducted with the help of a technique called Activity Based Costing (ABC) estimates the revenue running to a company, minus the costs increased.

✓ Customers are classified into different profit tiers—Platinum, Gold, Iron and Silver.

✓ There are three basic factors for retention of customers—adding financial benefits, adding social benefits and adding structural ties.

✓ In relationship and service marketing strategies are focused on the moment of truth or the service encounter revelations.

✓ Value is a quantification of what the customer will get minus what the customer has to pay hence, $V = B - P$

✓ Value Profit chain is based on value equations, for customers employees, partners and investors.

✓ Opportunity Cost is the cost of serving the defectors is very important for any analysis of profitability.

✓ Customer Defections shows the signs of deteriorating stream of value from the Company to its customers.

CHAPTER REVIEW QUESTIONS

1. What do you mean by lifetime customer value?
2. Narrate the savings in customer retention for a cellular service provider.
3. Explain the evolution in value-centered thinking.
4. Explain the hierarchy of customer behaviors in detail.
5. Elucidate the customer-product profitability analysis.
6. Describe the various levels of profitability analysis.
7. Narrate the episode configuration matrix.

8. Describe the value-chain analysis.

9. Explain the value-profit chain and its implications.

10. How do you analyse customer defections?

11. Explain the measurement hierarchy

12. Devise a hypothetical customer balance sheet and the value flow statement to a relationship banker

---

CASE STUDY
FCS AIRLINES-MARKETING RELATIONSHIP FOR PROFIT

BACKGROUND

The Federal Charter Service (FCS) was started in the year 2000 with a view to provide quality and value added services to passengers from all over the world to Kerala. It is estimated that nearly 10 million Keralites are settled in several parts of the world which include the US, UK, Singapore, Germany, France, Switzerland and so on. The state is also receiving a substantial inflow of non-resident Indians (NRI) remittance from the Gulf, European and American countries besides its tourism receipts. The state has been witnessing a boom in its hospitality sector, (thanks to the increasing chartered flight tourism services) since 1997. The NRI Keralites themselves had mobilised the money for setting up the first privately owned international airport (at Nedumbassery in Cochin) in India in 1998 (which in itself revealed the interest shown by the NRIs in developing the air transport business to Kerala to handle the heavy passenger traffic to the state). Taking into account of all these factors the FCS in 2001 decided to expand its network in a global manner including the Middle East and Europe. As a part of it, the FCS acquired new aircrafts and changed its name to FCS Airlines.

The FCS Airlines concentrated mainly on marketing. Even the airline's name and its logo —a stylised Maharaja sitting in a house boat— decorating the aircraft's dark blue tail fin became very popular on the routes it operated. The goal was to create a distinct airline service that would be international in scope but Indian in outlook.

Most importantly, the top management, having realised the importance of customer service in a highly competitive world, decided to enhance its in-flight services. As a part of that, they made their cabin crew, the prime link between the passenger and the airline, realise their importance in the airlines' business prospects and launched programmes to make them more customer-friendly. The idea was to utilise Kerala's real resource—the natural hospitality of its people—as a competitive advantage. Similarly, the FCS also became the first airline to introduce "snoozers" (fully reclining seats) in the aircraft. Since the company did not belong to IATA (International Air Transport Association), the FCS's management went against the rules by serving free drinks, offering free movie headsets and other extras. Research conducted later had shown that, when all other things were equal, passengers responded most to the appeal of high quality in-flight services.

The "Kerala Girl"—the personification of Kerala's tradition and friendliness—was realised as the model of an FCS stewardess and it became a reality only after painstaking and intensive recruiting and training procedures. For their 'good looking' and 'caring' factors, the girls were given above average wages and high status in the company. They were given a maximum of three contract terms of five years each and were also provided the possibility of promotions to senior jobs after their 15 years tenure.

An extensive advertising campaign was designed to promote these stewardesses, dressed in hand-woven light coloured silk sarees (lengthy dresses made from the traditional silk fabric and designed by the Paris couturier Balmain). These distinctively uniformed women became the symbol of the airline's mission to deliver the high quality personalised service. The male flight attendants were more conventionally dressed in light blue blazers and black trousers.

Research studies conducted later revealed that the appearance of their inflight cabin crew had the most lasting impact on passengers. Travellers reported that their beautiful uniform and charm were, in reality, all that the advertising had promised, and that the inflight service was as good as, or rather much better than, any other service.

The top management was equally concerned with the services on the ground. In 2002, a subsidiary company, the Kairali Airport Terminal Services (KATS), was formed to perform the ground handling, catering, and related tasks. Later, it started offering its services on a contract basis to other carriers that had operations in Trivandrum.

The FCS's consolidated financial results for the fiscal year ending March 31, 2003 showed a revenue earnings of Rs 44.95 crore. The number of passengers carried was three lakh and the load factor was only 78.3 per cent. The FCS preferred non-price forms of competition such as better service, more destinations, more frequent schedules, and newer fleets. With the entry of other world players into the region, however, pricing has also become an important feature.

The airline's fleet of two Boeing 747s and two Airbus 310s was the youngest fleet among all international carriers, with an average age of 4.75 years, compared to an industry average of around 10 years. The company had two new aircraft on order and another one on option. The management was convinced that the sate-of-the-art aircrafts were not only more attractive to passengers and helped staff provide better service, but also offered other advantages such as greater reliability and lower fuel consumption. The FCS network linked 63 cities in 12 countries, and soon it would fulfill a long-held ambition to serve the East Coast of the India with transatlantic service from Frankfurt and New York.

MAINTAINING THE CUSTOMER CREDIBILITY

Recognising that the most exciting years were now over, the top management continued to stress the importance of the FCS's customer credibility and service culture. The underlying principle was that the customer who came first should be carried through all levels of the organisation. The way the customers were handled at each point of contact was analysed with paramount importance. The company policy stated that if a trade-off had to be made, it should be done in favour of the customer. For example, contrary to the practice at other airlines, no customer was not allowed to be downgraded for a FCS Airlines senior executive who wanted a special seat.

The underlying philosophy was to enable the staff to place themselves in the customer's position. A lot of training time was thus experientially based. Executives at key positions were sent on special missions to find out the way other airlines handled their customers. Special delay simulation games groomed staff on ways to cope with the delay situations, a major complaint often received from the passengers.

One principle that was highly expected of the FCS staff was the aspect of 'flexibility' in their dealings with the customers, even if it required more time and effort. The management constantly reiterated that the customers should not be forcibly told to behave in a stipulated manner (simply because it suited the company). [For instance, some passengers would like to eat as soon as they boarded, while others preferred to wait. The customers should not be pigeonholed, they often changed their minds. They might come on board intending to sleep and then decide to watch a movie after all. On long hauls, flexibility was especially important. Most passengers had individual habits that corresponded to their travel agendas, which could include sleeping at the beginning and working later, or *vice versa*.]

The staff had learned that the customers were much more satisfied when given a choice. Offering more meal variations automatically reduced the number of unhappy people. Menus, typically changed by other airlines not more than four times a year, were altered every week on the FCS's high frequency flights. The information technology enabled the chefs to fine-tune their menu and immediately withdraw any dishes that were poorly received. Although there were marginal costs associated with such tactics, management firmly believed that these efforts would distinguish the FCS Airlines from its competitors. A service productivity index (SPI) was computed each quarter in order to assess the service quality standards. The multilingual in-flight survey was conducted to categorise the customer impressions on key issues; followed by a compilation of this information along with (a) the data on punctuality, (b) baggage mishandled/recovered per 1000 passengers, and (c) the ratio of complaints to compliments addressed to the management.

As soon as a complaint relating directly to a specific in-flight experience was received, the crew members could be temporarily taken out of the system and given special training. The cabin crew members were released from their flight schedules three or four times a year to meet with the training experts. Senior cabin crew members would meet every Monday morning for the feedback and exchange sessions with the service support personnel. One "ritual" practiced was to address the crew from the control center just before the takeoff about topical issues, special promotions and other issues relevant to the services.

BASELINE—CUSTOMER AND PRODUCT LINE

The product line was divided into two classes of travel: (a) the business class (accounting for 15 per cent of passengers) and (b) the economy class(accounting for 85 per cent of the passengers). The nature of flights varied in length, from less than one hour to over 13 hours for non-stop flights to Europe. Exhibit 1 shows the percentage breakdown of the airline's daily flights by the number of hours and the amount of overnight travel. On an average, the load factor was somewhat higher in the economy class (close to 80%) than in the business class. The top management believed that the business passenger market held the future for the airline—both in numbers and the yield. The expectations of these particular segment of customers, as the FCS marketing executives knew, have been constantly rising and their needs have changed considerably since the previous decade. Research revealed that the business travellers:

➢ tended to be impatient and resented having to wait;

➢ wanted to have the facilities found in airport lounges—from showers to fax machines—also available in the sky;

➢ disliked wasting time on board and wanted to be occupied throughout the flight.

EXHIBIT - 1

DETAILS ON DURATION OF FCS FLIGHTS

	Up to 2 hrs	*2 - 4 hrs*	*Beyond 4 hrs*
Flights	60%	18%	22%
Revenues	25%	25%	50%
*Mainly during day	All	60%	25%
Mainly during night		40%	75%

* depending on whether it goes through midnight of the ....ginating point.

In order to tap the market, the FCS management decided to introduce several technological innovations which included the installation of small TV screens at each business class seats, offering passengers video entertainment and the installation of satellite-linked air-to-ground telephone service.

New Initiatives

Mr Vinod Madhavan an MBA from the Harvard Business School was appointed the vice-president, marketing, FCS Airlines in September 2002. He has got 20 years of experience in formulating the marketing strategies for major airlines, including the Singapore Airlines and British Airways.

Vinod defined the level of customer relationship to include:

➤ The media through which the contacts take place. (e.g., e-mail, telephone, snail mail contacts)

➤ The frequency of contacts (and timing may be an important element here)

➤ The point of contact (which part of your organisation)

➤ The scope of each contact—what subjects are covered

➤ The information exchange in each contact

➤ The outcome of each contacts which is the next step for further contacts

➤ The cost of each contact to the customer (which include both physical and human resources efforts).

In most cases, the customers have an idea about the minimum acceptable and desired levels of relationships. If the customers already have an experience of dealing with the FCS, there may also be a perceived level—the level the customer would perceive that he/she should receive. The perceived levels contrast with the actual levels, which is a statement from the FCS point of view as to what relationship actions were definitely carried out.

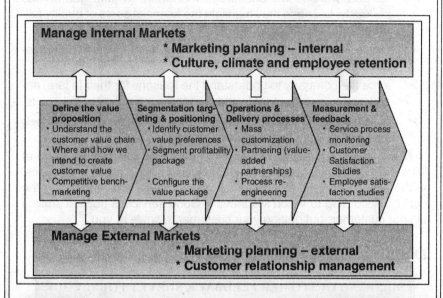

Fig. 7A The Relationship Management Chain*

Source: Jagdish N. Sheth and Atul Parvatiyar (ed, 2002), *Handbook of Relationship Marketing*, California, Sage Publication.

Figure 7A describes the relationship management chain in detail. Here it is obvious that the firm has to establish relationship both with the external and the internal markets. A few customers would have threshold levels of satisfaction and dissatisfaction. The relationship standards, which fall below the threshold, should be strongly criticised, but once within the threshold, the performance should be taken for granted. There may also be a band of relationship attributes within which they are more or less indifferent.

Service Guarantees

As a part of relationship building process (to be specific—the mutual trust, credibility and commitment), the FCS has chosen to offer customers an unconditional guarantee of satisfaction, promising an easy-to-claim replacement refund or credit in the event of dissatisfaction. Vinod Madhavan argues that such guarantees are powerful tools for both promoting and achieving the service qualities, as these guarantees would:

➢ force the FCS to focus on what their customers want and expect in each element of the service

> set clear standards, telling customers and employees alike what the FCS really stands for. The payouts to compensate customers for poor service will encourage managers to take guarantees seriously, because they highlight the financial costs of quality failures

> require the development of systems for generating meaningful customer feedback and action on that

> force the company to understand the reasons for their failure, encouraging them to identify and overcome the potential fail points

> build marketing muscle by reducing the risk of the purchase decision and building the long-term loyalty

Many organisations, known for their excellent service, are good at listening to both their customers and their customer-contact employees. In the airline services, the customer plays a major role in defining the quality. According to Vinod Madhavan "Good service is not just smiling at your customer, but getting your customer to smile at you."

EXHIBIT 2

SHOWING CUSTOMER FEEDBACK SURVEY FORM YOUR OPENION ON TODAY'S FLIGHT

1. Name (Surname first) : Mr./ Mrs./Ms.
2. Your Flight:
   (1) Flight Number _____ From _____ To _____
   (2) Date _____
   (3) Seat No._____
   (4) Class of Travel   Club Premiere ☐   Economy ☐

		Excellent	Good	Average	Poor
1. FREQUENT FLYER PROGRAMME	Are you a member of our "Frequent Flyer" programe? If yes, how do you rate the programe?	☐	☐	☐	☐
2. ACCESSIBILITY	(a) Accessibility	☐	☐	☐	☐
	(1) Reservations	☐	☐	☐	☐
	(2) Inquiry	☐	☐	☐	☐
	(3) Airport	☐	☐	☐	☐
	(4) Tele Chek-in	☐	☐	☐	☐

	(b) Reservations	☐	☐	☐	☐
	(1) Staff efficiency	☐	☐	☐	☐
	(2) Staff courtesy	☐	☐	☐	☐
3. AIRPORT SERVICES	(a) Check-in procedures	☐	☐	☐	☐
	(1) Ease in finding the Check-in counter for this flight	☐	☐	☐	☐
	(2) Time taken in queq to reach the counter	☐	☐	☐	☐
	(3) Grooming of the Ground Staff	☐	☐	☐	☐
	(4) Staff efficiency	☐	☐	☐	☐
	(5) Personal attention at Check-in counter	☐	☐	☐	☐
	(b) Boarding Procedures	☐	☐	☐	☐
	(1) Boarding announcements and procedures	☐	☐	☐	☐
	(2) If your flight was delayed, how well was it handled	☐	☐	☐	☐
	(c) Your overall satisfaction with our airport staff and services	☐	☐	☐	☐
	(d) Time taken for baggage screening	☐	☐	☐	☐
4. INFLIGHT	(a) Service	☐	☐	☐	☐
	(1) Friendly welcome/ greting at the time of boarding.	☐	☐	☐	☐

	(2) Help during embrakation phase (guidance, hand laggage & stowage)	☐	☐	☐	☐
	(3) Courteous and professional service	☐	☐	☐	☐
	(4) Grooming of the cabin crew	☐	☐	☐	☐
	(5) Cabin crew announcements: Clarity/ Content	☐	☐	☐	☐
	(b) Your overall satisfaction with our in-flight service	☐	☐	☐	☐
	(c) Reading material	☐	☐	☐	☐
	(1) In-flight magazine (Jet wing)	☐	☐	☐	☐
	(2) Selection of newspapers/ magazines	☐	☐	☐	☐
	(d) Cockpit crew	☐	☐	☐	☐
	(1) Announcements: Clarity/Content	☐	☐	☐	☐
	(e) Others	☐	☐	☐	☐
	(1) Temperature in the cabin				
	(2) Cleanliness of the cabin				
	(3) Cleanliness of the washroom				
		Veg.		**Non-Veg.**	
5. FOOD	(1) Type of meal enjoyed on this flight	☐	☐	☐	☐
	(2) Quality (taste) of the meal	☐	☐	☐	☐

	(3) Quantity of the meal	☐	☐	☐	☐
	(4) Persentation (eye appeal) of the meal	☐	☐	☐	☐
	(5) Appropriateness of the menu for the time of day	☐	☐	☐	☐
	(6) Your overall satisfaction with your meal	☐	☐	☐	☐
	(7) Did you receive the type of meal you requested for, at the time of making your reservation?	Yes ☐	No ☐	Did not request	☐
6. OVERALL EXPERIENCE	How do you rate your total experience with Jet Airways on this trip	☐	☐	☐	☐

If you rate us as average or poor in any of the attributes, please give us your suggestions to improve

> *Frequent Flyer Programme* _____
> *Accessibility* _____
> *Airport Services* _____
> In-flight _____
> Food _____
> *Overall Experience* _____

Exhibit 2 shows the improved customer feed back form issued during the journey. The company offers simplified procedure for business class travelers and speedier check-in process, with the boarding passes and baggage tags being automatically encoded and printed at the check-in. The boarding pass included seat allocation and gate information, and confirmed the special requests such as the vegetarian meals. A Telecar system was also introduced to take the baggage from one terminal to another within three minutes. It was then manually sorted and handled. If an urgent flight connection had to be made, this fact was communicated to the staff in advance so that the baggage could be taken by a trolley to the waiting aircraft.

PASSENGER RESERVATIONS AND GENERAL SALES SYSTEM

a. Pre-Flight Experience

Like most other carriers, the FCS Airlines depended heavily on the general sales agent to sell its services. However, in 2003, the airline initiated its own computer reservation and check-in system, the DASHCOM. When reservations were made on the FCS Airlines by the travel agents, a wide variety of special meal options, reflecting the travellers' health and religious needs, were also offered. The special meal requests were forwarded to the catering department which received a print-out of all such requests for each flight. The special meal request was linked to the seat allocated to the passenger.

b. In-flight and Post-Flight Experience

The ground services department was responsible for the ground handling of passengers' baggage, cargo and mail at all airports in the FCS network. Comparatively, it is easier to control the quality of service in the air than on the ground. The key decisions are made at the corporate office and implemented on board. The airports, on the other hand, are difficult to control as most of them are too crowded, with too few gates and counters. However, advanced technology could play a key part in this regard.

While the in-flight service staff typically provides the customers with some pleasant offerings—free headsets, free newspapers, free drinks, free meals, free movies—the ground service staff have a much tougher time (as they deal in tickets, excess baggage fees, or they say you cannot have the seat you want). It should be reminded at this point that thirty per cent of all the complaints relate to seat assignments, while another 20 per cent to aircraft delays. The handling of these 'delay situations' could create a big impact on the customer opinion. The passengers would become really unhappy when the staff is not in a position to provide any information, help them find seats on alternative airlines, or obtain hotel rooms when they are delayed overnight. The baggage losses also accounts for about 20 per cent of total complaints.

THE CASE

Mr. Vinod Madhavan is working hard to improve in-flight services and trying to find answers to the questions such as:

1. What technology-based services should be developed to improve the customers' experience in the air?

2. Whether an "office in the air" concept would actually work? To what extent should more comfort and entertainment be provided?

3. How could the business class facilities be differentiated from the ones in economy?

4. Most importantly, how could all these ideas be consolidated and effected so that the FCS Airlines would be the technological leader in civil aviation? Will Mr. Vinod Madhavan be successful in improving the FCS Airline Service? Discuss

INFORMATION TECHNOLOGY ENABLED MARKETING

"Knowledge is a process of piling up facts; wisdom lies in their simplification."

Alexander Graham Bell

Learning Objectives

After reading this chapter you should understand:

- Database marketing and some of its features such as data design, data ware housing.
- Meaning of the term 'holding the data'.
- The importance of customer database in relationship marketing
- The usage of database for public utility services
- The meaning of digital revolution
- The importance of technologicalship marketing

INTRODUCTION

The 'relationship' between a customer and a business enterprise is character-ised by the strength of the relationship, the continuity of the relationship and the multiple dimensions involved in the relationship. From a marketing point of view, it means, among other things, (a) that the buyer is known to the seller by his/her name, (b) that the buyer's geographic location and other identifying characteristics are known, and (c) that the seller can communi-cate directly with the buyer. These dealings should be of sufficient 'duration',— a factor which differentiates them from mere transactions. The providers of mobile phone service and banking services, for example, have always been involved in relationship marketing.

In the world of relationship marketing, the buyer and the seller become interdependent. The relationship entails mutual expectations and obligations. If the product carries a warranty, the buyer registers the purchase with the manufacturer, thereby establishing the basis for marketing relationship.

True relationship marketing practice requires a fundamental shift in attitude towards viewing the customer as a partner and a business asset to be managed for long-term profitability. The sale should not be viewed either as a conquest or as the end of the marketing process, rather it should be construed as the beginning of a relationship with the customer. The information technology (IT), which includes the telecommunications, data storage and retrieval technologies, and the world wide web, have created a revolution that has shifted the business firm's orientation from production efficiency back to the customer needs. Since the IT methods also permit direct, personalised communication with the individual customer, the "high-tech" marketing could also be labelled as "high touch" marketing. The IT could draw the customer closer to the company, build a relationship, and reduce the probability of customer defection.

Nowadays, the companies foresee their best profit opportunities in exploring their customer base, which implies selling more products and services to their existing customers rather than trying to find new customers for their products. The concept of relationship marketing has thus made a shift in the focus of business enterprises from a product and a product-centric view of the business towards a customer-centric view advocated by the marketing concept. The purpose is not to sell what the company has made, but to offer products and services that are tailored more precisely to the customer needs and wants.

The customer relationship marketing does make sense in selected situations, wherein the potential value of future transactions with the same customer over a period of time is higher. The life-time value of the customer must be high enough to support the marketing investment required. Besides, the potential value of the relationship marketing is a function of the relative ease of identifying and reaching the target customer. It could help if the purchase is planned rather than made on impulse, and it should involve a substantial degree of product differentiation.

8.1 DATABASE MARKETING

In relationship marketing, there are good and bad customers. The **good customers** are those: (a) who value the best practices of the company, (b) who are attracted by its value propositions, (c) who value the relationship they have with the firm as an asset in their personal life or business, and (d) who are willing to pay fairly for the resources committed to solve their problems. A true, long-term buyer-seller relationship develops when the marketer knows the name and characteristics of the customers, including the history of transactions. Besides, there should also be the potential for a two-way communication so that the marketer could direct the communication at specific individuals rather than the anonymous consumer in the mass market. Similarly, the potential customer could respond in a proper manner and the marketer can then tailor its response accordingly.

The important aspect in database marketing is to understand the customer in a comprehensive manner, and for that the company should maintain a proper customer database. The **customer database** is an organised collection of comprehensive information about individual customers or prospects that is current, accessible and actionable for such marketing purposes as (a) lead generation, (b) lead qualification, (c) sale of a product or service, or (d) maintenance of customer relationships. In short, the **database marketing** is the process of building, maintaining and utilising the databases (on the customer, products, suppliers, and resellers) for the purpose of contacting, transacting, and building relationships. The database marketing is an interactive approach to marketing, which uses the individually addressable marketing media and channels (such as mail, telephone, and the sales force).

The salient features of database marketing include:

➢ Extending help to a company to reach its target audience;

➢ Stimulating the customer demand; and

➢ Recording and maintaining an electronic database of the customer, and all commercial contacts, so that the business firm could improve their future contacts and devise a more realistic marketing strategy

In interactive marketing, each customer is a subject of record in the database that provide the customer's or the prospective customer's personal details and other contact information. This information would include the personal characteristics, media usage patterns and purchase histories, including a record of previous contact with the company. The content of the data file would be customised to the specific needs of the marketer and the type of business involved. The database of customer information, when combined with sophisticated analytical techniques makes possible substantially better and precise segmentation strategies. It would also be possible to monitor the changes in these segments over time (the old segments decrease in size while other segments grow), and manage the customer profitability of each segment.

Virtually every company knows that 80 per cent of its revenue comes from 20 per cent of its customers. It is not uncommon to find that as many as 30 per cent of customers are unprofitable (in banking, it is known that the number can be as high as 45 per cent). Measuring the customer profitability requires data that relate both to revenues and their costs. The revenue measures on a customer basis include: (a) the total volume of purchases, (b) prices paid, and (c) the profit margins on those purchases. The cost measures include not only the cost of producing the product or service, but also all the associated costs of serving the customer such as order entry, inventory, packaging, transportation, applications and engineering assistance, selling time, credit, billing, post sale service and product collection, repair and disposal. It is usually easier to identify the revenue measures than the cost measures, given the difficulty of assigning the costs of many activities to the specific customers.

The principle of 'learning by doing' is implied in the process of database marketing. It provides most of the marketing information required by a business enterprise. Besides, each database marketing action also generates new information as the database marketing campaigns seek responses, which in turn could provide the lead for new information. It is up to the markets to ensure the value of such information.

Functions and Applications of a Database

The functions of the database includes the following:

> Targeting the design and marketing of products and services with greater precision and accuracy;

> Promoting the benefits of brand loyalty to the customers at risk from competition;

> Identifying the customers most likely to buy new products and services;

> Increasing the sales effectiveness;

> Supporting the low-cost alternative to traditional sales methods;

> Making the marketing function more accountable for its results;

> Improving the link between advertising and sales promotion, product management and sales channels;

> Improving the customer service by ensuring that all relevant information is available at any point in the service relationship; and

> Coordinating different aspects of marketing as they affect the individual customer to achieve full relationship marketing.

The customer database have a broad range of applications. These include:

> It could customise the service approaches and communications of a business firm (e.g. hotel chains), thereby increasing the customer retention rates.

> It could be employed to structure the various marketing programmes (like a 'preferred card programme' in a super market chain) which could generate higher revenues through price discrimination.

> It enables a shift from the third degree segmentation (or self-selection) to first degree segmentation, which implies the creation of customised offerings based on the customer characteristics and behaviour.

> ➤ It employs observation rather than inference (about customer needs and behaviour), as the observed shopping and purchasing behaviour are more powerful predictors of future buying behaviour.

Sources of Data

The database marketing system normally utilises most of the customer information available within a company. However, the system organises this information in a form different from the operations databases, from which much of this customer information is likely to be drawn. However, some new information is likely to come from the internal sources, such as the direct sales force. This proprietary data is one of the most valuable assets.

Basically, there are two types of data sources, internal and external. The internal and external data sources are listed in Exhibit 8.1.

EXHIBIT 8.1

SOURCES OF DATA

INTERNAL DATA SOURCES

- ✓ Customer files
- ✓ Order records
- ✓ Service reports, complaints, etc.
- ✓ Merchandise return records
- ✓ Sales force records, technical engineers records.
- ✓ Application forms (e.g. for credit, insurance, promotional benefits).
- ✓ Market research
- ✓ Sales enquiries, general enquiries, queries
- ✓ Warranty cards

EXTERNAL DATA SOURCES

The external data include the compiled and direct response lists from sources outside the company. Also included are the classificatory data (e.g. census data and their derivations), which provide ways of enhancing other external and internal data. The types of information on the database include:

> ➤ Customer information (both of a customer or a prospective customer), i.e. information on the ways of accessing the customer (e.g. name, address, telephone number) and on the nature and general behaviour of the customer (psychographic and behavioural data).
>
> ➤ Transaction information, i.e. information on commercial transactions between the firm and the customer, e.g. orders, returns, complaints, and service enquiries.
>
> ➤ Promotional information, i.e. information on the types of campaigns (tests and rollouts) that have been launched and the persons who has responded to them, and the final results in commercial and financial terms.
>
> ➤ Product information, i.e. information on the type of products that have been purchased, the frequency and quantity of purchase, the time and place of the last purchase
>
> ➤ Geodemographics, i.e. information about the areas where the customers live and the social or business category they belong to.

Source: www.crmguru.com with permission

The selection of data to be included on the database is made according to the revenue stream and the feasibility criteria mentioned above.

Characteristics of Database Marketing

1. Each actual or potential customer is identified as a record on the marketing database.

2. Each customer record contains information (used to identify the likely purchases of particular products and how they should be approached) on:

   ➤ Identification and access (eg. name, address, telephone number)

   ➤ Customer needs and characteristics (demographic and psychographic information about customers, the industry type and decision making unit information for the industrial customers)

   ➤ Campaign communications (whether the customer has been exposed to particular marketing communications campaigns)

   ➤ Customer's past responses to communications done as a part of the campaigns

   ➤ Past transactions of customers (with the company and possibly with the competitors).

3. The information is made available to the enterprise during each communication process with the customer. This enables the firm to decide on how to respond to the customer needs.

4. The database is used to record the responses of the customer to the firm's initiatives. (e.g. marketing communications or sales campaigns).

5. The information is also made available to the company's marketing policy makers which enables them to decide:

    ➢ the target markets or segments appropriate for each product or service.

    ➢ the marketing mix (price, marketing communications, distributions channel, etc.) appropriate for each product in each target market.

6. The firm could utilise the database to ensure the development of a coordinated and consistent customer approach strategy. This step is vital in relationship marketing.

7. The database could eventually replace most of the market research. The marketing campaigns are devised in such a manner to provide the most relevant information that the company is seeking.

The growth of database marketing has been facilitated by:

➢ the powerful processing capability and the immense storage capacity of state-of-the-art computers; and

➢ the manner in which the telecommunication technology is harnessed to make the customer and market data available to the wide variety of staff involved in the marketing and sales offices.

Advantages and Disadvantages of Database Marketing

The one-on-one marketing, which directs the customised offerings to individual customers, has provided an additional thrust to database marketing. It has employed the database to capture the interactions between a firm and its customers at each point of time, and utilises the data analysis to search for patterns in these interactions. These patterns provide the most attractive potential customers besides providing clues in customising the products, pricing and promotions of a product. When utilised in the proper manner, the database marketing could provide insights into the customer's buying behaviour across the product categories, so that the companies could devise their programmes and plans to the "whole customer", than the customer seen only through the narrow view of their own products and brands.

The limitations of customer database marketing include:

> The cost incurred in setting up the software and hardware requirements has made the database marketing expensive in its establishment.

> The database often demands new skills and organisations, from new analytical and decision-making skills in sales and marketing to a revamped information system organisation that could support the entirely new class of users.

> The database marketing depends on the data quality (While the observational data is powerful, the corrupted observational data could be 'powerfully misleading'.). The quality also depends on the quality of analysis and the extent to which the databases are linked.

> Till now, the database marketing has been primarily used as a tactical tool. A few striking counterexamples notwithstanding, its main goal has been to efficiently acquire customers, and not to maximise the customer asset value or to inform the management of the total marketing system.

Types of Data

Transaction data The past transactions are one of the most important indicators for deciding the nature of likely future transactions. Therefore, the transaction data should include the information on each customer's past purchasing patterns. For this purpose, the details of each purchase should be logged, and the information should include not only the obvious 'identifying' details (like "who bought the product? When? how? etc.), but also the associated marketing data (at what price, from which promotion etc.).

In the consumer markets, the transaction data could serve much more an effective basis for selection (than the geodemographic variables) in establishing the needs of existing customers in relation to a new product. However, the widespread availability of geodemographic data that are comparable to the individual customer data is changing this situation. A consumer products company with limited or no transaction data available could start the process with a campaign based on the geodemographic data and this data will normally be organised in a national file based on the electoral roll.

The transaction data could be employed to enhance the nature of the file further and provide some of the bases for demographic classification. However, this could create problems of matching the addresses to the census information. If any internal or research data specific to the market is available to assist in developing a profile of prospective users, it could be utilised in creating a 'scoring module' or 'directory' for selecting the target customers from the national file. Similar arguments should also apply to the publicly available databases on business markets.

Product Data If the company has a wide product range, the product classification would be highly problematic, and a numbering system that suits the requirement of the database marketing should be adopted. Such a system allows the grouping of like products in an easy manner. However, in a business enterprise having a single product, this would not pose a major problem as each of the transaction is either treated as a sale or a return.

Promotion Data If the effectiveness of the promotions is to be measured, and if the promotional planning is to benefit from the analysis of the past, the documentation of the past and present promotions is essential in some detail (right down to which the customers were subject to them, and the media and the contact strategy used).

8.2 PROSPECT DATABASES

The prospects are not customers, and the firm requires different marketing tactics to influence their behaviour. Therefore, the companies should separate the prospect databases from the customer databases. The prospect data fall into two categories: (a) profile data and (b) casual data.

Customer Profile Database*

The profiling involves the process of obtaining detailed information about the customers (prospects). This information could range from the demographic data (such as family size) to personal data (such as hobbies). The results of profiling help a firm to determine the best messages to convey, the products to target, and the communications to avoid.

Main categories of profile data (say, for a shopping mall like shopper's stop) include:

1. Customer sales potential;
2. Customer characteristics (such as demographic, lifestyle and industry classification data);
3. Summary of customer acquisition, retention and add-on-selling measures;

Source: www.crmtoday.com with permission

4. Organisational/product charts of various shops and key personnel (business-to-business);

5. Influences and specifiers for the visit; and

6. Customer attitudes and motivation to the shop.

The sales potential is one of the most valuable elements of the customer or the prospect profile. The data element should also include the customer's potential sales volume, and not just the actual purchases. This information also provides insight into the customer's profit potential. The analysts compute the sales potential in different ways, depending on the market under consideration. The industrial or business-to-business (B-to-B) firms often use the firm size and the industry type as the surrogates for the sales potential. The firms could obtain estimates of the customer potential from industry trade associations or the third parties.

The profile database should also contain the demographic data. For consumer products, these data usually include the life-style information. The industrial firms typically include the firm size and the industry classification in their demographic data, besides the personal information about the customers, the organisational charts and other pertinent details.

The attitudinal data is important as they indicate the manner in which a customer evaluates the firm. The databases that contain the attitudinal data help the firms to identify these customers and to design the marketing programmes aimed at affecting their attitudes. So far, only a few firms have tracked the attitudinal data because of the cost and difficulty involved in collecting such data. However, with the advent of the Internet, the cost of customer survey has declined drastically and it will continue to do so.

If a firm could understand the data-driven marketing and the process of business optimisation, then it would understand the basic driving forces involved in all the customer retention-oriented programmes.

Value Migration Within a Company Database

Figure 8.1 depicts the value migration of customer data collected by the company in a dynamic setting. Here, we could observe the diametric migration of state database (like date of brith, marital status), from a generic to a customer-specific level.

This, in turns would generate more value to the company in their future transctions and customer relationship.

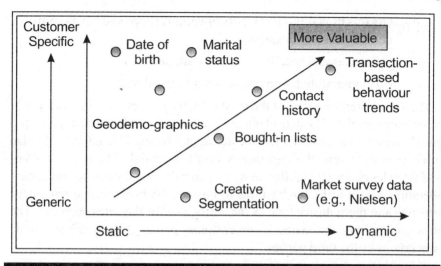

Fig. 8.1 Value Migration within a Company Database

Casual Marketing Databases The casual marketing databases capture the data on the marketing programmes offered to the individual prospects and customers. These databases are extremely complex to create, as it involves a lot of difficulty in tracking the marketing activities at the individual customer level. However, these databases are extremely valuable as the information they carry could significantly improve the marketing efficiency and effectiveness.

Table 8.1 depicts the recommended elements of a casual marketing database. To track these data, the companies should possess the ability to match the marketing activities to the customers (or prospects, as the case may be), and in many cases should have a disciplined sales forces that are willing to complete the sales call reports. It should be underlined that the firms that are not committed to track the required information about the marketing activities are definitely at a disadvantageous position.

Table 8.1 **Example of Casual Data**

Data Element	Internal/ External Source	Source
Sales calls per customer prospect	Internal	Sales force call reports
Product or service offers	Internal	Marketing
Pricing to customer	Internal	Accounting
Promotional offers	Internal	Marketing

Holding the Data

Another characteristic of the database marketing systems is the constant vigil maintained on differentiating the information that is 'useful', and the data that is 'nice to know', but not very useful. Special computer programmes are employed to separate the external data from the proprietary data and also for separating the data from different proprietary sources. The problems arise when an individual or a company is listed in different ways in different databases (or even in the same one). If the different databases are combined, the customers may be listed more than once. Depending on how important the reduplication is, the computer may be asked to list the entries where the duplicate entry is suspected, for manual correction.

Data Quality

The data does not stay fresh always. It becomes stale, as the contact on which it is based recedes into the past (For instance, people change addresses and jobs; companies shift their offices; job titles change; new companies emerge while companies go out of existence). The errors can occur either by commission or omission. Therefore, special exercises are required to check the validity of the data and/or update them. The planning that has to be done for the maintenance of the database thus constitute an important element in relationship marketing. The questionaire mailing can be an effective, but costly way of improving the data quality.

The quality of the data drawn from a database depends mainly on:

> the levels of credibility of the source data; and

> the relevance and appropriateness of the individual information (names, addresses, telephone numbers, job titles) available.

The data quality is measured based on the surveillance audit conducted on them. The quality of the information would also depend on the quality of staff engaged in the customer-contact (sales, telemarketing, retail branch, etc.). The staff should understand the value of high quality information and the importance of their feedback in improving its quality.

8.3 DATA WAREHOUSES AND DATAMINING

The market savvy companies are all the more enthusiastic in capturing information from a customer, every time he comes into contact with any of its departments. The touch points include: (a) the customer purchase, (b) the customer requested service call, (c) an online query, or (d) a mail-in rebate card. These data are collected by the company's contract center and organised into a data warehouse. The company personnel would analyse the data, and inferences would be drawn about an individual customer's needs and responses. Through data mining, the marketing statisticians would extract the useful information about the individuals, trends and segments from the mass of data available. The **data mining** involves the use of sophisticated statistical and mathematical techniques such as the cluster analysis, the automatic interaction detection, the predictive modelling, and the neural networking. The telemarketers could make a proper response to the customer inquiries only if they have a total picture of the customer relationship.

Database and Data Sources for Retention

To manage the retention process, a firm should understand the factors that influence the repeat-purchasing decisions, which include: (a) the expectations, (b) the actual experience, (c) the perceived value, and (d) the satisfaction involved. If it is perceived that every interaction between the firm and the customer (or prospect) affects the customer's attitude and his satisfaction with the firm, then the fact underlines the importance of tracking all customer (or prospect) interactions. Although the interaction with every customer or prospect may not generate the revenue, each one could be linked to an expected or potential monetary value in the future.

Table 8.2 Example of Customer Interaction Data

Customer Interaction	Data Tracked	Functional Area Responsible
Customer complaint	Complaint resolution	Customer service
Sales (end user)	Sales	Accounting/ Channel member
Market communication	Advertising sent Promotions sent Sales force calls	Marketing/Sales
Shipments or delivery operations	Fulfillment time/ Delays	Logistics
Product	Satisfaction Performance	Quality control
Invoicing	Billing	Accounting
Channel member (firm)	Sales Profits	Accounting

Source: www.customer equity. com.

8.4 MEASUREMENT IN DATABASE MARKETING

In the mid-1980s, the Coca-Cola spent nearly $4 million to develop a new Coke brand, failing to understand that the new formulation was not good enough to overcome the buyer loyalty for the 'classic' Coke taste. The buyer loyalty was predicted on some factors in the 'classic' Coke valued by the buyers which was apparently absent in the new Coke, the fact which the Coca-Cola failed to assess or realise. What the Coke had seen and focused on was the Pepsi product that was gaining the customers.

Often, the analysts of a firm spend too much time worrying about the 'absolute' numbers, refered to as the customer life-time value. In fact the focus should really be maintained on the change in the 'relative' numbers over time rather than the absolute numbers. It is not nearly as important to know the absolute value of a customer as it is to know whether this value is rising or falling, often called the customer life-cycle. The knowledge and understanding about the *customer life-cycle* is the most powerful marketing tool that a firm should possess.

The customers in the aggregate tend to follow similar behavioural patterns, and when any single customer deviates from the norm, it could be perceived as a sign of trouble (or opportunity) ahead. For example, imagine a situation in a cellular firm, where the new customers, on an average, calls the customer service 60 days after they start dealing with the firm. Suppose an individual customer calls the customer service 5 days after he starts dealings with the firm, this customer should be perceived of exhibiting a behaviour far outside the norm. The situation could be perceived either as a potential problem, or as an opportunity. Among the major questions that should be sought out at this juncture should include: (1) Whether the customer has any difficulty in understanding the advanced services on the phone? (2) Whether the customer is happily inquiring about the addition of more services? In either case, there is an inherent opportunity to increase the value of the customer, provided the firms possess the ability to recognise the opportunity and react to it in a timely manner.

It should be kept in mind that the concept of the 'average customer' is a myth and in fact, the business process involves different customer groups, each exhibiting their own kind of 'normal' behaviour. (For example, the type of media or the offer made to attract the customer could create a dramatic effect on the long-term behaviour, or the customers who arrive in the business process along the same media and offer would tend to behave in similar ways over time.) The tools available to identify and differentiate the customer segments using the behavioural metrics are discussed at length in the following sections. The measurement of latency (the number of days until the customer service call) serves as the "trip wire", a raising of the hand by the customer, to say to the marketer, "I'm different. Pay attention to me". It is the duty of the marketing behaviourist to determine the next course of action. Metrics like the latency provide the framework for setting up the capability to recognise the opportunity for increasing the customer value.

The raising of the hand by the customers and the reaction by marketers is the feedback loop at the center of the relationship- or life-cycle-based marketing. It's a repeating 'action-reaction' feedback cycle. The customer raises the hand, the marketer reacts. The customer provides the feedback through the action—either they cancel the service, or they add service. The marketer reacts to this action, perhaps with a 'win-back' campaign, or with a 'thank you' note.

A constant conversation (mostly non-verbal) and an ongoing relationship with the customer is essential to sustain the interaction process. This relationship proceeds as long as there is value for both the customer and the marketer. If the customer takes an action and there is no reaction from the marketer, the value begins to disappear for the customer, and they may defect. When the value disappears for the marketer (the customer stops taking action / providing the feedback), the marketers should stop spending the incremental money on the customer.

In fact, much of the profitability typical of the high ROI customer marketing techniques originates from the knowledge on weeding out the non-profitable/unwanted customers. Most of the decreased profitability in any marketing programme is the result of over-spending on unsuitable targets with lowered returns. However, if the marketers tend to look at the results in the aggregate, or if they are looking at demographics-based segments to measure the behaviour-based outcome (like purchases), they are more likely to miss some important details and thereby arrive at a mistaken judgement. For example, certain segments may return Rs120 for each Rs100 spent, while others may lose Rs 5 for every Rs100 spent, even though the campaign as a whole may return Rs15 for each Rs100 spent. When a firm trying its level best to encourage the customer to buy something, they are looking for a behaviour to occur. The reliance on demographic segmentation to understand the results of such a marketing campaign could be totally misleading. If a firm tries to create a 'behaviour pattern', the behavioural should be applied as the yardstick to measure the element of success.

Analytical Models in Database Marketing

The database marketing helps the firm in performing certain important marketing analyses like the decile analysis and the RFM analysis. Besides, it would also help in constructing customer defections tracking tools like the

RS matrix and the logit model. These toppics are discussed in the following section.

Decile Analysis The decile analysis is the most common and simplest procedure that could be adopted for retention targeting. The decile analysis determines the relative profitability and sales of different customer segments. The method also reveals the individual customers that are most valuable. The deciles are the groupings of customers computed by ranking each customer according to (a) his/her purchase, or (b) any other variable of interest, such as the profitability, and simultaneously grouping these customers into 10 per cent segments. There is nothing magical about the groups of 10 per cent as some firms prefer even the 5 per cent and one per cent groupings.

Typically, the top three deciles of customers represent anywhere from 60 per cent to 80 per cent of the firm's sales and profits. The advantage of decile analysis is that it is extremely easy to construct and execute.

However, it has several disadvantage. Firstly, it is very limited in scope. It does not (a) capture most of the information available from the customer database, (b) discriminate between new and old customers, or (c) determine the customers that have the highest potential to increase their purchases.

RFM analysis The RFM framework is an effective method for summarising and interpreting the complex purchase data. In general, the RFM analysis is a simple but useful way of categorising the customers (which makes it useful for determining the customer life-cycles). As explained in an earlier part of this book, the RFM model tracks the customers through their purchase histories, and subsequently categorises these customers into cells with the similar purchase sizes, frequencies and timing. The analysis further attempts to predict the future customer behaviour of each 'cell'. This type of modelling requires the use of decision trees, which are simple to understand but laborious to compute. Once the analysts predict the future purchase levels, they can compare them with the costs to calculate the retention equity. The important summary statistics for retention include:

> the number of current customers;
> the number of customes defected;
> the percentage of customers defected;
> the duration-adjusted defection rate; and
> the duration-adjusted retention rate (the number of current customers *minus* the duration-adjusted defection rate).

The typical defection and retention rates are the average rates, influenced equally by the retention rate of newer customers and the retention rate of customers who have had longer relationships with the business firm. The companies should also measure the ratio of the lost customers to new customers as it could indicate whether or not a firm is filling its pipeline with the new customers as rapidly as it is losing them.

The RFM analysis is highly predictive as it focuses on the actual buyer behaviour and not on the demographic type or the industry code. However, the RFM analysis has its own drawbacks. Firstly, it cannot easily incorporate the product affinity or the customer demographics. Secondly, it would be less useful for infrequently purchased goods, as the ability to predict in those cases diminishes in a significant manner. Third, the RFM analysis ignores the reference value of a customer. Specifically, this refers to the positive or negative impact that a customer could have on other customers. The MCI's "Friends and Family" promotion is an example of this type of value.

The RS matrix The RS matrix (a tool similar to the RFM matrix) provides the easiest way to target the defectors. The basic idea of the RS matrix implies that the customer's sales rate and recency could reveal the repurchasing possibilty of a customer.

The construction of the RS matrix should include the customers who have made at least three purchases and computation of three statistics for each of these customers. These statistics include:

1. Recency (the time elapsed since the customer's last purchase);
2. The sales rate of the customer per period (total time since a customer's first purchase *divided* by the number of times purchased); and
3. The number of periods that would elapse until the customer is likely to make a repurchase (the second statistic *divided* by the first statistic)

If the recency of the customer is greater than the third statistic (that is, if the customer has not bought within the predicted amount of time), then the customer is likely to defect.

The RS matrix is a relatively simple system for identifying the defectors and has many of the advantages that the RFM matrix possess. It is easy to interpret and construct. If a product or service has a moderately frequent and regular purchase cycle, the RS matrix can quickly identify the defectors.

Logit model The statistical modelling is a more sophisticated way to predict the defectors. The logit model is a commonly used statistical model that helps in identifying the variables affecting the probability of an event.

The logit models depend on the specific independent variables. For instance, while measuring the defectors, the possible *independent* variables should include: (a) the ratio of the purchase cycle to the time since the last purchase, (b) the number of purchases; (c) the total amount spent by the customer in the purchase; (c) the changes in the price; and (e) the changes in promotional activity.

Other variables include: (a) the number of different products or services purchased by the customer, (b) the specific customer service problems, (c) the change of address, or (d) any other indicators that could cause the change in the customer buying behaviour. The benefit of a logit model is that it could include the explanatory variables, which makes it significantly more powerful than the RS matrix.

8.5 TECHNOLOGICALSHIP MARKETING

The general relationships based on IT, enable the organisations to address and integrate the overall customer and company performance requirements. As such, the partnerships should consider the long-term objectives as well as the short-term needs of the participant organisations, thereby creating a basis for the mutual investments and rewards. The building of relationship-based technology (T), therefore, should address the means of providing regular communication and information-sharing among the participants (organisations or consumers) so that they could (a) evaluate the progress, (b) modify their objectives, and (c) accommodate the changing conditions. In short, the twenty-first century organisations should be managed on the basis of facts rather than on instincts or feelings. If the IT provision is kept as the basis for business relationship, the information systems group (IS) should be kept as the catalyst in managing and utilising the powerful IT structures.

The technologicalship marketing provides a viable means for making the concept of relationship marketing a reality. The IT tools should be applied to provide the relationship-building credibility and opportunities. It is very obvious that nowadays the organisations and people (consumers) are finding it difficult to separate the 'relationship' from the IT. This type of new relationships could be otherwise called the 'technologicalship' (relationship based on using information technology). The effective use of relationship based on IT encourages the establishment of long-term relationship marketing with the customers, suppliers, competitors, and others in the organisation's external environment.

In simple worlds, the technologicalship marketing implies the process of marketing through the application of technology tools. Here most of the marketing activity would be based on technology and a desire to make a relationship work. For instance, the online marketing permits for one-to-one marketing, the most important loyalty-building benefit of online marketing, as it gives the companies the ability to establish an enduring relationship with the individual consumers.

The McDonald's McFamily, on America Online, is a good example. This site reinforces the idea of McDonald's as a parent's best friend. The parents can get information on the latest happy meal or nutritional information about McDonald's products. But even more valuable is the community that the McDonald's has created. The parents could not only talk directly to McDonald's, but even with experts and other customers on a whole range of parenting issues—from the ways of keeping the family healthy and safe to the ways of spending more quality time with their kids. The application of an effective IT structure would also allow each linked firm to perform in a more elaborate manner with less investment. Besides, it affords new market opportunities for the channel members, suppliers, consumers, etc. Overall, the emergence of IT relationships and alliances have encouraged the use of new practices and technologies by organisations to share more real-time information and thus, reduce the business uncertainty.

The differences between traditional marketing and technologicalship marketing depend upon the nature of the technologies used to substitute for physical proximity (Exhibit 8.2).

EXHIBIT 8.2

CHARACTERISTICS OF TRANSACTION MARKETING AND RELATIONSHIP MARKETING			
Category	*Traditional Marketing Assumption*	*Relationship Marketing Assumption*	*Technological Marketing Assumption*
Marketing Environment	1. Marketing rules are very clear, defined and constant	Relatively defined and constant	Dynamic, driven by technological advancement.
	2. Market is bound by countries and regions	Relatively bound	Boundaries by default
	3. Market niches are difficult to identify	Easy to identify	Generally larger, creates additional niche business opportunities. They

			are easily identifiable and accessible
	4. A firm and buyers are involved in a general marketing. Arms-length and interpersonal contact	A dayd relationship face-to-face, close interpersonal contact based on commitment and trust	Firm and buyer in a specific target market. Personalised tacts ranging from distance to close
	5. Corporate push marketing (the business defines the place and time) dominates	Corporate push and customer pull marketing: customer defines the place and time	Customer pull marketing
	6. Too high cost advertisement	High cost of advertising and relationship building	Low cost of advertisement relationship building
	7. Low information system enabled marketing	High information system eabled marketing	Highly information system enabled marketing. Marketing groups become important
Marketing Sucess Factors	1. Transaction/ sales volume volume and creating new customer are considered a success	Keeping the existing customers, retention is considered as a success	Transactions, attracting new customer as well as keeping the existing one is considered as success.
	2. Focus on product quality	Customer satisfaction	Customer satisfaction technology like EC, IT advance
	3. Awareness of the product/ service considered as a success	Relative aware-ness but perceived values are considered as success	Relation awareness but very high perceived value is essential for success.

	Quality of the product and promotion mix are used for product differentiation.	Customer orientation creativity, long term close relationship, adaptation are used for differentiation.	Innovation, Technological medium and mode of delivery (through Internet) are considered.
	4. Low customer interactivity	High customer interactivity	Very high customer interactivity
Organisational Position	1. Decision focus on product/ brand and 4 Ps	Relationship between firm in a net work of individals and firms	Product/brand and customer in a target market as well as low to use IT advances and capabilities to create the exchange relationship
	2. Marketing drives product development	Relationship drives	Marketing and information system drives
	3. Separate and detached marketing group	Marketing group exists as umbrella organisation	Marketing group highly integrated with technology, relationship and organisation net work
Customers Perception	1. Customers are less knowledgeable and informed	More knowledgeable and informed. Their feedback could be accessed in an immediate manner	They are more aware and well informed. Feedback could be more immediate and easy to access
	2. Consumer behaviours and expectations are less practicable	Relatively Predictable	New customer behaviour, expectation and interests are being created and could be better monitored
	3. Customer are considered as a group/sector	Group of Collaborators	More of an individual nature and offers customised physical and virtual products

Source: www.ebsco.com and www.managementfirst.com

The success in designing and running the technologicalship marketing depends on developing or applying technology (in the broadest sense) to manage the relationships between the involved parties in question. These relationships would have to be managed differently as long as the technology provides anything short of a total replication of physical presence. Chapter 9 gives a detailed information on the CRM and the web- based technologies widely used for relationship building

8.6 COST EFFECTIVENESS OF MAKING OFFERS THROUGH DATA-DRIVEN MARKETING

The data-driven marketing and sophisticated statistical methods allow the firms to drive down the costs of making offers by matching the customers with the appropriate products. It would increase the number of offers that could be made for the same cost, and hence increase the maximum add-on selling rates.

Prof Blattberg *et. al* (2001) has emphasised six basic changes to the marketing strategy in this regard:

1. The marketing strategy, tactics and execution should become customer centric, and not product-centric.
2. The firm should manage a customer life-cycle. The marketing mix varies by stage in the customer life-cycle.
3. The firm should manage a portfolio of customers which should be balanced across the acquisitions, retention, and the add-on selling stages.
4. Since the marketing output of the firm is quantifiable, the marketing should be managed using the appropriate customer equity measures, and costs balanced against the financial returns.
5. The firm should communicate change in the asset value of its customers through the customer equity flow statements and the customer assets should be measured through the measurement of the life-time value.
6. The firm should organise around the customer acquisition, retention and add-on selling.

CONCLUSION

The new technologies have radically altered the ways in which many service organisations deal with their customers. The most powerful force for change today comes from the integration of computers and telecommunications. The digitisation allows text, graphics, video and audio to be manipulated, stored, and transmitted in the digital language of computers. The faster and more powerful software enables firms to create relational databases that combine the information about customers with details of all their transactions. The firms could utilise these databases for (a) insights into new trends, (b) new approaches to segmentation, and (c) new marketing opportunities. The technological change affects many other types of services too, from airfreight to hotels to the retail stores.

The application of technologies to create more customer added value and to facilitate the coordinating of networks, is of particular importance for a modern organisation and its networks. Jeffrey and Sviokla (1995) has referred to this aspect of IT application as the 'market space' (or virtual world) to distinguish it from the physical world of the marketplace. The managers have to look to the 'market space', IT, to create added-value with information. They have to integrate the activities of the physical world with those of the 'market space' (virtual world) in order to create and extract value in the most efficient and effective manner. A well-integrated application of technology and staff alongwith operations that could respond to the customer needs, encourage the customers to use a whole range of products/services of firm rather than confine to just a few. The data-driven marketing approach explained in this chapter is expected to define the future trend in this regard.

CHAPTER REVIEW QUESTIONS

1. Discuss the concepts of database, data design, data warehousing and data mining.
2. Explain the term 'holding the data'?
3. Narrate the importance of customer database in relationship marketing.
4. Explain the various sources and types of data in detail.
5. What would you measure in database marketing of a new generation bank in India.
6. List the five important ways of using the database for a public utility service firm like Reliance Infocomm.
7. Discuss about the emerging trends in relationship marketing in the Indian scenario with examples of your own choice..
8. Explain the concepts of digital revolution.
9. Narrate the importance of technologicalship marketing. List its advantages over other forms of relationship.
10 Critically examine the feasibility of facilitator in technologicalship marketing suitable for a marketing research firm in India.
11. Comment on the changing nature of marketing in this millennium. Also evaluate the various forms of technologicalship

marketing that could be applied for successfully crossing over these changes in Indian context.

CASE STUDY
TESCO: A RETAIL CUSTOMER DIVISIBILITY CAMPAIGN

BACKGROUND

The Tesco, one of Europe's largest and most data-advanced retail chains, is one company known for proper gathering and application of in-depth customer information to optimise its customer share. Its customer database contains not only the demographic and life-style data (including the total dollars spent on food items in stores and the customer response to its promotions and other programs), but also specifics about its customers' interest in, and use of, a diverse range of other food-related services and non-food products and services.

THE CAMPAIGN

The company has leveraged on the customer data drawn from its loyalty programme to diversify into the attractive banking and financial service sector. With this aim, the Tesco along with the Dunnhumby launched a two-tier "club card programme". Under this programme, the first tier is meant for gathering the invoice data straight (though it gives only one point for every pound sterling spent) that could be redeemed for vouchers up to 150 points. The second tier, targeted for frequent spenders, is more innovative. Here the customer acquires a key per $38 spent. Fifty such keys makes the customer a key-holder and 100 such keys gives him the status of a premium key-holder. The key programme offers discounts, invitation for prime events and so on. This aims at seeking the change in the behaviour pattern of the customers towards the company products. The Tesco also launched an internal marketing programme for building their capability for supporting the campaign (Exhibit 1).

EXHIBIT 1

THE GOLDEN RULES

The Golden Rules	Do you do it?	What difference Does it make?
1. Determine which groups of customers Tesco wishes to serve, taking into account		

their potential life-time value and their propensity to be loyal or defect. Then identify, using research or feedback, the different relationship requirements of different groups, where appropriate, allowing the customers to select themselves into these groups.

2. Recognise that the Tesco customers' views of their relationship with you may be very different from that of the firm, and in particular that the customer's perceived transaction period is usually much longer than the actual contact, and that there may well have been several attempted contacts or considered contacts before the actual one.

3. Attune the overall business processes and customer management processes to the customers' relationship requirements.

4. Make it easier for the customers to access the company, and then to identify and learn the script for managing a relationship with Tesco.

5. Make it easier for the customers to give information (e.g. about needs and problems), or ideally, anticipate the information and collect, if it suits the customer best, perhaps confirming it when appropriate.

6. Make it easier for the customers to extract information and help from the

Tesco (e.g. about how you could help them, the status of their case) or ideally, anticipate their need for information and give it to them when it suits them.

7. Educate the customers the ways of extracting the best from Tesco.
8. Help the Tesco staff in providing the best service to its customers by an appropriate mix of empowerment of staff, empathy with the customers' motivation, information support and the training and development of customer handling scripts.
9. Let the customers take control when they want
10. Treat customers specially who believe they have a special relationship with the firm
11. Reduce the error rate in the customer transactions as close to zero as possible
12. Create a physical or technical environmental that makes the customers feel the right mood / at home while doing business with Tesco.

Using the information derived from its loyalty card programme (which has millions of members) and appended externally-generated demographic data, the company conducted targeted research and developed profiles of customers who would be most interested in the basic banking services (as well as other options, such as car loans, pension savings programmes and auto, home, and travel insurance).

A NEW BEGINNING

Within four years, the Tesco raised its market share from 13 to more than 17%, and 75% of its current sales are accounted through this programme. The memebership has crossed 10 million and the average spend per customer per visit is $38.70. The Tesco, with over 900 stores in Europe and Asia, has determined that it could acquire a financial services customer for less than half of what it would cost a bank to do the same. This has invariably become a highly profitable cross-sell opportunity for them. Additionally, the service has been perceived of by customers to be of high value. The success of its financial services programme has encouraged Tesco to become even more innovative in applying the customer insights and to build on the trust and equity created in their stores. A couple of years ago, the company parlayed its off-line customer data to become the world's largest online grocery and sundries home delivery service. The Tesco has almost one million registered customers and processes over 70,000 orders per week. The division is quite profitable and had over $600 million in sales during 2003. Additionally, the Tesco uses its customer information to target and segment the communications to the millions of its loyalty programme members having infinite demographic, purchase, and life-style profiles. The add-on selling based on the data gathered has immensely benefited the company for leveraging its product profit base.

The loyalty-card programme is tracking several hundred million in-store purchases per day. The company developed 5,000 customer "needs" segments, with each segment receiving the personalised coupons. The Tesco could create up to 1,50,000 variations of its promotion and reward statement mailings each quarter. This provides the opportunity to create divisibility in outbound customer communications. The result has been tightly targeted messaging and marketing opportunities, giving Tesco the ability to address individual customer requirements, by the purchasing situation. Its coupon redemption rate is 90 per cent (something unheard in the marketing history).

IT-ENABLED CAMPAIGN

The Tesco launched two types of online promotion through the interactive advertisement. The consultant Jim Novo was hired for explaining the impact of tracking the customers.

The consultant explained the situation with the help of a chart (provided above). He said, " ... Ad #1 starts at 20% of customers having purchased in the past 30 days, and in 6 months, falls to less than 5%. Ad #1 also seems to be headed even lower in Recency; these customers are losing even more potential value as time goes on. Ad #2 starts at 15% of customers having purchased in the past 30 days and falls into month 3, but then starts rising in later months, ending up higher than it started, and is still rising. The customers from Ad #2 might end up having greater potential value than the customers from Ad #1 over

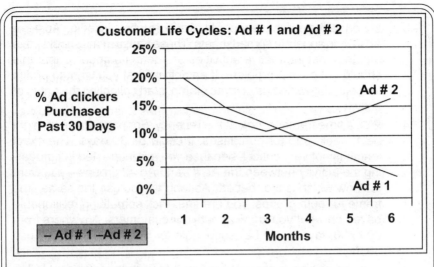

Customer Life Cycles: Ad # 1 and Ad # 2

% Ad clickers Purchased Past 30 Days

— Ad # 1 — Ad # 2

Months

Source: www.jimnovo.com
Ad #1 Starts with Higher Recency, but has Shorter Lifecycle than Ad #2

the longer term. So it could be that, after looking at the life-cycle of customers from Ads #1 and #2, you may find even though Ad #1 looks best based on recency at a point in time, Ad #2 creates the higher potential value customers when the recency is looked at over time."

"It would appear that the customers from Ad #2 may take a little longer to make a purchasing decision, but become more valuable customers over the long run. This is a very common occurrence in the customer behaviour and if you are not tracking it, you won't know it is happening, leading to poor decisions about the profitability of your ad campaigns"

The standard approach to RFM analysis is a "snapshot" method, measuring the customer at a point in time. These new methods make use of the RFM parameters over time in unique ways, and are not dependent on purchase amount (monetary) as the original RFM model is. The result of using these methods is very high ROI marketing campaigns and site designs. Let us use the recency to compare the potential value of customers coming from two different ads (Ad #1 and Ad # 2) that ran at the same time, for the same duration.

1. Identify the groups you want to compare for potential value. In this example, it's the customers who clicked on either of the two ads, Ad #1 or Ad #2 (two groups).

2. Decide which activity is most important to you for these groups. If you're a publisher, probably the log-ins or page views are the most important. If you are selling merchandise, you would use purchases. For this example, we will use the purchases. An example using visits (or log-ins, if you don't track visits) is given below.

3. Import all the purchase records of people who clicked on Ad #1 or Ad #2 into separate spreadsheets. These transactions should have a date; most interactive activities are date-stamped so that this should not pose a problem. If an activity that you want to profile for potential value has no date stamp, start collecting the dates of activity.

4. Pick a time frame to look at the recency. For page views, it might be 1 week; and for purchases, it could be 30 days. The exact length is not very critical, because you are interested in comparing the activity between the Ad #1 and Ad #2 groups—you want to know which is the "better". As long as you use the same time frame for both groups, you are fine. Pick something reasonable based on what you know about your customers. Anywhere from 30 to 90 days would be reasonable for the purchases; let's use 30 days.

5. Sort the purchase records for Ad #1 from the most recent to the least recent, and find out the percentage of the people, who has clicked on Ad #1 and made a purchase, and have made at least one more purchase in the past 30 days. Count back 30 days using the transaction dates, total the number of customers making a purchase, and divide by the total people in the spreadsheet. Perhaps it is 20%.

    Note: The software that comes with the book will automatically aggregate the multiple transactions by the customer and sort customers by their most recent transaction.

6. Run the same analysis for people who clicked on Ad #2 and made a purchase. Let's say only 15% of these people have made at least one purchase in the past 30 days.

7. A higher percentage of people who clicked on Ad #1 are recent, active and purchasing, when compared with Ad #2. This means that Ad #1 generates customers with higher potential value. You need to take this into account while analysing the success of the ads. If you go through this process for customers grouped by the product they bought first, you can determine which products generate new customers with the highest potential value. After going through this process for customers grouped by the area of the site they visited most, and the areas which generated the highest potential value customers could be found out. If you go through this process for customers grouped by the demographics or the survey data they provide, you could determine the data points which could define the customers with the highest potential value.

Mr Novo further explained, "This is a simple example of how companies with experience in managing the remote shopping customers find ways to maximise the sales and minimise the expense. The customers, through their actions, tell them which route is the most profitable to take. The most recent customers for any particular activity are always the ones most likely to repeat that activity, and so have a higher potential value. Thereby one could track the multiple activities for the same customer groups. In the first example, you found customers who clicked on Ad #1 and made a purchase are more recent on purchases, so they have a higher potential value on the activity "purchases". But what about the recency of the people who clicked on the ads for visits? If they keep coming back, they could be of some future value."

Mr Novo further explained how this recency study might look.

1. Visits / log-ins: For example import all the visits (or log-ins if you don't track visits) into two separate spreadsheets of people who clicked on Ad # 1or Ad # 2 (the date stamp is required).

2. Pick a Recency cut-off. Again, we are interested in a comparison, so the number isn't critical. Let's use 1 week.

3. Sort each spreadsheet from the most recent to the least recent and find out what percentage of the people who clicked on Ad #1 have visited (logged-in) at least once in the past week, as was done above for the purchases. You might come up with 10%.

4. Run the same analysis for people who clicked on Ad #2. You might come up with 30% who have visited / logged-in at least once in the past week.

Note that this method is based on the actual facts of customer behaviour and not on speculation or the "best guess" theories. The behaviour of the customer is the most accurate yardstick for assessing the potential value. Once you complete studies like these, you could organize all the business practices around the potential value of the customers they generate. If the money is allocated away from activities that generates low potential value customers, and instead to generate higher potential value customers, your marketing become more profitable over time.

THE CASE

1. By using the data gathered from their loyalty programmes and selectively adopting the divisibility campaign and product development research, Tesco has shown the ways of reaping the financial and relationship benefits. In this context make an attempt to compare the strategies followed by the Tesco and the Shoppers' Stop (refer Chapter-2 case study) and design an integrated divisibility campaign for the online store subhiksha.com

Source: Michael Lowenstein, CPCM, CRM NETWORKS and www.crmguru.com with permission

OVERVIEW OF CRM AND WEB BASED TECHNOLOGIES

Learning Objectives

After reading this chapter you should understand:
- How CRM is applied in relationship marketing.
- The concept of customer divisibility and its relation to CRM.
- The importance of relationship values in the management of customer relationship.
- The various types and levels of CRM.

INTRODUCTION

The current business environment has been characterised by a dynamic mix of growing competition, new and emerging channels of communication and relationship, changing consumer attitudes, increasing demand for customer intelligence, and a need for faster dealings and developments in the market.

Under the relationship marketing concept, the focus has shifted from the one-time transactions to ongoing relationships. The purpose of marketing is not confined to the process of making a single sale; rather it involves 'creating' a customer. The sale is not the end of the marketing process, but the beginning of a relationship in which the buyer and seller become interdependent. Under the customer relationship management, the customers are viewed as assets, and evaluated according to their long-term profitability (revenues minus cost-to-serve) and not just the sales volume. The product or the service enters the customer's 'use system' and the customer becomes a source of both the financial support and ongoing requirements for the business.

9.1 EVOLUTION OF 'RELATIONSHIP' CONCEPT

The focus of customer relationship management is organised around the idea that the buyers and sellers could do business along a continuum from pure transactions to totally integrated alliances and networks. At one end, the buyer-seller interaction is controlled exclusively by the market forces, while at the other, the control is strictly internal and bureaucratic, within the organisation of the buyer-seller relationship itself. In the middle, there is a complex interplay of market and bureaucratic controls governing the relationship. Six stages could be identified along this continuum.

1. Pure transactions;
2. Repeated transactions /simple relationships;
3. Long-term buyer-seller relationships;
4. Strategic partnerships;
5. Strategic alliances and joint ventures; and
6. Network organisations.

A **pure transaction,** which occurs in a perfect market, could be defined as the one with a very large number of competing sellers, each selling an undifferentiated product, and a set of buyers with perfect information about all the product offerings, including the prices. The consumer preferences are given, exogenous to the process. In this perfect market situation, no seller could influence the desires of any buyer. The only variable is the price and the buyer is a profit- or utility-maximiser, seeking the lowest price. Each transaction is a completely independent event, not influenced by the consideration of the past or future transactions. In this context, the market forces of supply and demand set the price.

Perhaps the best example of a pure transaction in the real world is the purpose of an agricultural commodity. The repeated transactions are common in the marketing of services and packaged goods. The marketing effort is devoted towards differentiating the products, building the brand awareness, creating the brand preference and customer loyalty. The repeat purchases show that the relationship has progressed beyond the assumption of the economist's model and the pure transactional.

The **repeated transactions** represent the beginning of a relationship. The products are differentiated and the consumers have preferences. With repeated transactions, a critical element has entered the equation, 'trust'. The familiarity of a brand name or sales person contains an implicit promise of (a) a consistent product and services performance, (b) quality, and (c) purchase experience that would meet the expectations.

The consumers are creatures of 'habit' because of this implicit trust factor (we have our favourite soft drink, restaurant, convenience store, financial advisor, hotel chain and newspapers because we trust them). The trust factor is the fundamental building block of relationships.

The present day customers have become more difficult to please with offers that would have pleased them in the past. Many business firms have realised the fact that the customers are smarter, more price-conscious, more demanding, less forgiving, and are approached by many competitors with equal or better offers. The challenge here is not to create the satisfied customer, but to produce delight and loyalty among the customers in a manner that the competitors cannot achieve. In this context, the **CRM** could be defined as *the process of managing the detailed information about individual customers and carefully managing all the customer "touch points" with the aim of maximising the customer loyalty.*

Further, the marketing information system of a company must give an accurate and up-to date picture of the acquisition and retention of its customers. The most relevant management report in this regard is the customer inventory. The *customer inventory* shows the customer gains and losses, which could be classified in various ways; (e.g., by the type of customers or the type of product typically bought. The concept of customers mentory is dealt in detail in the last chapter.) For this reason, it is very important to have the 'benchmark' figures from the company customer database prior to the introduction of relationship marketing, so that the benefit could be demonstrated against this benchmark, besides maintaining a true perspective of the costs and benefits of the relationship enhancement.

To make the concept clearer, let us have a look into the ways of Taj group of hotels in attracting their consumers. The Taj group publicises the availability of its services through appropriate advertisements. The advertisements are aimed at luring the prospective customers to try the offered products and services. The advertisements and other efforts made by the marketing personnel to inform the prospective customers about the attractive features of their offering result in customers availing of the company's services. If the customers are satisfied with their hospitality, they continue to enjoy the same and remain loyal customers. If, on the other hand, they are not satisfied, they would not patronage the company services. This leads us to a thought that the advertisements and other marketing initiatives, though extremely useful in attracting new customers, are not sufficient to retain them.

The satisfaction of the customer, followed by the resultant 'delight' factor, is essential for the retention of customers and for continuing the sales of the products and services of the company to these customers. The customers would now have a wider choice and hence they would only buy the products and services that could satisfy them fully or meet all their expectations. The customer satisfaction and the corresponding loyalty factor, which was earlier important for the company only from a 'success' and 'growth' perspective, is now essential even for its survival.

The quantum of investment required by the company in building the loyalty factor without making much of a compromise on the profit and cost factors are important points of concern for a business enterprise. For this purpose, the investment in customer relationship building should be distinguished into five different levels.

Levels of Relationship Building

> **Basic marketing**: Here, the salesperson simply sells the product.

> **Reactive marketing**: Here, the salesperson sells the product and encourages the customer to call if he or she has questions, comments or complaints.

> **Accountable marketing**: Here, the salesperson telephones the customer to check whether the product is meeting the expectations. The salesperson also ask the customer for any product or service improvement suggestions and any specific disappointments.

> **Pro-active marketing**: Here, the salesperson contacts the customer from time to time with suggestions about improved product uses or new products.

> **Partnership marketing**: Here, the company works continuously with its large customers to help improve their performance. (General Electric, for example, has stationed engineers at large utilities to help them produce more power in USA.)

9.2 RELATIONSHIP VALUES

The companies seeking to expand their profits and sales should spend considerable time and resources searching for new customers. To generate the leads, in this regard, the company resorts to several measures which include (a) advertisements in the media that will reach new prospects; (b) direct mail and phone calls to possible new prospects; (c) participation of sales people in trade shows where they might find new leads; and so on. All these activity produces a list of suspects.

The next task is to identify the good prospects out of these suspects, by interviewing them, checking on their financial standing, and so on. Then it is time to send out the sales people. The aim of relationship marketing is to produce the high customer equity. The **customer equity** is the total of the discounted life-time values of all of the firm's customers. Clearly, the more loyal the customers, the higher the customer equity. Rust, Zeithaml, and Lemon has distinguished the three drivers of customer equity as:

> Value equity,
> Brand equity, and
> Relationship equity

Value Equity

The value equity is the customer's objective assessment of the utility of an offering based on the perceptions of its benefits relative to its costs. The sub-drivers of value equity are: (**a**) quality, (**b**) price, and (**c**) convenience. Each industry has to define the specific factors underlying each sub-driver in order to find the programmes to improve the value equity. An airline passenger might define the quality as the seat width, while a hotel guest might define quality as the room size. The value equity makes the biggest contribution to customer equity when the products are differentiated, and when they are more complex and needs evaluation. Most importantly, the value equity drives the customer equity in business markets.

Brand Equity

The brand equity is the customer's subjective and intangible assessment of the brand, above and beyond its objectively perceived value. The sub-drivers of brand equity are: (**a**) the customer brand awareness, (**b**) customer attitude towards the brand, and (**c**) the customer perception of brand ethics. The companies employs advertising, public relations, and other communication tools to affect these sub-drivers. The brand equity is more important than other drivers of customer equity, where products are less differentiated and have more an emotional impact.

Relationship Equity

The relationship equity is the customer's tendency to stick with the brand, above and beyond the objective and subjective assessments of its worth. The sub-drivers of relationship equity include (**a**) loyalty programmes, (**b**) special recognition and treatment programmes, (**c**) community-building programmes, and (**d**) knowledge-building programmes. The relationship equity is especially important where the personal relationships are given greater prominence, and where the customers tend to continue with the suppliers either out of habit or inertia.

In short, the customer relationship management is a strategy composed of applications, technology and products that fulfill the various requirements of a business enterprise. These requirements include:

(**a**)   Enabling the customer to have a consistent view of the enterprise, regardless of the way the customer contacts the company. This improves customer satisfaction and customer retention.

(**b**)   Enabling the front office staff to perform the sales, service and marketing tasks more efficiently as a team, increasing efficiency and reducing costs and

(**c**)   The CRM describes a strategy used to manage and report the customer/prospect/partner/contact interaction with the enterprise contacts including the sales, marketing, billing and customer service and support.

9.3 CRM AND RELATIONSHIP MARKETING

As the Internet gains increasing penetration in both the workplace and the home environment, the consumers are acquiring greater access to financial and product information. The Internet has emerged as a powerful marketing channel to target the potential customers, and the emergence of advanced digital television technology (like the interactive televisions) would further create an enormous change in the behaviour of both the consumers and service providers.

The new sales channels would also offer the consumers more choice regarding the place and time of their purchase. Besides, the new 'push' technology would allow the companies to adapt their products to target new market segments. The industry trends are suggesting a polarisation between the more complex and the less complex products; and this trend is being driven by the regulators and the consumers who are demanding more simpler products.

However, in practice, it has been proven that only a few business firms have their business functions fully cut out along the lines of an ideal CRM concept. The major hurdle spotted in this regard is the lack of experience in using the customer data to run a business enterprise. For instance, a company dealing in financial services should really understand the expectations of a customer to satisfy him/her, and thereby enhance the customer relationship.

The accurate and current information at the POS is essential in this regard, and the electronic channels should provide an ideal opportunity for intelligence gathering. The advancements in technology in the fields of 'data warehousing' and 'data marting' are making these applications, which were formerly dealt in a separate, stand-alone manner, to an integrated system that encompass the whole of management and business information.

The use of enterprise-wide CRM systems would fuel the growth of market-oriented financial service providers. Many people had expectations that they could just "automate" their marketing. However, human experience and inputs are an important constituent in the proper handling of customer data.

9.4 CRM STRATEGY

As it has been stated in the beginning, the CRM is an enterprise-wide strategy for presenting a single face to the customer. The CRM could respond to issues relating to the customer data sharing, besides providing a seamless contact and fulfillment experience for the customer. The CRM front-end applications usually integrate with the back-end systems such as the accounting and manufacturing for a true enterprise-wide solution.

To create and sustain the true customer loyalty, it is vital that the companies should have a single window of the customer across the organisation, besides having a sensitive and actionable profile of each customer and his/her evolving needs. In many ways, the CRM is the operational face of the one-to-one movement. The CRM also bears the business philosophy required to accomplish the one-to-one marketing vision.

Classification of CRM According to the functionality of the software tools, the CRM could be divided into:

 a. **Analytical CRM:** This implies the use of data modelling and profiling to accomplish the CRM goals

 b. **Collaborative CRM:** This implies the tools that should not be used while directly engaging and interacting with the customers

 c. **Operational CRM**: This implies the 'back end' systems, which unify the business operations and deliver the products.

The CRM should be the architecture for each purpose, while the furnishing required to make the architecture work would be provided by the customer data. The core of CRM effectiveness lies in the deep and reliable customer information. In other words, the companies should know as much about each customer as possible, and, in many cases, much more than they have known at present.

Focus of CRM The three main areas that the CRM systems should maintain their focus are the

 ➤ sales,
 ➤ customer service, and
 ➤ marketing automation

The **sales**, also called the sales force automation, includes: (**a**) field sales; (**b**) call center telephone sales; (**c**) third-party brokers, distributors or agents; (**d**) retail marketing and (**e**) e-commerce (which is also referred to as the technology-enabled selling).

The **customer service and support** includes: (**a**) field service and despatch technicians, (**b**) Internet-based service or self-service via a web site and (**c**) call centers that handle all channels of customer contact (and not just voice).

The **marketing automation** differs from the other two categories as it does not involve the customer contact. The marketing automation focuses on analysing and automating the marketing processes. The marketing automation products include the following: (**a**) *Data-cleansing tools*: Data analysis or business intelligence tools for ad hoc querying, reporting and analysing customer information, plus a data warehouse or data mart to support strategic decisions; (**b**) *Content-management applications* that allow a company's employees to view and access business rules for marketing to customers; (c) *Campaign management system*, a database management tool used by the marketers to design the campaigns and track their impact on various customer segments over time. Depending on the company goals, the tools it chooses would be integrated across the main areas of sales, services and marketing.

The technology involved in the automation process includes (a) databases, (b) data warehouses, (c) servers and other hardware, (d) telephony systems, (e) software for business intelligence, (f) workflow management and e-commerce, (g) middleware and system administration management tools.

EXHIBIT 9.1

SIMPLE CRM (SCRM)–THE PRACTICAL CRM PACKAGE

The latest package for SMEs in CRM is the Simple CRM (SCRM). This is a low-cost simple software. The SCRM could be even implemented using the resources from spreadsheets to the simple DOS-based cash register systems. The only requirement is the ability to capture the customer transactions and attribute them to a specific customer ID.

Ideally, Simple CRM works with inputs of customer database of the company. Here the company has to select prospective customers and identify the customer groups (present and potential) with a view to maximise the frequency of availing the service. This can be done in there stages. In the first stage the company attempts to measure the defection rate and service standards through gap analysis in the second stage, the firm attempts to provide a retenturn programme to the defectors by utilising the outcome of stage one. The third stage will provide the impact of such retention programmes in the day to day through business feedback analysis.

Simple CRM Stage I

Measure: Evaluate the current customer retention situation, both with the "hard numbers" economic analysis and "soft numbers" review of policy and procedure.

The steps involved in this stage include:

➤ Defining customer defection and finding the exact customer defection rate

➤ Quantifying the defection rate in real profit

➤ Ranking current customers by the likelihood to defect

➤ Reviewing the existing customer-facing policy / procedure

➤ Evaluating internal service standards

➤ Creating a blueprint for highly valued service

Simple CRM Stage II

Manage: Implements customer retention marketing and training programmes to the defection rate and recapture lost customers profitably

The steps involved in this process include:

➤ Initiating high ROI on ongoing customer retention marketing programme based on customer's likelihood to defect rank and customer value

➤ Initiating defected customer recapture programme

➤ Initiating customer-centric toolbox—rights, customer retention statement and job descriptions

➤ Setting service quality measurement standards and tracking

➤ Imparting training:

➤ Dazzling and delighting customers

Simple CRM Stage III

Maximise: Creating a feedback loop for continuous employee learning on "what will work and what will not"

The steps involved in this stage include:

➤ Optimisation of customer retention marketing programme; continuous learning feedback loop which drives programme improvement over time

➤ Optimisation of defected customer recapture programme; this feature also has a continuous learning feedback

➤ Optimisation of complaint handling and resolution system for lowest loss / least expense tradeoff

In Simple CRM, the marketing and customer service share the same set of customer value metrics, making evaluation and accountability for customer retention and value a team effort

Source: www.crmtoday.com with permission

9.5 IMPORTANCE OF CUSTOMER DIVISIBILITY IN CRM

As it was stated earlier, the essential underpinning of CRM is the customer data. To strategically apply the customer data to a CRM programme, the marketer should have a thorough knowledge about the ways of identifying, gathering, storing, managing, sharing and applying the knowledge for creating the highest levels of customer value. A major, strategically differentiating opportunity for the actionable data is the customer divisibility.

A study by Gartner found that 75 per cent of the leading companies are incapable of creating a unified view of the customer. Most of the challenges in the organisational performance originate from the maintenance of customer data which include (**a**) lack of data availability, (**b**) poor storage and management, and (**c**) ineffective sharing and usage. This implies that the mere positioning of the systems in place for data management, is not sufficient enough for a better customer management. Rather, the companies should become more data-focused and customer-centric and should have a proper understanding of the real value and impact of customer information. The company should also have a disciplined plan for sharing and utilising the data to make the company more customer-centric.

If the company is proficient in gathering and applying the information and is going beyond the transactional relationships to provide the genuine, customer-perceived value, the promise represented by having "divisible" customers could become a reality.

Evolving from Customer Segmentation to Divisibility

Generally, the companies perform the segmentation process by demographics, life-style characteristics, or the recency-frequency-purchase (RFP) profiling (which we have already explained in the beginning of the book). However, the customers tend to be more complex than that, having different needs and requirements for different purchase or service usage situations.

Customer divisibility

First, let us define what we mean by "divisible". The business firms typically develop the basic customer segmentation for use in their sales, marketing, and customer service activities. Usually, the firms perform this segmentation by demographics, lifestyle characteristics, or the recency-frequency-purchase (RFP) profiling. However, the customers, having different needs and requirements for different purchase or service usage situations, tend to be more complex. Therefore, the companies, even while gaining some improvement in their customer processes through better segmentation, would still be competitively vulnerable until they possess a real insight into the customer needs, problems, expectations and complaints. This insight would yield fruit only if the customer information is shared and applied at the right time and in the right way.

The customer divisibility could be accomplished only if the firm have a thorough knowledge about its customers and optimises the value for them. More than the one-to-one relationships, this involves an understanding of the customer's changing needs, along time and place. Globally, only a few smart companies have made dramatic strides in building the customer value. These companies could retain their customers and thereby achieve substantial profits in their business process.

One example of an industry that practices the customer divisibility on a fairly large scale is the gaming business in the US. This industry is both highly competitive and advanced in the ways of gathering and utilising the customer data. The 'loyalty cards' enable the gaming companies to overlay the casino play with the changing customer profiles. (The data for the loyalty cards will be first generated when the players become the customers and later updated at the cashless slot machines and the gaming table.) The data acquisition and maintenance is done in a very serious manner in this industry, since the gaming facilities typically derive the profit from the gambling machines and tables, shows, hotels and restaurants, and they find it really valuable to address the needs of the customer at each venue.

Naturally, the needs, expectations and requirements of the customer may vary according to the place of his activity (for example it will be different when he is at the gaming table or the restaurant). It will be the same customer in both locations, however that one customer has become divisible. The purchase and relationship dynamics of this customer are different in each location, and therefore the casino/hotel should have the customer insight that's appropriate, in real time to the extent possible, to optimise the customer's overall experience.

One of the successful global example for the divisibility campaign is from the Tesco, the largest e-tailer in Europe. The Tesco could create up to 1,50,000 variations of its promotion and reward statement mailings each quarter. This provides the opportunity to create the divisibility in the outbound customer communications. By utilising data in the loyalty programmes and selectively conducting the loyalty and product development research to reap the financial and relationship benefits of having divisible customers, other companies should also be able to divide and conquer their customer segments.

Banking on Customer Divisibility—A Case Study of Royal Bank of Scotland*

The Royal Bank of Scotland (RBS) is a financial services company famous for generating efficient customer data and applying it for optimal effectiveness. Building on the groundbreaking customer loyalty research that it had

---

Source: www.crmtoday.com with permission

conducted several years ago, the RBS had begun applying the value-centric relationship programmes that were largely simple from a very early time. These programmes mostly relied on the hands-on telephone and personal communications protocols maintained by the bank service and the sales staff. Since the Royal Bank has nearly 3.3 million customers, such labour intensive approaches were found highly challenging. Similarly, its findings about the customers themselves created major challenges as the bank has found it difficult to break its customer base into clear-cut segments. As a consequence, the Royal Bank modified its typical one-to-one approach to build the customer groups from the individual interest basis.

The Royal Bank's customers are divisible, that is, capable of being in multiple segments at any point, and this depended on the ways that were adopted for categorising the customers for loyalty building. These facts–the intensive use of staff for customer loyalty purposes and Royal Bank's insights regarding customer segmentation–required still further innovation to build on its early relationship successes.

For the purpose, the Royal Bank adopted a software solution that enables its marketers to execute the personalised and multichannel offers to the individual customers. The software also enabled the company to automate the event-driven campaigns. This was done in a two-stage process.

First, the bank tested the creative material on the representative customer groups. Secondly, when the trigger criteria have been met, the bank would send a print campaign to the relevant customers within 48 hours. The company has developed 5,000 customer "needs" segments, with each segment receiving the personalised coupons.

Several other organisations would also have arrived at the same conclusion and design their customer programmes and protocols accordingly, provided they had a comprehensive data about their customers akin to that of the RBS.

EXHIBIT 9.2

EXPERIENCE OF SAS INSTITUTE, THE LEADING CRM SOLUTION PROVIDER*

The CRM solutions of SAS Institute, USA offers various tools that could enable the companies to set targets and respond to the customer needs. These tools enable the companies and organisations to organise and access the customer data from all sales points including the e-commerce systems, and transform these data to knowledge about their customer behaviour and thereby build more profitable relationships with them.

Source: www.crmtoday.com with permission

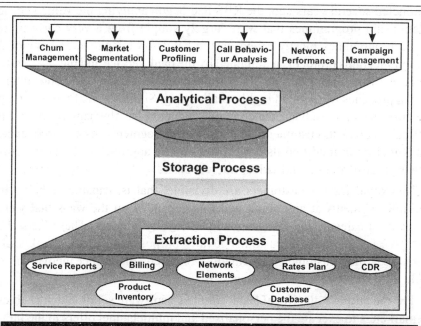

Fig. 9.1 Analytical, Storage and Extraction Process

According to the analysts of the CRM sector, the development of the customer-centric strategies should depend on a complete analytical CRM system, which allows the utilisation of the data that could be produced by the operational CRM systems. The CRM analytics comprises all types of programming that could analyse the data about an enterprise's customer and presents it in such a manner that helps in taking better and quicker business decisions. The CRM analytics could be considered a form of online analytical processing (OLAP) and may employ the data mining. (Please refer Fig. 9.1 for details such as analytical, storage and extraction process.) In this way the desired "single view of the customer" could be achieved, as each organisation would be in a position to provide the necessary information to all points of contact with the customers. These points are also known as the points of sale (POS) and the points of contact (POC).

SAS Data Warehouse

The CRM solutions of the SAS Institute utilise the exceptional structure of the SAS data warehouse as well as the necessary data concerning the customer-centric solutions that are collected and analysed from this environment. The data warehousing is being used by the operational systems of a company for the collection of data which is relevant from a customer's point of view (namely, the net and invoicing system), and are organised in such a way that helps in easy analysis.

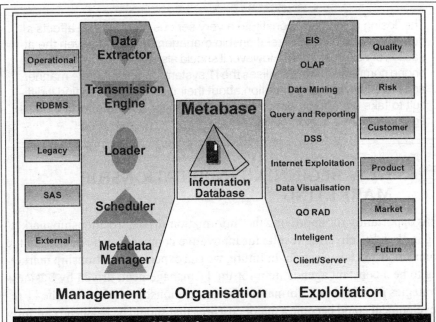

Fig. 9.7 *Interlinking of Metaphase*

The data mining enables a firm to recognise its most important clients as well as the products and services they wish to buy. The solution contains a template, which is based on data mining methodology of the SAS Institute, but it has been adjusted specifically for the management of customers allowing the marketing professionals to have direct results in the data mining procedures concerning the loss of customers. The solution also contains the Rapid Result Service through which the SAS along with the company, (a) could focus on the specific project of access in the customer data (b) predict which among them could be utilised to discontinue their collaboration with the company, (c) estimate their value and (c) detect the factors that lead to such a decision.

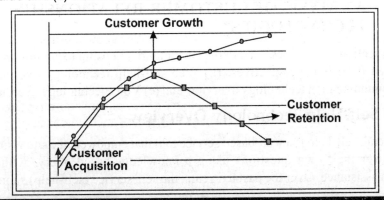

Fig. 9.8 *Relationship between Customer Retention and Acquisition*

> The 'losing customers' constitute a very serious problem that affects all domains of the customer relationship management (CRM), even the attraction of new customers. However it should also be noted that the mobile phone companies, which utilises the IT systems in an elaborate manner, and have invaluable information about their customers, even find it difficult to take advantage out of this information for a more effective management of their customer list.

9.6 NEW BEGINNING IN RELATIONSHIP MARKETING

This opportunity for improving the 'information-driven' relationship marketing is already delivering results for innovative companies who have seen the connection and taken action. In future, we can expect the relationship marketing to be a constant agenda item for the IT management, driven by business strategies premised on information-driven relationship marketing. The IT redevelopment could become a major cost area that should be balanced carefully with the benefits.

The rate of technological change in the marketing environment is an important factor that affects the relationship marketing success. The relationship between the rate of effective IT utilisation and the relationship effectiveness would be positive. Since marketing through the Internet is highly effective in meeting the requirements of the customers, companies are going electronic to communicate with their customers, create an awareness of their product and, perhaps, make a profit. A new class of web-based technologies have entered the market which have promised to make it easier, faster, and cheaper to develop such comprehensive relationships.

9.7 ANALYSIS OF CUSTOMER RELATIONSHIP TECHNOLOGIES*

In this section, the currently available customer relationship technologies are analised from four perspectives: **(a)** Web self-help technology overview; **(b)** Communication technology overview and **(c)** Voice technology overview.

Web Self-Help Technology Overview

In general, self-help is a web-based service tool that empowers the site visitors to answer their own questions using a knowledge-based query, without human assistance. Over the past ten years, the self-service (self-help) support

Source: www.crmtoday.com with permission

environments have evolved from file transfer protocol (FTP) or web-based online libraries and frequently asked questions (FAQ) to sophisticated artificial intelligence systems where a virtual online representative or technician is available through the web. (It should be noted that although they are primarily used in an external manner, the self-help tools may also be used internally by companies serving as a knowledge base for customer service representatives who rely on them while answering customer questions in e-mail and other interactions.) This evolution has been driven by (**a**) the available technology, (**b**) the complexity of the problems submitted, and (**c**) the customer segments served.

As defined, the self-help tools provide, through a simple and clear interface for the web visitor, a web form field, where the user can ask a question in plain language. Entries could also be navigated through a tree-based (or similar) set of questions and answers. From a company standpoint, the self help tools should also provide an authoring and workflow mechanism for the creation and publishing of self-help articles, tracking of resolutions and hits, and integration with backend and other relationship systems.

At the core of the self-help system is either a natural language processing engine or an artificial intelligence programme. Both types of engines are more than just word-matching systems. They use unique algorithms to review user's question(s) based on the context, word order and word meaning. The result is an accurate answer to a multitude of questions.

More broadly defined, the self-help can also be understood as any of the following:

> **Traditional FAQ**: Typically posted to a web page in a static environment and maintained by a webmaster.
>
> **Web site searches engine:** Searches all web site pages or a subset of them based on key words.
>
> **Interactive FAQ:** With natural language processing, an "engine" can more accurately present the correct answers through complex algorithms from a repository of available content.
>
> **Collaborative community:** Company-sponsored (and monitored) user forums and bulletin boards where the customers can help each other answer the product questions (mostly post-sales issues).

Advantages of the Self-help Service

The advanages of self-helps service include:

> **Dynamic content**: The contents of the knowledge base are limited only by what is thought will not be asked. Therefore, the

self-help tools are often very robust covering a wide range of topics, and should be constantly updated by adding new articles, and removing articles determined by the user survey as incomplete, incorrect, or not relevant.

Good coverage: Many topics could be covered and many users could access the tool.

Low cost: Relative to other electronic interaction channels, the cost of purchasing, implementing, and administering is low.

Disadvantages of Self-help Service

The disadvantages of self-help service include:

Mixed resolution rate: Some questions, due to their nature, may not be answered.

No engagement: No human follows up or clarifications. (What-you-see-is-what-you-get.)

Impersonal: The service does not easily recognise user or the patterns of users.

Communication Technology Overview

The e-mail, the most prolific of communication technologies adopted in the recent times is the e-mail because it is (a) cost effective, (b) efficient, (c) universally available and (d) could be easily personalised. The e-mail has revolutionised the personal communication. The e-mail could take very different forms: one-to-one for customer service or sales interactions, one-to-many for mass marketing (and even one-to-one for direct marketing given the appropriate tools). The traditional e-mail technology tools such as the Microsoft Outlook have been popular for personal communication, but due to the dramatic increase in the use of e-mail as a communication tool, business enterprises now require more powerful technologies designed to operate with a "one-to-many" communication model in the mind.

Advantages of e-mail based CRM system

The advantages of e-mail based CRM system include:

Better interaction tracking and personalisation: By using an eCRM system, companies could not only personalise the e-mail responses and follow-ups, but also track the history of the relationship with that particular customer.

Better resolution rate: Being able to personalise and track e-mail lends itself to higher customer resolution rates by keeping track of the customer history and inquiry status, as well as being able to follow-up as necessary in order to resolve any outstanding issues.

Relatively low cost: The average cost for e-mail has been measured to be as high as Rs 25 for those companies not systematically managing the e-mail flow, and drops to Re.0.35 when the e-mail is fully automated.

Disadvantages of the E-mail Based CRM System:

Volume challenge: By offering an e-mail option to customers, the companies can "open their doors" to an e-mail deluge. By doing so, they implicitly state that the customer e-mail will be answered in a timely and accurate fashion.

Response time challenge: As a corollary to the volume challenge, the e-mail response time often vary depending on the workload. Even the best eCRM systems need to be staffed adequately.

Advantages and Disadvantages of Web-Forms as an Interaction Channel

Advantages

Data collection: Allows collection of structured, relevant and complete customer data.

Form: The structured data enables the company to make a rapid response to the customer queries.

Low cost: Inexpensive interaction channel.

Simplicity: Easy to use.

Disadvantage

Privacy: The customers will not use the web forms, if the data collected is too intrusive and does not match the perceived benefits expected from providing the information.

Process Points for Implementing with Best Practices

Although web forms are relatively easy to create, certain steps should be followed to extract the maximum utility out of them. These guideline include: (a) Length, (b) Relevance and (c) Integration

Length The forms should be as short as possible.Though the purpose of the firm should be in eliciting the maximum possible information about the user, the form should be unobtrusive, uncomplicated and short.

Relevance In order to keep the web form short and simple, only relevant information should be collected. While much of the information is "nice to know," collect only "the need to know data".

Integration Collecting information about customers and targets is useful, but unless the rest of the organisation could share the knowledge, the data has not achieved its full usability. It should be ensured that the data collected from web forms could be integrated with the information collected from e-mail, chat, and voice interactions.

As the online companies struggle to convert the surfers into buyers and offer the top-notch customer service, one of their realisations is that the online business does not offer the "human" experience. In the brick-and-mortar world, the employees are on hand to welcome the shoppers to the store, provide on-the-spot guidance and useful information, and be a friendly face when the customer has a service inquiry or complaint. Until recently, companies operating in an Internet environment did not offer such luxuries. However, with the advent of chat technology, the online customers could now reinvent the "human" experience.

The Chat

The 'chat', developed as result of the "interactive" requirement of the Internet, is one of the most revolutionary technologies available. As a technology, it allows real-time interaction with the customer, and its application is extremely valuable as a technology for replacing the dependence on telephone as an instantaneous method of communication. The evolution of chat, in its short history, has been profound.

Currently, the chat comes in many gradations. These include:

Active Chat: With the click of a button, the user could interact with the service representative for a real time session in answering his queries.

Pro-active chat: The service representatives could utilise this technology to monitor the web surfers on a site in real time, and initiate a session with a specific surfer to attend his/her specific questionnaires.

Browsing: While serving a customer in chat, using the collaborative browsing features of a chat session, the specific pages could be pushed to a surfer for special promotions or to direct them as an answer to his/her question.

Collaborative Browsing: Leveraging on the chat technology, the service representative could (a) help the customer in filling out an order form, or (b) procure the required information (as in the case of a survey) in whatever web form the data is required for the enterprise

Remote Desktop Control. At the farthest reach of the chat technology is the ability for a surfer to turn over the control of his/her desktop to a service representative. This technology is extremely valuable in a technical support environment, where it could be easier for someone to remotely diagnose and fix a user's computer than attempt in talking to the end-user through the fix.

With the advancements in the chat technology, the service representative could provide a higher level of personalisation than any web-based interactive technology (like self- help, web forms and the e-mail) through (a) a proper recognition of the types of pages that the surfer has visited, (b) addressing the surfers by name and (c) understanding the surfer's history if he or she has interacted with the company before.

Advantages of Chat Technology

Increasing Browser-to-Lead Opportunity Conversion
Proven 25 per cent browser to lead opportunity conversion when the customer is proactively engaged in chat.

Decreasing Shopping Cart Drop-out Rate
As many as 27 per cent of online consumers abandon the items they put into a "shopping basket", because they find filling out the forms too difficult.

Improving Customer Experience
Without being "pushy", the chat could add the 'personal touch' to the customer's web experience by using the real-time textual conversation with a staff trained to build solid relationships.

Best Resolution Rate
By responding quickly and accurately, a higher percentage of issues and questions could be resolved.

Good Potential for Interaction Tracking and Personalisation
Maintaining a record of all interactions provides the information required to further personalise the future interactions.

Potential for Browser Push/Drive
Leading chat applications allow the Net representatives to "push" pages to surfers (i.e. automatically take them to a web page without the surfer having to click to that page).

Disadvantages of Chat Technology

Call Volume Management Challenge
If the companies deploy the reactive chat, there is the potential issue of many surfers requesting the contact at a single point of time.

Time Management Challenge Once a surfer is engaged, research has shown that he/she at times would prolong the conversation (one primary reason for this being the fascination with the technology) even though the genuine questions have been attended to. The companies must find a way to politely disengage from such unproductive interactions without hampering the self-respect of the surfer.

"Big Brother" Syndrome Some surfers may get spooked or rather feel uncomfortable with the proactive chat and the practice of pushing web pages.

Relative Cost Because of the limited volume that could be managed and the potentially lengthy interactions, the chat is not viewed as a cost-saving relationship channel. However, because of the sales, the cross-sell, and up-sell implications, it is viewed as a revenue-enhancing tool. An impressive return on investment is still quite possible.

Process Points for Implementing with Best Practices

Many chat implementations have started emerging successful as many business firms have recognised the value of utilising chat as a powerful technology in its customer relationship programmes. In addition to this vision, there is a checklist of items that the companies should consider to best leverage the benefits of chat. The companies that are willing and are capable of sharing the hard-gained chat interaction experience are still few. Some of the tried and tested process points for chat are as follows:

> ➢ Use a distinct button to distinguish the chat service on the web site.

> ➢ Place the hours of availability with the chat button, unless it is $24 \times 7 \times 365$.

> ➢ Carefully position the chat button on the site in areas most directly related to revenue, as the chat is a more expensive resource and should be deployed strategically.

Voice Technology Overview

Using the telephone as an interaction channel is a well-established practice throughout all companies regardless of the size, vertical industry, or the business model. The relationship between costs, returns, customer satisfaction, and infrastructure are relatively well understood. However, presently, the technology spawned from the Internet has added another layer of complexity to the traditional telephone channel. The catch-all phrase for linking the

Internet and the telephony applications is called **computer telephony integration (CTI)**.

The CTI, once considered a challenge of network technology, presently, is more approachable and provides the vital backbone functions for many call center applications, VoIP, and unified messaging environments (providing PC or telephone access, with one call to e-mail, voice, and fax). In the early days of voice-data integration, only large corporations had the resources to develop and deploy solid CTI applications. But today, as the need for a consistent, accurate, real-time view of the customer takes the center stage, as well as the ever-increasing advancements in technology come to market, the CTI has become more practical, affordable and useable.

The question remains, however, on the real importance of this technology, and the technical requirement of a business enterprise to include and integrate the voice technology with other electronic relationship channels from a process standpoint.

Advantages of CTI The advantages of CTI include:

➢ Good resolution rate.

➢ Potential for interaction tracking and personalisation.

➢ Personal attention and high service level

Disadvantages of CTI The disadvantages of CTI include:

Call volume challenge Until the customers are retrained to select the communication channel which best suits the situation (self-help, e-mail, chat, VoIP, phone), they often resort to what is most convenient, over what may actually be the most efficient. The sudden availability of voice could present a call-volume management challenge.

High cost To integrate voice with other electronic channels, it remains expensive and difficult to cost-justify for the smaller companies.

Burden on customer to initiate call Although the companies could achieve a 360-degree view of their customers, to utilise the voice channel, customers still have to initiate the call (assuming the voice is used for service-not marketing or sales).

Single copper line dilemma Since many voice-integrated lines still operate and will continue to operate on telephone lines, the customers still lack a dedicated Internet connections to operate the voice technology.

9.8   BEST PRACTICES IN MARKETING TECHNOLOGY

There are different flavours of technological applications available that promises a marketing automation. In general, most of these applications are suited only for a low-volume business enterprise, where the sales function is the primary driver for customer acquisition. On the other hand, some applications categorised for high volume campaign management are suited only for organisations where the marketing is the primary source of customer acquisitions. Yet another category is the applications that could provide the analytical and profiling tools.

The chosen package should provide the virtues of all the above applications. The application must tightly integrate with the service and sales modules and should seek to provide:

> ➢   A framework for automating the marketing processes,
> ➢   A campaign manager for conducting all types of campaigns, and
> ➢   Analytical tools for customer profiling and reporting.

As a suite application, the marketing applications should be integrated with the service and sales modules and support the following features:

(a) automated marketing process; **(b)** campaign mamagement; **(c)** graphic workflow; **(d)** customer profiling; **(e)** personalisation; **(f)** content; **(g)** affers; **(h)** scheduling eventsand mailing list; **(i)** responce management and **(j)** analitic tool.

Automated marketing processes   An 'adaptive rules engine' offers a framework of campaigns, targets, opportunities and orders, which could be utilised to streamline the creation, management, execution and tracking of the marketing processes in an organisation. This framework could be used to define a wide range of activities and accommodate the organisation-specific processes..

Campaign Management   The campaign manager functionality allows the automation of the flow of campaigns. It facilitates the campaign definition and planning using the (a) workflow, (b) customer profiling and segmentation, (c) personalisation of content and offers, (d) scheduling of events and mailing lists, (e) response management, and (f) analysis tools.

Graphic Workflow   A simple drag-and-drop text and graphics workflow could be used to create multiple campaign types. The workflow captures the logic of the campaign and enables the user to define, schedule, run, and manage the campaigns. It allows business enterprises to conduct a variety of campaigns such as loyalty programmes, seasonal offers, sweepstakes, cross-sell, up-sell, product launches, partner and channel schemes, trade show registration, newsletters, and so forth. The powerful graphical workflow allows the marketers to:

- ➢ Define multiple campaign types
- ➢ Conduct permission-based e-mail marketing
- ➢ Schedule multiple events and execute micro-targeting
- ➢ Schedule condition-based events
- ➢ Create manual actions (send thank-you notes)
- ➢ Test campaigns before the rollout
- ➢ Manage the campaign rollout
- ➢ Monitor targets in real time at each stage of a campaign
- ➢ Associate the cost and ownership with each stage

Customer Profiling, Segmenting and Targeting The customers could be profiled, segmented and targeted based on the demographic and psycho-graphic information available in the customer database. Any integrated solution should allow creation of static or dynamic mailing lists using a complex 'advanced query builder'. While the static lists are suited for targeting the niche segments, dynamic lists are used to target segments that require frequent updating.

Personalisation The mailers should support features such as attachments, graphics, hyperlinks, and support to multiple languages. In addition, they should also provide the ability to highly personalise mailers.

Content The mailers should be personalised to include the content specific to a customer together with the properties such as name, company and so on.

Offers The offers should be created with different discounts for different target segments.

Scheduling Events and Mailing Lists Scheduling events using the wait function based on date and time elapsed is another valuable feature to look for in the eCRM technology. It could also be utilised to schedule the mailing lists to participate in campaigns at pre-determined intervals.

Response Management A comprehensive set of features must track the response of customers. Based on the response the following activities could be undertaken: (a) sending another mailer, (b) moving a target to a different campaign, (c) changing the value of target parameters, (d) deleting a target, or (e) generating an opportunity or an order.

> ***Response to mailer*** The response to the mailer could be tracked on the basis of both the time taken for the response and the message body.

> ***URL and banner tracking*** Embedding the trackable URLs and

banners in mailers. When a customer clicks the URL or banner, the database automatically updates this information.

Web forms Inserting the web forms in a mailer. The information submitted in these forms is collated and sent as an e-mail to the eCRM solution. The solution then interprets the content and creates an interaction based on this information. This information is also saved directly in the integrated customer database.

Analytic Tool The campaigns could be analysed through a rich set of back-end metrics and reports. These reports would capture the number of people who have responded in a step (step efficiency), the number of people who responded within a list (list efficiency). They could also track the costs associated with each step, calculate the return on investment (ROI) for campaigns and specific steps, the success percentage, and the types of response actions taken. In addition, the click-through ratio, the cost per thousand (CPM) and the responses to banner ads, could also be analysed.

9.9 THE INDIAN SCENARIO

The Hindustan Lever Ltd. (HLL), one of the premier business enterprise of the country estimates that nearly 24 million households (out of the total 60 million households) of the nation will become online by the end of the year 2003. The HLL plans to have a Net strategy for each of its brands, around the three identified 'needs': beauty, food and health. Early initiatives in this regard have already been launched by the HLL which include (a) setting up of touch screen kiosks, called Lakme Beauty Zone and (b) a click on a 'Yahoo!' banner in the web which will ride the consumer to an 'Axe' game on *Hungama* site .

However, there are still no answers on the definite form of advertising that works best with this interface. So, the focus is on creativity. An international campaign that got the advertising fraternity buzzing was the one that Coke did with the Microsoft. Each time the user clicked on the 'Refresh' button on the MSN browser, a bottle of Coke popped up. The Indian scenario is considerably less hot, but a few bright sparks are emerging. A campaign by the Ogilvy & Mather for Fevicol is interesting. Every time a user clicks on a banner, a blob sticks to his browser for three minutes. Similarly, the HLL decided to use the banner option in a creative manner. Typically, a click through on a banner would take the user to the host's website; but in the Hall's banner on Yahoo! the user is transported to a game on the *Hungama* site. However, with online advertising solution agencies sprouting around the country, the Indian double clicks—the creativity and the market—is all set to make a quantum leap in the coming years.

A global survey carried out by one of the world's largest market information conglomerate has ranked India 32nd in terms of Internet usage. A survey carried out in 36 countries by the Internet research arm of Taylor Nelson Sofres, the world's fourth-largest market research firm, has revealed that 13 per cent of India's adult population accesses the Internet. Many firms believe that the figure would really grow in the Indian environment as the standard of living and awareness of technology are really in the upswing.

CONCLUSION

It has been realised from many vendors that the CRM solutions were developed for a single purpose—to help businesses to manage customer communications efficiently. These systems are client/server-based, with a focus on handling the workflow within the corporation, as well as on cost-reduction and resource allocation. By its nature, the CRM is an internal mechanism focused purely on automating the technical processes of sales and service. The communication channels likewise are limited to low-tech avenues such as storefronts, telephones and mail. Rather than providing the customer with an interactive experience, the CRM focuses on helping the internal groups that could handle the customer requests in a reactive way. The CRM limits the communications and information sharing to only two groups — the service representatives and the customers.

Unfortunately, the business issues are rarely so limited: customers, partners, suppliers, and company representatives need communication interaction and information to access across all parts of the organisation, and not just the service center. Even more limiting, because customers, partners, and suppliers have no access to information, they could not find the relevant information or solve problems themselves, resulting in a more service-intense, costly, less-satisfying relationship with the company.

The CRM's client/server technology has been able to create almost unlimited data warehouses. But, as applications began to address the sales force automation (SFA), customer profiling, product distribution, web-based interaction and e-commerce, these applications were developed as separate "information stovepipes" with little or no integration between the systems. As a result, valuable information remains untapped and non-integrated, and companies are missing out on the knowledge that they could gain by viewing and managing the enterprise-wide relationships. The complexity only increased as the bridges attempted to include various internal and external groups as well as multiple communication channels including the e-mail, the web, phone, and wireless aided protocol (WAP). When the Internet arrived, it sounded the death knell for client/server solutions that cannot scale to meet the exponential increase in interactions and information needs the Internet has unleashed. All of a sudden, the business enterprises must adapt to a new business model, and new solutions must be created for the new e-business economy.

When companies use the new technology to its full potential, it could provide effective market research to establish consumers' areas of interest, as well as to gather electronic information at the point of sale (POS) that providers do not currently hold in a usable electronic format. Many financial services organisations are moving towards the business models adopted by retailers—most of them have an inbred marketing and service culture and huge databases of customer information, allowing them to react quickly to changing market conditions. However, many are still reactive rather than proactive, with even some of the newer players not adapting to the changing market fast enough. To move towards a true market-led culture, the providers should establish their customers' requirements and incorporate these into their business development plans. In this chapter we have seen the practical uses of the CRM and its components. Managing the customer relationship is one of the uphill tasks of any organisation in the present global scenario.

CHAPTER REVIEW QUESTIONS

1. Discuss the application of CRM in relationship marketing.
2. What do you mean by customer divisibility? How is it related to CRM practitioners?
3. Narrate the importance of relationship values in managing the customer relationship.
4. Explain the various types and levels of CRM in detail.
5. How do you adopt the simple CRM practices for a FMCG company in India?

CASE STUDY
NEW eRM CHALLENGES IN SMOOTH CREDIT Inc.

BACKGROUND

The enterprise relationship management (eRM) demands a technology solution that enables companies to move away from a purely company-centric approach to one in which the participants inside and outside the company walls are considered equal. Kana is the one company today that could meet the demands of such an eRM strategy. The Kana's visionary developers have created an all-encompassing solution that leverages the web technology. As a result, Kana is the leading provider of Internet-architected eRM software, delivering a broad range of world-class, integrated e-business and interaction applications with a modular and scalable platform for both the Internet and Global 2003 companies.

For Smooth Credit, Inc., a leading indirect consumer lender, managing customer relationships is critical. The company does no indirect marketing, and relies solely on long-term relationship with its clients and the word-of-mouth advertising to bring in business. The Chennai-based company specialises in the direct sales market. The 115-employee company, which has about 46,000 credit customers, receives its credit business from about 600 clients across the country that sell items such as vacuum cleaners and cookware directly to consumers.

THE PROBLEM

In dealing with its clients, the company was facing several problems. According to Mahesh, VP, Operations, "The company's clients have different products, different needs, and different issues, and we did not have a system that would let different parts of our company know what might be happening with a particular client. "Primarily," Mahesh said, "..we wanted to create clear communication within the company. We wanted to track discussions, conversations, emails, and special programmes for each client — and we wanted the ability to create form letters. We wanted to be able to determine whether we had followed up on a problem or request." In addition, the company wanted to acquire the capacity "creating personal relationship" with its clients in an easy manner. Since Smooth Credit relies on the word-of-mouth to build business, it's important to know its clients intimately." We like to know the names of their family members, their hobbies, their interests, and what they've done in the past," Mahesh said, "so that we could send appropriate flowers, cards, and gifts." Such information, he said, had been recorded on paper and was not very accessible. "We needed a better profile of our clients at hand," he said.

SELECTING A CRM SOLUTION:

It may come as no surprise that the company decided that it should go for a robust customer relationship management (CRM) package. The company turned to consultants to help select the software. The Smooth Credit had budgeted Rs.10 lakh for the project, but the first consultant suggested a CRM product with a price tag twice that amount. A second consultant found Wintouch from Touchtone Corporation, a CRM product that met the company's budget.

Following a demonstration, the Smooth credit was satisfied by Wintouch, both in the performance as well as in cost factor. Critical to the decision process was the fact that Wintouch runs on the IBM iSeries. "That had been a sticking point with other vendors," Mahesh said. Touchstone, he said, easily wrote an interface to the company's legacy, and implementation "was smooth and simple as any implementation I've ever gone through." Wintouch was up and running within three months, "..and probably could have gone faster except that it was a busy time for us and we were slow getting information back to Touchtone." If issues arose, he said, "they were resolved within one or two days."

IMPLEMENTATION

With Wintouch in place, "the information that once was scattered throughout the system now is all in one location," Windfeldt said. The company could more easily track personal information about its clients. SAS solutions deliver personal web portals that offer customers, partners, suppliers, and the enterprise a global view of their interactions and relationships. This global view includes managing the full set of communications channels such as the e-mail, web, chat, instant messaging, telephone and person-to-person, as well the e-business applications to integrate the marketing, sales and service functions. This full-service suite enables the e-businesses to compete and succeed in today's global economy. The SAS's customers are proof of this claim: the SAS's solutions are found in more than 800 companies, including 8 of the 10 most visited web sites.

Today, customers, partners and suppliers demand more from the enterprise—more information, more access, more collaboration. The CRM, with its company-centric focus, could no longer meet these critical business demands. To build the profitable and enduring business relationships, every business needs a new business model. It's very clear that companies taking the eRM business approach would overtake their competition and sustain that advantage well into the future.

THE CASE

The Smooth Credit's employees have found Wintouch's activities function easy to use. "Everybody pulls up Wintouch first thing in the morning and can schedule their activities. Our staff really likes this, especially being able to assign tasks and then being sure that the task gets done. "A long-term benefit of Wintouch, Mahesh said, is that Smooth Credit will have a history of its relationship with each client. "Earlier, the historical client information was mostly recalled from memory, with no written record. The technical staff at Touchtone is capable of handling complex situations. They provided the best customer support of any software development project I've ever dealt with. And the nice thing is, you don't have to go through a help desk. When you call, you get right to the people who designed and built the system." Will Smooth Credit be able to deliver the goods? Also suggest the three-step strategy for implementing the eRM from the basics of people and technology front of relationship marketing.

10 LEARNING ORGANISATION

"If all of Coca Cola's assets were destroyed overnight, whoever owned the Coca Cola name could walk into a bank the next day morning and get a loan to rebuild everything."

Carlton Curtis, VP Corporate Communications, Coca-Cola

Learning Objectives

After reading this chapter you should understand:

- The meaning of organisational learning and its various processes.
- Vertical and horizontal learning.
- Internal marketing as the first step in CRM as well as the perquisite for external marketing.
- Learn about employee loyalty .
- Meaning of knowledge of market response.

INTRODUCTION

Peter Drucker has observed that many organisations would often make statements asserting that 'people are their greatest asset'. Yet, only few of them would really practice what they preach. Most of these firms still believe, though not consciously, what the nineteenth century employers had believed: "people need companies more than companies need them." However, it is a fact that the organisations should market the membership as much as they market their products and services. They have to attract people, hold them, recognise and reward them, motivate them, and above all serve and satisfy them.

Some executive recruiters advise that a change of job every three to four years is an absolute necessity for the kind of resume that will appeal to a modern corporation. (as long, uninterrupted stints with a single company would signal the narrow experience and lack of ambition of an executive)

10.1 LEARNING ORGANISATION

The **learning organisation** could be defined as an organisation dedicated to continuous improvement and to reinventing itself as the market conditions demand. In order to change productively, an organisation should be capable of

(a) foreseeing the changes that are likely to occur in the markets and (b) capture ideas and learn from the experience that is occurring "on its periphery". In the traditional, hierarchical, bureaucratic structure of a multidivisional functional organisation, these learning experiences are likely to be ignored, if not actively suppressed, by the normal routines, policies, and procedures. Such improvisations occur as people try to find solutions in an adhoc manner to problems that may arise in the normal course of events, without resorting to the old methods that are usually employed for dealing with them.

The concept of the learning organisation becomes increasingly important among the network organisations, as partners have more opportunities to learn from one another. In fact, the motivation for many strategic alliances is simply aimed to create a learning organisation, introducing change into the existing structure in order to develop and improve distinctive competence and to learn from the new partner in areas critical to developing and delivering the customer value.

The relationship-oriented firms base their competitive strategies on their strategic advantages. They recognise that the only way to reach and sustain superior productivity is to share its benefits, which encourages the employees not merely to stick around but also to apply their knowledge and drive productivity in an upward spiral. They consider the employee learning as a vital asset that allows companies to change and heal themselves. However, in practice, even with a core of loyal employees, the companies encounter immense barriers to change. This is because the most useful and instructive learning grows from the recognitions and analysis of failure; and most often failure 'resists' examinations.

Failures

There are two principal reasons why the organisations do not study their own failures. The first is bureaucracy, which is characterised by a structure perfectly designed to conceal the mistakes, and an attitude totally disinclined to seek the real cause mistakes out and lay them bare.

The second is an almost universal fixation with success. The companies seldom do the "failure analysis", but rather would like to get preoccupied with success. By studying the elements of successful strategies and understanding the factors that make these strategies really work, the companies could adapt them to win new victories in new circumstances. Similarly, by observing the triumphs of other companies, a business firm could occasionally pick up an insight or a useful idea.

Take the phenomenal success of *In Search of Excellence*, first published in 1982. The book, based on theories that the authors had developed by studying the high performance companies had sold nearly 5 million copies. Its research included (a) a painstaking analysis of data covering a span of twenty five years, and (b) a who's who of business leaders who had contributed and endorsed the ideas mentioned in the book. Unfortunately, two-thirds of the "excellent" companies mentioned in the book are close to extinction. Now, how on earth could this have happened? Success breeds success, how could *In Search of Excellence* turn out to be a castle built on sand?

Only systems analysts could provide a suitable answer for this. According to them, when a system is working well, it's impossible to explain the real cause of its success. Its success rests on a long chain of subtle interactions, and it's not easy to determine which links in the chain are most important.

10.2 LEARNING AS A PROCESS

The concept of organisational learning applies to the implementation of the relationship marketing concept. First, the market intelligence function should be committed to (a) understand the customer needs, (b) define specific areas that require improvement, and (c) identifying the "best practice" wherever it is occurring throughout the organisation and in other companies.

The organisational learning occurs in the creation and management of strategic alliances with the customers and other partners. It is inherent in the definition of an "adhocracy" culture, where it is externally focused and capable of quick and flexible response to a changing market. The organisational learning is seen in the progression from a mass production to mass customisation.

The learning organisation is part of Jack Welch's concept of General Electric (GE) as a boundaryless organisation in which barriers between the company and its customer environment become permeable and the walls that separate the functional areas of the business break down. It continues in the GE process called "workout", where the traditional ways of doing things are actively challenged as a first step in finding ways to improve. The "re-engineering" is an attempt to make the organisational learning occur in a planned manner.

Slater and Narver Model of Learning Process

Historically, Slater and Narver articulated a model of the learning organisation that is centered on market intelligence. They draw a distinction between the most common form of organisational learning, the *adaptive* learning (the process of acquiring knowledge within the constraint and assumptions of the organisation) and the *generative* learning (the process by which the organisation actively questions the established beliefs about customers, mission, capabilities, and strategy). Only generative learning could create new ideas of the world.

The knowledge development involves three processes:

    a.   Information acquisition

b. Information dissemination and

c. Shared Interpretation

The last two processes distinguish the organisational learning from individual learning. The organisation could learn from its own direct experiences. Learning from the experience of others includes many techniques which include benchmarking, re-engineering, customer visit programmes, marketing alliances, strategic partnering with vendors and sellers, and formation of networks. Most of these have already been dealt in detail in the earlier chapters.

The knowledge developed as the result of organisational learning leads to behaviour change resulting in improved customer satisfaction, sales growth, new product development success rates, and profitability if it is combined with an entrepreneurial culture.

Slater and Narver conclude their learning organisation with the findings of relationship between corporate culture, innovativeness, market orientation, and corporate climate, and provide the evidence of the impact of organisational learning on business performance.

Key Factors Influencing Organisational Learning

There are several keys to organisational learning. The *first* is to understand that the fact that the true mission of any business is the creation of value. The *second* key to organisational learning is to grasp the value of failure. Only by measuring their failures could the organisations unlock the doors to real learning. The *third* key to effective learning is to ensure that the right people in the organisation learn to identify and correct the failures, whose frequency and severity would constrain the company's capacity to reach higher levels of value creation. *Finally*, the best place to start monitoring failure is to watch the defection rates for targeted groups of customers, employees and investors. This practice will identify the hot spots that require attention in the firm's value creation system.

Explicit and Tacit Knowledge

As you are aware, the knowledge takes several forms. At the most basic level, It could be differentiated into "explicit" and "tacit" knowledge. The explicit knowledge is more easily captured and exchanged. It is relatively simple, observable in use, often schematic in nature, documented and relatively easy to communicate. It resides near the bottom of the "organisation learning hierarchy".

The tacit knowledge, on the other hand, is complex, hard to observe in use, rich and often undocumented, hard to teach, and difficult to communicate even by the best technology. Most often it is not shared without a culture of learning and specific incentives provided by the leadership.

10.3   VERTICAL AND HORIZONTAL LEARNING

There are only two ways to improve the learning curve: (a) a vertical steepening of the curve, or (b) a prolonged climb by increasing employee loyalty. Steepening the curve is mainly a matter of "vertical" interventions like process redesign or automation. The vertical interventions are important opportunities, and the companies should pursue them. In essence, by enabling people to be more productive than their years of experience would normally allow, such interventions create precocious employees. But vertical investments accomplish little, unless they are combined with a second strategy of horizontal investment to increase the loyalty so that the employees will stay and climb higher on their learning curves

The personal productivity of the individuals in a company is the product of *how hard they work* and at times, *how smartly they work*. To some extent, it is possible to use the fear and insecurity factors to drive people to work harder. But the plain truth is that talented people work hard, when (a) they are proud of what they are doing, (b) their jobs are interesting and meaningful, and (c) they and their team members are recognised for their contributions and share in the benefits. How smart a person works depends very much on training, but the fact is that the vast majority of training comes on the job. If employees are not loyal to a business long enough to learn and use their learning, they and their company will never achieve the superior productivity.

Conversely, the improvements in employee loyalty and duration are much harder to match, for a human resource system is built on intangibles, subjective inducements, and circumstances peculiar to one company. These include: the hiring strategies, the career paths, training, compensation and measurement. Properly coordinated, these intangibles could be the source of a sustainable productivity advantage that the competitors would strive in vain to duplicate.

10.4   INTERNAL MARKETING AS A FIRST STEP IN RELATIONSHIP MARKETING

The management of people within the organisation is a key task for any organisation. The organisation's staffs are its prime resource, and human resources management is the professional approach in finding and developing the right people. Central to a successful relationship marketing strategy is the management of the customer/service provider interface. The employees should understand their role in the service exchange, and the human resources management provides the programmes and strategies to ensure the highest standards of customer care.

The **internal marketing** could be defined as a new way of treating the employees like the external customers through proactive programmes and planning, by delivering both the satisfied and loyal employees and customers. The internal marketing also covers issues, which are traditionally linked with other areas in organisations and the implementation of training programmes designed to enhance organisational performance should highlight the following aspects:

➢ Knowledge of the firm's product/service mix

➢ Pride in the firm itself, and individual jobs

➢ Awareness of opportunities for new service and business development, and

➢ Specific marketing skills.

There is no great difference in terms of marketing technique between marketing to the external and the internal customers. The distinction lies in the strength and types of the very different forces at work like the targets, incentives, skills, motivation, etc. It is clear, therefore, that the internal marketing is concerned with more than treating the employee as a customer, rather it means that the organisation should constantly endeavour to develop programmes and strategies for enhancing the employee satisfaction in much the same way as external marketing plans which are continuously updated and improved to meet the external customer demands.

The concept of internal marketing has its origins in conventional marketing theory and the marketing concept itself. The internal marketing addresses employees (or the internal market within an organisation), whose participation and role is recognised as being critical to the levels of service quality and delivery. However, the internal marketing is now being seen as more and more essential for all organisations striving for marketing success.

10.5 INTERNAL MARKETING AS A PREREQUISITE FOR EXTERNAL MARKETING

Internal marketing is required to ensure the support of traditional non-marketing people. They have to be committed, prepared and informed, and motivated to perform as part-time marketers. As Jan Carlzon of SAS noticed, "only committed and informed people perform". This is not applicable for the back-office and frontline employees alone. Rather, it is, of utmost importance that the supervisors, and middle-level and top-level managers are equally committed and prepared.

The *internal marketing concept* states that "the internal market of the employees is best motivated for the service mindedness and customer-oriented performance by an active, marketing-like approach, where a variety of activities are used internally in an active, marketing-like and coordinated manner".

The internal marketing as a process has to be integrated with the total marketing function. The external marketing, both the traditional parts of it and the interactive marketing performance, starts from within the organisation. As compared to transaction marketing situations, *a thorough and ongoing internal marketing process is required to make relationship marketing successful*. If the internal marketing is neglected, the external marketing would suffer or rather fail in its performance.

Major Considerations in Internal Marketing

i.   Every employee and every department or division within the same company have roles as internal customers and internal suppliers. In order to ensure high quality external marketing, every employee and department within a service company should provide and receive excellent service.

ii. It is necessary for people to work together in a way that is aligned with the organisation's stated mission, strategy and goals. It is a critical element within the high contact service firms, where there are high levels of interaction between the service provider and the customer.

The Role of Internal Marketing

If it is possible to ensure that the staff of a firm (a) are committed to the goal of guaranteeing the best possible treatment to its customers; (b) are motivated; and (c) could find themselves participating actively in achieving the organisation's goals and, if it has been realised that internal marketing is the key to establish these factors, then the potential for long-term success is evident.

The customer service is one of the most crucial aspect of an organisation's competitive advantage and the internal marketing could create a definite influence in enhancing this aspect. The internal marketing is attracting increasing attention and growing recognition as an implementation tool for adoption by all organisations. The most advanced systems for developing the marketing plans and strategies are worthless if the plan fails at the implementation stage.

Key Areas of Internal Marketing Application

The core areas where the internal marketing could play a key role include:

Management of change, where the internal marketing could be used to place and gain acceptance of new systems, such as the introduction of information technology and new working practices, and other changes.

Building corporate image, where the internal marketing's role is to create awareness and appreciation of the company's aims and strengths, as all employees are potential company ambassadors.

Strategic internal marketing, which aims at reducing the interdepartmental and interfunctional conflict and developing the cooperation and commitment required to make the external marketing strategies work.

10.6 ROLE OF THE EMPLOYEE IN INTERNAL MARKETING

The customer perceptions of quality are frequently influenced directly by the actions of service personnel. The levels of satisfaction or dissatisfaction could be governed by (a) the way in which the service personnel deal with the specific needs and requirements of customers; (b) the steps taken by the service personnel in the event that some aspects of the service goes wrong; and (c) the service which goes beyond the customer expectations (this includes the personal actions of an individual employee).

Staff Selection and Recruitment

The internal marketing recognises those employees and potential employees as customers of the organisation's internal market, and the consideration of their needs and wants in the same light as those of the external clients. The marketing activities should be applied in these internal markets in the same way as it is done while marketing to the external clients. The human resources management function could support, advise and guide the line management in this area. The programmes designed to generate interest in the organisation (through sponsorship and public relations, for example), could also be applied to attract the people who share the organisation's ideals and standards.

Requirements for the Job

The service employees frequently have significant personal contact with the customers and the responsibility for satisfactory service delivery lies on the individual's shoulders. The conflicting demands from the customers and management over the time spent on personal service versus efficiency and productivity need a careful handling.

Training and Development

Training is required in more than one level. At its basic level, it should impart knowledge about a particular aspect of the organisation or job while at a broader level, it gives focus and direction for the future to employees and also plays a communications role within the organisation. The training could be carried out in any number of ways. Workshops, team briefings, formal presentations and structured programmes are commonly used, together with work shadowing, job exchange schemes and project management. The different modes of training are more suited to different training and development needs.

10.7 WINNING EMPLOYEES'S LOYALTY

The cornerstone of human resource management is the employee value, and not a vague set of concepts or actions with unmeasured outcomes. It is enhanced through policies and practices that build continuity and commitment among the employees. The outcomes that could be measured are of primary concern here. The high rates of employees' turnover may be costly, though extremely low rates may also result in the cost of a different kind.

Thus, the employee continuity would have its downside as well. Overtime, the employees would reach peaks in job satisfaction and productivity, after which the effort might wane, attitudes toward customers harden, and revenue and profit production decline. When this happen despite an organisation's efforts to provide stimulation through continued training, new assignments, and other incentives, the individual and the organisation may best be served by severance of the relationship. Such "planned turnover' is a fact of life in all organisations.

The employee satisfaction and productivity follows varying patterns over the life of an association with the organisation. For example, the study conducted by the Service Management Group (SMG) found that in a multi-unit retail chain of companies, the satisfaction level of a new employee is usually found to be nine on a scale of ten after one month of employment. The satisfaction level dips to a level of six after five to eleven months of employment. For those remaining on the job, however, the satisfaction levels begin as a steady incline to a level of 9 after 4 years or more. This suggests the importance of measuring and understanding the employee satisfaction and productivity cycles so that appropriate efforts could be developed in a timely manner to help employees through the "troughs" in their job experiences and thereby averting some amount of planned turnover.

According to Frederick F. Reichcheld (1996), the satisfaction surveys are a far less accurate test of satisfaction than the behaviour. Research conducted in several business enterprises has shown that 60 to 80 per cent of the customers who defected had said on the survey, done just prior to defecting, that they were satisfied or very satisfied.

Some companies have tried to overcome this problem with an increase in the sophistication of their satisfaction measures. For instance, ninety per cent customers of several business enterprises in the home loan, personal loan sectors claim to be satisfied, but only 40 per cent come back for another deal. Yet most finance companies are still investing more money into refining their satisfaction surveys than into developing the reliable loyalty measures.

While every company's strategy is unique, the loyalty master Frederick F Reichcheld (1996) believed that they could build their employee relationship strategies on the following elements:

1. **Finding the right employees:** The successful loyalty-based business enterprises tend to be as selective in their choice of hires as they are in their choice of customers. They look for people with character who share the company's values, recruits those with the talent and skills to achieve the levels of productivity that make for a satisfying, long-term careers.

2. **Earning employee loyalty:** The loyalty leaders invest heavily in the development and training of their employees and construct the career paths and organisational structures that enable them to make the most of their education and abilities. As employees stay on, they get better at their jobs and become better acquainted with their customers. The employee loyalty and customer loyalty reinforce each other, making jobs more satisfying and thereby further increasing the potential for superior customer value. The loyalty leaders share the resulting productivity surplus with the employees in the form of higher compensation, which feeds back into the growing loyalty spiral.

3. **Gaining cost advantage through superior productivity:** The productivity surplus that grows from better customer and employee loyalty reduces a cost advantage. The employees may earn better salaries – often 10 to 50 per cent higher than their scale.

10.8   THE ECONOMIC MODEL

In the course of studying a range of industries over more than ten years, Bain (1996) has developed a generic model of the seven economic effects associated with the employee loyalty.

1. **Recruiting investment**   Most of the costs of hiring are obvious: recruiting fees, interviewing costs, relocation expenses, and so on.

2. **Training**   Giving the newly hired, a foundation for productive work which often involves formal classroom training as well as on the job training. The wages paid during the training period yield little or no contribution to the firm. While good companies continue to invest in training, even for their most experienced people, the expense is more than offset by the free training that the senior employees could provide to their junior colleagues. In other words, for the creation of loyal employees, training ceases to be a cost and becomes a net benefit.

3. **Efficiency**   On the simplest level, the employees learn to work more efficiently as they give experience on the job. Their increasing efficiency means that they require less supervision, which brings additional efficiencies. On top of these gains, however, it is important to remember that the efficiency is the product of *how intelligently people work* times *how hard they work*. As a general rule, the employees stay with the company because they are (a) proud of the value they create for the customers, (b) pleased with the value they create for themselves (c) more motivated and work harder.

4. **Customer selection**   The experienced salespeople and marketers are much better at finding and recruiting the best customers. In the life insurance business, for example, the new business persistency is much better for the experienced agents than for the trainees, In many cases, the policies written by the new agents have such low persistency, and they represent a net loss for the company

5. **Customer Retention**   Many research studies conducted by Bain (1996) in banking, brokering and auto service has revealed that long-term employees create higher customer loyalty. Even in manufacturing, where the employees rarely meet customers, the long-term employees could produce better products, better value for the consumer, and better customer retention

6. **Customer referral**   The loyal employees are sometimes a major source of customer referrals as in the mutual funds and insurance business in India.

7. **Employee referral**   The long-term, loyal employees often generate the best flow of high caliber job applicants. This not only raises the average quality of new recruits, but also cuts the recruiting costs.

The profit and growth are linked directly to customer and employee satisfaction and loyalty. They are driven by the value delivered to each of the several important constituencies, including customers, employees and shareholders. There is a growing body of evidence to support all these claims. According to James L. Heskett *et. al.*(2003),

Profitability of change (POC) = Dissatisfaction (with status quo)

×

Quality of the model for change

×

Quality of the process for change

The product would be greater than the cost of change (COC)

POC > COC (to those who must endure it)

Those who have been successful in managing the change have either benefited from an already high level of dissatisfaction among members of the organisation or have been able to foster it, often through restructuring, layoffs, ultimatums, or benchmarking against more successful competitors and others. It is often the most distasteful step in the process. The critical roles of leadership and management are those of identifying and fostering the value-building cultures, values, visions and strategies, while implementing the change-reinforcing processes intended to establish and align the three components of the performance trinity.

10.9   MARKET-DRIVEN ORGANISATION

Michael Porter's widely known work, *Competitive Strategy*, provided a structured approach to the analysis of strategy, with primary emphasis on the so-called external aspects of strategy encompassing the source of an organisation's leverage in its relationship with other players in its competitive environment. Whether or not it was Porter's intent, this was accompanied by only limited attention to culture, values, organisation, or change-inducing processes, even though no strategy would be complete or even achievable without them. Generally, the configuration of such market-driven organisation is the nested relationship of the firm's culture, capabilities and processes in the structure of the firm.

Features of a Market-Driven Organisation

a. **Strategic focus on the market**   The organisation is configured to focus on delivering superior customer value. This strategic theme is the central tent pole around which all the elements are orchestrated and connected. This ensures that all functional activities and investments are part of an overriding business model focused on the market.

b. **Coherence of elements**   This is achieved when all the elements of the organisation– culture, capabilities and configuration-complement and support each other. Conversely, the incoherence leads to 'disconnects' in strategy and implementation, creating lapses that the customer is usually the first to see.

c. **Flexibility**   Since the markets change, the configuration should not be a straitjacket, that inhibits trial and error learning and continuous improvement. The challenge for a market-driven organisation is to devise a structure that could combine the depth of knowledge found in a vertical hierarchy with the responsiveness of the horizontal process teams. Otherwise, even the best-aligned organisation will ultimately find itself out of step with the market and face expensive "retooling" of its organisation to meet the new demands.

The market-driven firms are adept at anticipating and acting on market shifts and emerging opportunities ahead of its competitors. Thus, the General Electric saw the potential in augmented services much earlier than its market rivals and diversified their operations to sectors as wide as the locomotives and factory automation, while the British Airways became a leader in providing an inflight experience that reduces the burden of long flight journeys. Both firms have recognised that their offerings were susceptible to the inexorable forces of commoditisation as the competitors catch up, and that the customers would buy the expectations of benefits and solutions to their problems.

The market-driven firms are focused not just on attending the needs of the customers, but also on anticipating the moves of rivals in the market. A continuing point of contention is whether a firm could act both as a customer- and competitor-oriented firm at the same time. The market-driven firms are especially adept at (a) anticipating the moves of their competitors, (b) anticipating both the moves they initiate and their reactions, and (c) spreading this information throughout the organisation. The firms that lack this capability are often caught by surprise when attacked by a competitor. The early indicators may have been scattered through out the organisation, but no one pulled the clues together to sense a pattern.

Shared Knowledge Base

Few organisations could match Honda's ability to learn, remember and act with agility. Their experience provides instructive guidelines for designing a market-driven memory.

Among the major features of the Honda organisation include:

> The key learning unit is the multifunctional team, which is embedded in a compressed organisational structure that observes few hierarchical distinctions. The absence of hierarchy and seniority makes it easier for ideas to be judged on their merit rather than on the basis of conventional wisdom. When teams are disbanded, their members are soon assigned to new programmes, which hastens the percolation of knowledge through the organisation.

> The team members are able to build the careers with promotion prospects that are based on the mastery of an area of expertise. These are not blinkered specialists, as they have ample opportunities for brief rotations into other functions. Thus, as soon as a team is formed, it has a gateway to the collective knowledge of

Honda through the team members' personal knowledge and networks of colleagues with similar expertise.

➢ The teams are guided by a deeply held belief that it is not possible to comprehend a market by relying solely on second hand reports. The design teams are expected to be in the field regularly to gain shared insights, and

➢ Failure is not stigmatised, which encourages the teams to experiment. For example, 90 per cent or so of the experimental research projects that Honda estimates fail the first time when they are analysed for lessons on what to avoid and the results are pooled for possible use in future projects.

10.10 CULTURE, CAPABILITIES AND PROCESS

The capabilities that distinguish the market-driven organisation are (a) the market sensing, (b) the market relating and (c) strategic thinking.

The Marriot Hotels consistently receives high ratings from business travellers and event mangers for their quality service all over the world. The Marriot is certainly as capable as Hyatt, Hilton and others at selecting good sites, opening new hotels smoothly, and marketing them well. This begins with a hiring process that systematically recruits, screens, and selects from as many as 40 applicants for each position and continues through every hotel operation. (For example, the maids follow a 66-point guide to arrange the bedrooms.) The effective management of these linked processes, within an organisational culture that values thoroughness and customer responsiveness, creates a distinctive capability that gives the Marriot employees a clear guidance on the ways of providing excellent customer service.

The capabilities are further obscured because much of their knowledge component is tacit and dispersed. This knowledge is distributed along four separate dimensions which include

➢ the accumulated employee knowledge and skills that come either from technical training, or along the experience gained with the process.

➢ the knowledge embedded in technical systems, comprising the information in linked databases, the formal procedures and established "routines" for dealing with given problems or transactions, and the computer systems themselves,

➢ the management systems and

➢ the values and norms that define the content and interpretation of the knowledge, transcend individual capabilities and unify these capabilities into a cohesive whole.

The organisation's culture is embedded within each capability.

The value is defined, developed and delivered to customers. The response to this value from the market leads to activities required to maintain and strengthen it, which ultimately lead to a renewal of the value proposition. As the firms move from a make-and-sell to a sense-and-respond model, these loops and value cycles will become even tighter.

The market sensing depends upon an open-minded inquiry rather than looking for information to confirm the pre-existing beliefs about the market. The next stage in this learning process involves the dissemination of information generated by these inquiries and absorbing the insights into the collective mental models of how the market behaves.

These mental models help make sense of the information, ensuring that everyone pays attention to the essence and potential of the information. A hallmark of a market-driven firm is a broadly shared assumption about their markets that assures the coherence and timeliness of strategies that anticipate rather than react to market events.

a. Sensing the market

The market-driven organisations use many devices to open their collective "mind" to new information that could help anticipate the emerging opportunities and competitive threats and more accurately forecast the nature of market response to a change in strategy. These devices include:

> ➢ Creating a spirit of open-minded inquiry,
> ➢ Carefully analysing the competitor's actions,
> ➢ Listening to staff on the front lines,
> ➢ Seeking out latent needs of both the internal and external customers,
> ➢ Active scanning of the periphery of the market, and
> ➢ Encouraging continuous experimentation.

The capability for market sensing is part of a learning process. The organisation collects information about the market to become more aware of the opportunities to create value. The firm learns how to position itself to take advantage of these opportunities. But great "senses"- even with effective mental models that don't limit the view of the world—are not enough. The information that is gathered by the sensing process must be processed into knowledge that could be accessed when required. To establish a continuous process of learning, the organisation should devise a way to capture and retain the information and knowledge it has collected. The entire organisation should have the capacity to access this knowledge in a quick and efficient manner. The advances in information technology have made the process of designing and building these shared knowledge bases on a large scale in a much easier manner. (Fig 10.1)

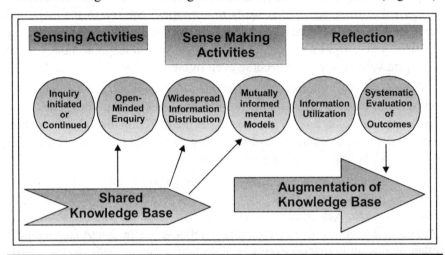

Fig. 10.1 *Market-Driven Processes for Learning About Markets*

Source: Frederick E. Webster Jr. (2002), Market driven management, New Jersey, John Wiley & Sons, Inc.

The Honda's ability to learn as an organisation and to remember this collective experience, depends on having this memory reside within the individuals, but remain at the service of cross-functional teams. The choice of what to learn is guided by a widely shared vision of Honda's competencies, markets and strategy. A shared vision has a very positive influence on the capacity to learn, because people are encouraged to expose their ways of thinking and seek new ways of thinking in order to reach the future implied by the vision.

Market-driven organisation can take two important steps to develop a shared knowledge base:

➢ Build systems for synergistic information distribution that are accessible throughout the organisation to assure that relevant facts and insights are available when and where they are needful, and

➢ Track strategic knowledge about the market structure, response and value creation that contribute the perspectives required to develop the informed decisions.

The market boundaries are defined by the competitors and customers. The market-driven firms utilise the potential customers and competitors to define the boundaries of the market rather than relying on pre-existing definitions of the market. This definition will be jointly informed by customers' perceptions of "substitutes-in-use", and the assessment of present and prospective rivals who have the capability to serve the needs of the target competitors.

b. The Knowledge of Market Response The decisions to launch a new product, change a pricing structure, invest in more salespeople, or cut an advertising budget have one thing in common. They are risky and often irreversible choices that depend on sound assumptions and beliefs about the shape of the relationship between the change to be made and the response of the market. If these judgments goes wrong, the strategic moves would become ineffective or turn counterproductive. Knowledgeable judgments require deep insight into the consumer acquisition and usage experience.

The firms in service industries are finding that the employee satisfaction has such a close relationship to the customer satisfaction—and eventually customer retention—that it can almost stand as a proxy. Such proxy measures are valuable, for they provide a continuing report on the management. What sets apart the market-driven firms is the priority that they assign to a few common indicators that reveal "the where", "the how" and "the when" factors of making money. They know that "what gets measured gets managed" and that their customer portfolio is an asset to be managed like any other asset. There is no surefire recipe to say what belongs in this part of the knowledge base – it all depends on what drives the performance. Building a customer base and brand equity is a long-run process of (a) raising awareness, (b) inducing trial and usage as a precursor to gaining customer loyalty, and then (c) tightening the relationship. Finally, the companies should hold on to their knowledge about the ways of learning so that they could build their shared knowledge base in a continuous and consistent manner. This helps to improve the learning competency and avoid lapses in memory from management turnover and sub-contracting.

EXHIBIT 10.1

> **FUNCTIONAL AREA STANDARDS WHICH SUPPORT THE GROWTH OF A PRO-ACTIVE LEARNING ORGANISATION**

> ➢ **Market research standards** Greater ability to identify potential for increase revenue among existing customers
>
> ➢ **Business and marketing planning** More coherent plans to address new revenue opportunities, due to higher quality and relevance of information, leading to higher success rate with launch of new products, greater matching of distribution channels to customer needs, etc.

> ➤ **Retail Customer standards** Ability to market additional products to existing retail customers, whether at retail or through mail order, due to quality of customer information.Higher sales volumes of existing products due to ability to target promotions·
> **Marketing Communications standards** Greater effectiveness of communicating with customers and prospects, leading to higher revenue for the given cost.
>
> ➤ **Product marketing standards** Reduced costs of selling, due to better attunement of channels to customer needs, leading to ability to capture higher market share through lower prices.
>
> ➤ **Inventory standards** Lowers the stock-outs and therefore quicker inflow of revenue and reduced loss of sales to competition due to improved sales forecasting.

Source: www.crmguru.com with permission

CONCLUSION

Learning organisation explores the idea that the human mind is evolving and that the quality of awareness experienced by the individual will be intimately related to their position on this evolutionary trajectory. In particular, the quality of awareness is related to the development of the model the individual has of their self. On these foundations, it is suggested that the learning organisation concept could be thought of as the lowest of a three-stage conceptual hierarchy of learning-wisdom-enlightenment. The wisdom could be thought of as a special case of learning culture that is of a higher order than a general learning culture because it provides the conditions for understanding the reality rather than the increased sophistication of representational systems that is a characteristic outcome of other learning environments. The enlightened organisation could be thought of as an ultimate goal or a condition in which the reality is known

The wise organisation will have structures, strategies and a culture (beliefs, attitudes, values, and goals) that support learning in the direction of the second mode of knowing. An enlightened organisation could be conceptualised as a goal rather than a learning or transitionary stage which the learning and wise organisations are meant to represent. The goal is to understand the reality. According to Wilber (1996) the social, economic and cultural characteristics of a society moves from a culture of wisdom towards knowing the reality or becoming enlightened. The intellectual capital oriented companies like TCS must develop human mind for their organisational excellence. A learning organisation could also have the wisdom of capturing the market by monopolising its customers not the product or service!

CHAPTER REVIEW QUESTIONS

1. Explain organisational learning as a process.
2. What do you mean by vertical and horizontal learning?
3. Elucidate internal marketing as a first step in relationship marketing.
4. Describe internal marketing as a prerequisite for external marketing.
5. Discuss the role of the employee in internal marketing for a hotelier.
6. How do you win the employee's loyalty.
7. Explain market driven organization, shared knowledge base and sensing the market in Indian context.
8. Illustrate market driven processes for learning about pizza markets in India.
9. What do you mean by the knowledge of market response?

CASE STUDY
HOTEL SAMUDRA-LEARNING EDGE FOR BUILDING RELATIONSHIP

BACKGROUND

In 1981, the Department of Tourism, Government of Kerala joined hands with the Kerala State Tourism Corporation Limited (KTDC) to develop a major deluxe beach resort hotel at Kovalam near Trivandrum, the capital of Kerala. The site located was approximately 15 kms away from the airport, railway station and national highway NH-47. The project envisioned the construction a of a central complex, in a style reminiscent of the early Spanish-Californian architecture, and 68 guest rooms and suites located in freestanding, two-story villas. The central buildings housed the guest reception area, the executive offices, a gift shop, beauty saloons, a grand ballroom (capable of seating over 500 diners and also divisible into three smaller rooms), other meeting rooms, two restaurants, and a cocktail lounge. The interior of the main buildings echoed the Spanish California theme, with exposed wood beams, rough textured stucco, tiled floors, wrought iron grillwork, hand-painted murals, and Spanish style furnishings. The guest rooms, by contrast, were furnished in the contemporary style. There were 68 deluxe rooms, 14 smaller rooms called parlours, and 8 suites. All rooms featured a balcony; all of them overlooking the Kovalam beach. Most rooms were within a few minutes walk from either of the hotel's two swimming and hydrotherapy pools.

By early 2003, the Samudra's executive committee made a review of the hotel's growth progress to date as it worked on developing a plan for the coming year. The occupancy rates and average room revenues for the first 12 months of the current year are shown in Exhibit-1, as are projections for the balance of the year.

HOTEL MANAGEMENT

Shyam Kumar, the general manager (GM) of Hotel Samudra reported to the senior vice president (VP) of KTDC (Hotels) who was located in Trivandrum. Mr. Shyam Kumar headed an executive committee consisting of himself, the hotel's resident manager, the directors of marketing, food and beverage (F&B) and personnel, the chief engineer, and the controller. This committee met weekly, although the GM often met separately with individual managers as the need arose.

Shyam's first exposure to the food and hospitality business had come 23 years earlier from working in for the Taj group of hotels. During college, he had worked summers at various resorts in Goa, a popular beach resort area in India. From the very beginning, he told a visitor as they walked into the cool of the hotel lobby, that he had planned his career to get exposure to all facets of the food and lodging industry. After college, he had worked for the Oberoi group in Mumbai, and then for the ITDC Ashok Hotel in New Delhi. He also worked for the Ambassdor Hotels, Madras and the Grant Hotels, Calcutta before joining Samudra in 1981 as the resident manager. Next, he became the GM of Hotel Mascot in Trivandrum, from where went to the UK on a three years deputation as the GM of the ITDC Hotels. He had taken up this assignment as the GM of Hotel Samudra in July 1999 after the completion of his deputation.

Shyam Kumar paused in the red-tiled lobby to exchange brief pleasantries with an uniformed hotel staff member. An old stone fountain splashed in the center of the lobby, surrounded by groups of lush potted plants, including a 20-foot palm tree. Beyond some rounded archways, several guests were checking in at the reception desk. The staff member excused herself to see if she could assist them. Shyam believes that internal marketing is the first step for marketing a beach resort as the destination is well promoted by the government. He identified the problems with staff capability and competency building measures to tap the revenue during the season

SHINING STAR CAMPAIGN

Shyam Sunder is seeing stars, because he is giddy about the organisation's innovative new campaign to reward the standout employees for their performance. The large, striking posters greet visitors to Martyris's cabin. The posters are advertising the Hotel Samudra's 'special thanks and recognition system' (Star) programme, a HR initiative aimed at rewarding the achievers across all levels of the organisation. "The purpose of this internal campaign is to create an association between our star performers and the brand, Hotel Samudra," says Shyam Sunder . Hotel Samudra is actively promoting the campaign across each of its 150 employees. As Shyam Sunder says: "It was time to recognise and reward our own stars." These stars are not the statesmen or tinsel town glitterati who grace the distinguished environs of the group's hotels, but to the organisation they are just as important.

The *Shining Star* campaign offers no cash awards or prizes. The recognition comes in the form of levels. Points could be picked up by employees for integrity, respect and regard for others, teamwork, environmental awareness, reliability, outstanding work, courage of conviction and initiative. The practical and useful suggestions that are beneficial to the company could also earn an employee point.

➢ Level 1 is the silver stage and it requires an employee to earn 120 points in three months.

➢ Level 2 is the gold grade and could be achieved by gathering 130 points within three months of reaching the silver level.

➢ Level 3 is top of the pops, the platinum standard. To reach this mountain an employee should procure 250 points within six months of reaching the gold level.

➢ At 510 points and beyond an employee would become part of the chief operating officer's club.

➢ An aggregate of 760 points or more would elevate the employee into the supreme grade at the corporate level, the managing director's club.

An interesting facet of this web-based initiative is that while it helps the employees earn the merit points for acts of excellence, it puts pressure on the review committee— comprising the general manager, the training manager and the heads of different departments—to respond within 48 hours of a suggestion being made. If the committee fails to get back in time the employee earns 20 'default' merit points. The employees could earn merit points through guest compliments, compliment-a-colleague forums and suggestion schemes.

The programme encourages them to work together and compliment each other. Important as the initiative is, it hasn't been linked in any way to the regular performance appraisal system for employees.

The programme has picked up momentum and is expected to raise motivation levels in the company, not to mention the obvious spin-off, the enhanced customer satisfaction. "We have noticed [since the campaign was launched] that a large number of employees have started working together in the true spirit of teams," says a satisfied Shyam Sunder . "There are stars all around us and this will eventually help us value our human capital. Many employees go that extra mile to dazzle the customer. The 'Star programme' is linked to customer delight; it is based on the premise that happy employees lead to happy customers. The employee recognition is, hence, directly linked to customer satisfaction. It is a recognition for the people, of the people and by the people.

By October 2003, as the Kovalam beach resorts entered the peak season, cumulative financial results have started showing that Hotel Samudra was in line with the projection of its budgeted revenue figures. The executive committee was busy developing plans for 2004 as well as working hard to increase the bookings for the months through Christmas. The financial projections for 2004 included a cost budget for each of the 12 months in the fiscal year. As they reviewed the experience of the resort's opening year to date, Mr. Shyam Kumar addressed the question of the monsoon season. "Are we going about marketing the monsoon season in the right way?" he asked the other members of the executive committee. "Should we be approaching the problem differently or should we even be opening at all?" After reviewing the experience of the festival season during the August-September and considering the latest projection for the Onam (festival of Kerala) seasons, he also suggested that the executive committee should devote greater emphasis to attract domestic business executives and corporate houses in those seasons. Finally, he stressed the goal of a five-star rating for the resort. "All of us at Hotel Samudra have got to think five stars, and our operating and marketing plans for 2004 should reflect this goal".

ACTION PLAN

Shyam sunder suggested six major categories of technique used in developing the capability for relationship marketing for serving global customers in Hotel Samudra ,Kovalam. These techniques include:

1. **Strategy development:** This implies the development of an overall approach to managing customers, which will reflect the overall corporate and marketing strategy. This link is important as significant investments and changes in many policy areas, processes and structures are required, in developing the relationship marketing

capability and a link back to corporate strategy may be important to justify the investment in the senior management.

2. **Customer information strategy:** This implies the data identification, collection analysis and interpretation to enable the detailed strategy to be determined with confidence.

3. **Planning and internal marketing:**

This includes:

> ➢ Drawing together all analyses to produce a case for changing the way Hotel Samudra manage its customers, plus the associated investment and profit implications, and

> ➢ Developing a project plan to manage and monitor.

> ➢ Selling the concept to Hotel Samudra staff at all levels within an organisation.

The message and the selling 'levels' to different group (e.g. the field sales force, finance director) will be vary according to the group positions.

4. **Capability development:** This involves the development of

> ➢ the processes, media, systems and organisational infrastructure (organisation, staff recruitment, training etc), to support relationship marketing and

> ➢ long-term business culture change.

Together these factors would build the capability to deliver the customer management strategy at the point of contact with the customers.

5. **Programme development:** This involves the planning and development of marketing programme and other tactical activities, which are designed using the customer and market data

6. **Implementation of marketing programmes in the market:** This includes the factors of monitoring and control, and feedback to objectives and strategies.

1. Will Mr Shyam Kumar succeed in marketing Hotel Samudra among global tourist?

2. Comment what needs the hotel to focus on external marketing as the manager overlook such concepts in his programme.

3. Prepare a relationship marketing programme for hotel Samudra and send it to Mr Shyam Kumar.

INTEGRATED RELATIONSHIP MARKETING STRATEGIES IN THE MILLENNIUM

"I have found the most important thing to do is decide what you're about, decide who you are, what you hold as important, and what you value. Make sure that whatever you're doing about becoming more of what you really are and not about plans and strategies that have financial gain as the starting point."

Scott Livengood, Chairman, CEO, Krispy Kreme

Learning Objectives

After reading this chapter you should understand:
- Learn more about analysis of service gaps and gap matrix.
- Learn about customer value adding process.
- Formulate relationship strategies.
- Strategies for nektionship Improvement.

INTRODUCTION

The twenty-first century is witnessing rapid changes in the world (by any criterion) at a pace faster than what we had witnessed in any of the decades of the past century. We are living in a time that has variously been called the Information Age, the Knowledge Economy, and the Age of Discontinuity. A predominantly resource-based economy has been supplemented by the one based primarily on knowledge and information. The service economy, with the information technology (IT sector) at its core, now accounts for more than half of the employment and consumer expenditures in virtually all of the developed countries. The knowledge economy of the twenty-first century will reward most handsomely those organisations: (a) that are best capable of acquiring, developing, and sharing knowledge; (b) that performs more than merely 'learn', (c) that 'remember' both its success and failures; (d) that connect seemingly unrelated information to predict the future, and (e) that engage their employees in the acquisition and utilisation of ideas for new products, services, processes, and solutions that could transform the individual as well as the collective work experience.

11.1 PREPARING FOR A RELATIONSHIP MARKETING STRATEGY

The continuous improvement is applied more to 'processes' than the 'products', although product improvement also came as a by-product of this process. The new concern for process improvement emanates from the realisation that the supporting service bundle in a business process is as important as the physical product in defining the customer value and also in the redefinition of the business as a service business.

The commitment to continuous improvement led to the development of a relatively new discipline called "re-engineering". The re-engineering has been defined as a fundamental, radical rethinking of the business from the ground up. These are all aspects of an organisation's core shared values, other wise termed as the core of its culture.

The outstanding employers regard the organisation culture as their "brand." The communication of this brand to the existing and prospective employees is regarded as a high-priority activity.

Hardwiring

The term hardwiring is a term popularly used in the computer hardware and software sectors. However, as a concept it evolved from 'hotwiring'. The hotwiring is a practice where the ignition wire is brought into direct contact with the power source, bypassing the ignition key. This practice is commonly done when you have lost the key to the automobile or by those who try to steal automobiles. However, in the business terminology, hardwiring describes the conceptual part of a business strategy. This strategy generally links the business performance with that of the employees who handle the mission.

Therefore, by projecting the success of the strategy, in turn, could enhance both the confidence of the employees as well as the level of support which the company has extended to them in similar assignments. In reality, most of the companies adopt hardwiring to overcome the bottlemecks of systems formalities and procedures. This is also an example of management by exception (MBE). The hardwiring could be achieved at several levels:

> ➢ the transactional,
> ➢ the strategic,
> ➢ the cultural, and
> ➢ the organic

Each of these levels is most appropriate to a given organisation. Those organisations capable of achieving the organic hardwiring have achieved the most dramatic results from the process.

Fig. 11.1 Showing A Hierarchy of Initiatives

Source: James L. Heskett, W. Earl Sasser Jr. and Leonard A. Schlesinger (2003), *The Value Profit Chain*, New York, Free Press

The waste of organisational knowledge is the greatest deterrent to value creation. It results from the failure to develop information from the available data, and encourages the development of individual knowledge and capability, and facilitates the retention of such knowledge and its transfer from one part of the organisation to another. It is the most important challenge addressed by the leadership in any organisation competing primarily on the basis of information and knowledge for customer acquisition, retention and add-on selling. The situation is explained in Fig. 11.2.

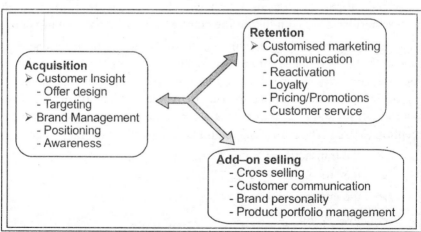

Fig. 11.2 Customer Value Adding Process

Source: www.customerequity.com

For the add-on selling company, the major imperative lies in developing a relevant set of offerings and bringing them to customers. The add-on selling organisation focuses on (a) cross selling expertise, (b) effective communication of its offerings and their benefits to consumers, (c) development of a coherent brand personality that could reach across multiple offerings, and (d) careful management of the offering portfolio. The portfolio managers should prevent the offering set from becoming (i) too broad (alienating customers with the irrelevant offers), (ii) unlinked (creating an offering set with a total value worth less than the sum of its parts), or (iii) too narrow (under-leveraging the potential asset value of the customer). The add-on selling company should have (a) a strong portfolio management and brand management groups, (b) a powerful sales organisation, and (c) a marketing function that focus on the identification of potential areas for add-on selling as well as for the establishment and maintenance of the umbrella brand.

What sets the market-driven firms apart is the priority they would assign to a few common indicators that reveal the 'where', the 'how' and the 'when' factors of making money. They know that "what gets measured gets managed" and that their customer portfolio is an asset to be managed like any other asset. There is no surefire recipe to predict the contents of a particular part of the knowledge base. The content will depend on the factors that drives the performance of the firm.

Nonetheless, few firms would achieve the superior long-run profitability without managing the following indicators:

➢ Value of the customer portfolio
➢ Rate of migration of value
➢ Return on marketing initiatives

Not all customers are equally valuable. Yet few firms know which of their customers are profitable and which of them are subsidised. Only the final results could serve as an eye-opener in this regard. Figure 11.3 shows the customer matrix for a bank, say the HDFC bank. Here the bank has segmented its customers by (a) cost to serve (where a high-maintenance customer would make fifteen or more visits a month to a branch), and (b) the risk-adjusted revenue (where low revenue would be below Rs. 500 per month, largely because they carried a small balance).

Cost of Serving					
Low		**Medium**		**High**	
Highly Profitable	**10%**	Quite Profitable	**3%**	Moderately **10%**	
Break Even	**20%**	Small Losses	**40%**	Big Losses **20%**	

| High |
| Risk- |
| Adjusted Revenue |
| Low |

Fig. 11.3 Customer matrix for a Bank

Value Migration

The value migration provides a useful framework for keeping track of the market forces that will shape the answer. The value migrates when the economic and shareholder value flows away from the obsolete business models towards new competitive offerings. A good strategic thinking requires early measurable signs of value migration before (a) the process begin to accelerate and (b) it is too late to combat. The useful early indicators in this regard include:

> Declining share among the 'leading edge customers'— the ones that influence opinions,

> Deteriorating quality of share, reflecting higher turnover rates, reduced participation in the growing segments, poorer profitability, and growing reliance on promotional discounts,

> Shrinking customers' share of their market (e.g., disk drives for mainframe computers)

> Profits from new products below the historic levels, because time-to-breakeven is longer while the life-cycles shorten

All these factors influence the acid test of value migration, which is a declining ratio of market capitalisation to revenues. This is the equity market's pronouncement of foreseeable trouble, and should mobilise the strategic thinking process to seek explanations and solutions.

There are many indicators of an expense-driven mindset. This thought process highlights the following questions:

> What is the sales forecast for next year?

> How many sales people can we afford at that sales level?

> Whether the expenditure on advertising, sales, promotion and so forth (as a percent of sales) is in line with our competitors?

> How can we cut these expenses?

> Are we gaining or losing share?

The strategic insights come to play when the marketing initiatives are foreseen as the drives of future revenue, and not the other way around. Building a customer base and brand equity is a long-run process of raising awareness, inducing trial and usage as a precursor to gain the customer loyalty, and then tightening the relationship. Finally, the companies should hold on to their knowledge about the ways of learning, so that they could build their shared knowledge base in a continuous and consistent manner. This helps in improving the learning competency and avoid lapses in memory from management turnover and sub-contracting.

11.2 STRATEGY FOR IMPROVEMENT

The strategy to improve the level of customer relationship is a simple four step process as described below:

a. Identifying the Customers

The first step is to identify the customers. An organisation, forming the strategy, would only list its external customers of all types. The list should include (a) the trade customers and actual users of the company's products and services, (b) the individuals who matter in case of institutional customers, (c) current customers, (d) past customers and (e) future or potential customers and (f) the competitors' customers. The list should also include professionals who may be not be direct customers (e.g. physicians who prescribe a company's products to their patients). The concerned regulatory authorities are also included in the list. With increasing awareness about the environment and social responsibility, the society in which a company operates is also considered its customer.

The list of past customers will be useful for finding out the reasons why they had deserted the company. Similarly, a list of the customers of the competitors will be useful to find out the reasons for prefering the competitors' product or services. A list of regulatory authorities is needed to ensure that the organisation does not lose sight of its statutory obligations. The preparation of a comprehensive list of all types of external customers of the company is the first step in the strategy to improve the level of customer satisfaction.

b. Identifying Customers' Needs and Expectations

The second step in the strategy is the identification of the requirements or the needs and expectations of the customers. In many companies, the opinions of sales and marketing personnel regarding customer expectations are mistaken for the customers' perceptions of their needs and expectations. One should guard against this common error as the real need is to understand the requirements of the customers as they understand them. This information has to be gathered straight from the customers themselves through surveys. The decisions would then be based on the data gathered and analysed in a scientific manner rather than on a gut feel or opinion or hunch.

For every category of customers, a different approach for gathering information has to be developed. The guidance from the experts has to be sought in designing the questionnaires and conducting the surveys. The customers should be requested not only to list their requirements but also rank the product or service characteristics in the list in the order of their importance.

For a quantitative survey, the customers should also be requested to provide the corresponding weightage to the various characteristics, but it does not give a very clear idea about the degree of preference of one over the other.

A higher ranking can be either due to a very small marginal difference between the two or a highly significant difference.

Thus step two of the strategy consists of (a) development of approaches, (b) designing of questionnaires and (c) conducting surveys to gather information on expectations and preferences of all categories of customers. The analysis of this data would provide the basis for conducting customer satisfaction measurement in step three of the strategy.

c. Measurement of Customer Satisfaction Level

The third step of the strategy consists of the measurement of the level of satisfaction of different categories of customers with the products and services offered by the company. The detailed information would serve as a base for desigining the company performance in meeting their expectations. The surveys for measuring customer satisfaction could also be utilised for updating one's knowledge about customer expectations and preferences or relative weightage for different product or service characteristics for further applications. It would provide comprehensive information about customers' perception regarding company's performance in meeting their expectations. It would also compare the company's performance with key competitors' performance in satisfying the customers. This information is the basis for taking action to improve customer satisfaction on factors ranked as important by them.

d. Developing an Improvement Plan

Step four of the strategy consists of making use of the information in developing an improvement plan for increasing the level of customer satisfaction, leading to enhanced competitiveness in the market place and excellence in customer satisfaction. It can be divided into four sub-steps or tasks as under: (a) analysis of gaps (b) solving customers' problems (c) preventing recurrence of problems and (d) going beyond customer satisfaction.

Analysis of Gaps The analysis of data collected in the first three steps would reveal several gaps—gaps between customer expectations and company performance, gaps between company's own perception and customers' perception about the performance and gaps between the company performance and the competitors' performance.

The company should refine and fine-tune its internal measures so that the gaps between the customers' perception and company's perception about its performance are minimised if not eliminated. The data on competitive position on different product and service characteristics and the level of importance of those characteristics are placed on a Gap Analysis Matrix (as shown on Fig. 11.4).

		LOW	HIGH
IMPORTANCE GIVEN-TO CUSTOMERS	**HIGH**	B	D
	LOW	A	C
		LOW	**HIGH**
		COMPANY STRENGTH	

Fig. 11.4 Gap Matrix

Quadrants of Gap Analysis Matrix

Quadrant A includes those characteristics of the product or service that are not considered important by the customers and on which the company is also not in a strong position. There is no need to be unduly worried about the company's low strength in these characteristics. They should not feature in the advertisement or sales promotion of the product or service.

Quadrant B includes those characteristics that are of high importance to the customers but the company is not in a strong position in meeting the expectations of the customer and/or where the company performance is lower than the competitor's performance. This quadrant indicates areas that requires an urgent need for improvement. Unless the company does something to improve its performance in these areas very soon, it is in the danger of losing market share to the competitors who may have strong position in those characteristics. **Quadrant B thus points to both the problem areas and the opportunities for improvement** requiring urgent attention.

Quadrant C includes those characteristics that are not of great importance to the customers but in which the company is strong. It is incurring cost on the items that are of little consequence to the customers. This quadrant provides opportunities to the company for reducing the cost without affecting the customer satisfaction levels. The strategy for the characteristics that fall in this quadrant, therefore, is to improve the profits by cost reduction. However if the company feels that the characteristics are likely to assume importance, then it could start educating the customers on the importance of the characteristics.

Quadrant D includes those characteristics that are of high importance to the customers and on which the company is also strong. Here it is necessary to maintain and if possible improve the company strength. The company should publicise these strengths through advertisements to attract more customers and increase the market shares. Even if the competitors are equally strong, the first company to announce their strength in these characteristics can gain a competitive edge. The strategy for the characteristics in this quadrant, therefore, is to maintain and improve strength, advertise the strength and keep constant watch on the internal measures for the characteristics to ensure that the competitive edge is maintained or enhanced. The 'south roaming facility' extended to the pre-paid credit segments of mobile phone users of AIRTEL is an example in this regard.

Solving Customers' Problems A good complaint handling system, should take care of customers' problems with proper care and necessary follow-up. The information collected during the customer satisfaction surveys and results of gap analysis generally have to be made useful for this purpose, if the firm does not have much data for customer complaints. The essential components any of such system include (a) a well-designed problem recording and rectifying process and (b) a well-trained and empowered employees to handle such grievances on the spot. In the presence of such systems/arrangement an organisation could convert a dissatisfied customer to a completely satisfied one and eventually to a delighted and loyal customer even.

Preventing Recurrence of Problems The information on customer dissatisfaction gathered through surveys should be shared with the employees so that they could learn about the causes of dissatisfaction and prevent the recurrence of problems. It is important that the employees should be made more customer focussed. The standards for customer service have to be set and deployed. The employees have to be trained to meet the set standards. The key processes involved should be standardised to meet the customer expectations consistently. Project teams should be set up for improving the processes that are currently not capable of meeting the customer expectations consistently. Once the processes are standardised and/or improved, they should be controlled and monitored by developing internal measures that enhances the customer satisfaction. Regular internal measurements would serve as an online estimate of the level of customer satisfaction.

Going beyond Customer Satisfaction In the competitive business environment, the company culture should be oriented towards delighting the customers. The policies and procedures of the company should be made customer friendly. The satisfaction of employees assumes a lot of importance in going beyond the customer satisfaction. The contended employees should be adequately trained, motivated and empowered to exceed customer expectations as one of the effective strategy for attaining customer delight. In view of this it is essential to conduct surveys to measure the employee satisfaction.

If employees are publicly recognised for providing outstanding service to delight a customer even at considerable expense to the company, others would follow the example. If the satisfaction level of customers is an important component of the system of appraisal of employees, employees will strive to delight the customers. Thus an appropriate recognition and reward system plays a very important part in creating the right culture in an organisation. The internal measurements that are related to customer delight have to be extensively used for controlling the processes and for appraising the employees.

Exhibit 11.1 describes the process of evolving a relationship strategy in the present business context.

EXHIBIT 11.1

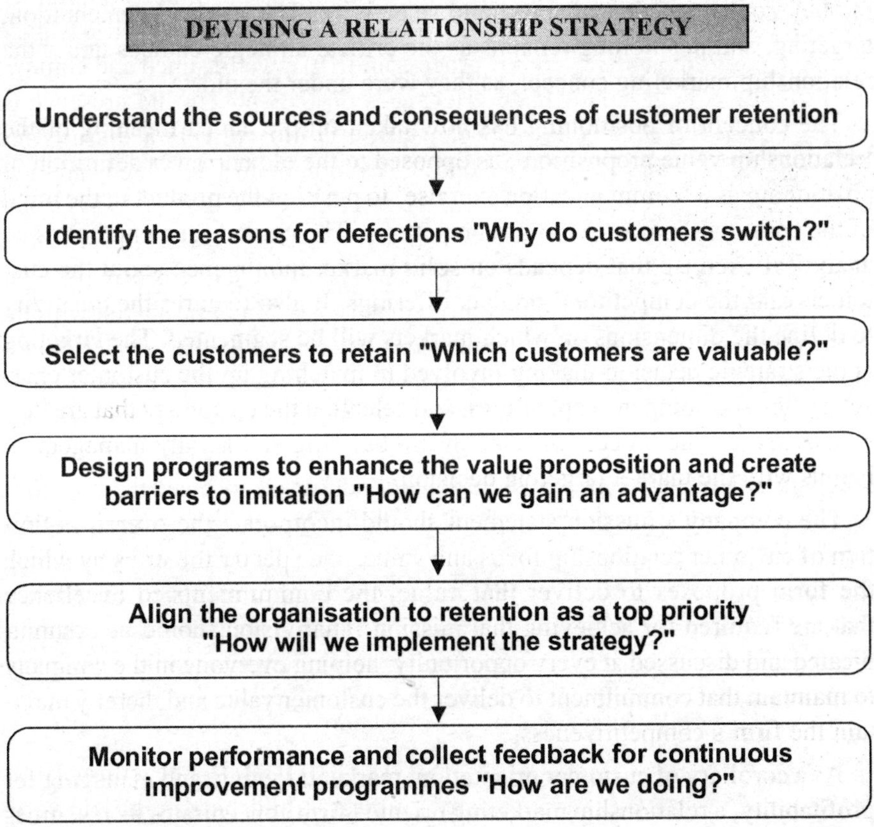

DEVISING A RELATIONSHIP STRATEGY

Understand the sources and consequences of customer retention

↓

Identify the reasons for defections "Why do customers switch?"

↓

Select the customers to retain "Which customers are valuable?"

↓

Design programs to enhance the value proposition and create barriers to imitation "How can we gain an advantage?"

↓

Align the organisation to retention as a top priority "How will we implement the strategy?"

↓

Monitor performance and collect feedback for continuous improvement programmes "How are we doing?"

11.3 GUIDELINES FOR IMPLEMENTATION

It is essential that from top to the bottom management, people should commit to a single overriding purpose for the business to create a satisfied and loyal customer by delivering superior value. The customer should be put on a pedestal above all others in the organisation including the owners and the managers. The customer orientation includes a commitment to customer-defined quality, innovations, and the value-driven concept of strategy. Here the underlying assumption is that the marketing is customer-centric, and not product or company-centric.

The market intelligence is absolutely essential to a relationship market-oriented organisation, and the source of knowledge could be utilised to improve, grow, and adjust to the changing market environment. The roots of this focus should be the capabilities and resources of the company, the factors that it could successfully link while serving the under-served market needs and wants. The customer selection is the critical strategic choice. The customers who cannot be served well by the company and are unwilling to pay the company for its capabilities could severely damage a business. Once again, the key concept is that of focus and selectivity. The market segmentation, targeting, and positioning remains as the critical strategic choices under the relationship marketing concept, as they were under the old.

The concept of positioning has now taken on the added meaning of the 'relationship value proposition', as opposed to the old narrower definition of positioning as a 'communication exercise' to position the product in the mind of the consumer in relation to its competitors. The market segmentation is an analytical exercise that depends on solid market intelligence about the customers and the competitors' product offerings. It also requires the creativity to define the dimensions on which markets will be segmented. The targeting is the strategic decision-making involved in matching up the customer characteristics and company capabilities, and selecting the customers that are best able to serve. The process of relationship building and loyalty management begins with the market targeting decision.

The company's mission statement should incorporate the overall definition of customer relationship focus and value, and specify the ways by which the form proposes to deliver that value, the commitments to excellence that are required for achieving that mission. That vision should be communicated and discussed at every opportunity, helping everyone in the company to maintain that commitment to deliver the customer value and thereby maintain the firm's competitiveness.

As a corollary of customer orientation, market targeting, and managing for profitability, a relationship marketing oriented firm concentrates its resources and energy on developing and maintaining the customer relationships and building customer loyalty. Most companies find it difficult to be in both types of business relationships at the same time—transactions with some customers and partnerships with others, unless through distinct strategic business units.

Building and managing brand equity is a key part of building customer relationships and managing customer loyalty. The **brand** could be defined as (a) a relationship with the customer, and (b) the meaning that surrounds the product offering. Brands are found in virtually every business category, both industrial and consumer, often in the form of the name of the company. The brands have value because they connote trust in the relationship between the producer and consumer. Building and managing brand equity depends on a total marketing programme that begins with creating brand identity and brand meaning, and ends with the defining of desired customers response to end relationships with the brand.

The marketing programme creates customer awareness, preference, and buying actions that lead to superior market results in terms of sales volume, market share, profit margins, customer loyalty, and repeat business. The brand equity provides leverage for all marketing expenditures including advertising, product development, and trade relations. Ultimately, the enhanced market performance creates cash flow, stronger earnings per share, high stock prices, and increased shareholder value. Without a brand, the company could never hope to earn superior returns. It remains a commodity business lucky to earn a return on its investment that covers its cost of capital.

CONCLUSION

Today, the customer-value delivery and satisfaction must be the shared responsibility of each and every individual in the organisation. The marketing is no longer a separate management function, but the market-focused leadership for creating superior customer value and profitability such as adoption of customer relationship management, innovation management, and value chain management. As we have stated in the book, the relationship marketing concept is a way of managing the present business professionally by delighting its customers. It focusses on distinctive human and non-human competences, value delivery, market targeting and the value proposition, brand equity, profitability rather than sales volume, and a customer-focused organisational culture. It requires hands-on involvement by management at all levels and in all functions, throughout the complex networks of strategic partnerships, to develop and deliver superior value to customers. It requires that everyone put the customer first. We hope the Indian business become more competitive by adopting this latest marketing practise. It is highly relevant to organise focus group, seminars and training programmes for the both corporate houses and academia extensively for promoting this business philosophy in India.

CHAPTER REVIEW QUESTIONS

1. Describe the customer value adding process for a supermarket chain like the Foodworld.

2. Devise a strategy for improvement for a hotelier.

3. What do you mean by gapanalysis? Explain the gap matrix.

4. Formulate a relationship strategy for the Reliance Infocomm

5. Explain the guidelines for implementing a relationship marketing strategy for an insurance service provider say, the ICICI Prudential.

6. How do you prepare the relationship marketing strategy for cellular service provider in India?

7. Explain the hierarchy of hardwiring of initiatives for an e-tailor say the fabmart.com

CASE STUDY
MYSHOP.COM—TRACKING FOR E-LOYAL CUSTOMER

inspiration

BACKGROUND

The e-commerce is one of the most exciting economic and technological trends of the recent pasts. It provides a new market place, more opportunities to sell and market the product and attain greater competitive advantage. In fact, the Internet has taken only 5 years to achieve a critical mass of 50 million users, which the radio took nearly 38 years to achieve, television 13 years and the local cable nearly 10 years. These figures suggest the rapid acceptance of the Internet as a medium of connectivity and commerce. The e-commerce encompasses the entire online process of developing, marketing, selling, delivering, servicing and paying for products and services. An online study conducted by brandquiver.com pointed out a good potential for business to consumer sites in India. Further, they observed that 70 per cent of the up-market netizens would go online shopping. Again, the study revealed that 60 per cent of the on-line shoppers had done purchase three or more times through the net.

According to Forrester Research Inc. survey, the global Internet trade is expected to reach $56.8 trillion in 2004 which is amounting to 8.6 per cent of the global trade. Incidentally, only 12 countries representing 85 per cent of world wide net sales and North America will grab nearly 50 per cent of the deal (about $3.2 trillion) in 2004. India has not, however, made much headway in e-commerce, where the world market is growing in an exponential manner.

EMERGING INFLUENCE OF E-COMMERCE IN INDIAN BUSINESS

After the liberalisation process, the domestic firms have been passing through a period of transition, from a seller's market to a buyer's market, from the rationing shortages to marketing of surpluses. In today's context, the information technology and business process have a truly recursive relationship with the strategy and process being driven more by the new possibilities that the Internet opens up on a regular basis. According to the NASSCOM survey, more than 81 per cent of PC's sold were driven by the need to access the Internet. About 23 per cent of the Internet users in India were females. The users, on an average, are estimated to be accessing the Internet for 6 hours a week, the maximum of them being in the 18- 24 age group (49 per cent).

It is a fact that the popularisation of web-based technology endeavours in the new millennium would result in (a) more effective performance (better quality, greater customer satisfaction, and better corporate decision making), (b) greater economic efficiency (lower costs) and (c) more rapid exchange (high speed, accelerated or real-time interaction) of Indian business. The business rationale for the use of electronic commerce is generally based on profit, revenue and cost. The firms use technology to either lower the operating costs or increase the revenue. Depending up on how it is applied, the e-commerce has the potential to increase revenue by creating new markets for old products, creating new information-based products and establishing new service delivery channels to better serve and interact with the customers.

My shop.com

A dynamic youth, Mr. Aravind after his graduation from the Indian Institute of Technology (IIT), Chennai, decided to set-up a web-based company called myshop.com. He explored the possibility of setting up an e-tailing firm with the assistance of Mr. David, a marketing professional and Mr. Ramesh, a chartered accountant. Logically, Aravind explored various options starting with digital and cyber marketing. Aravind is very well aware that the cyber marketing is not simply a one-shot deal, where a business throws together a web page on the Internet, hoping enough customers will find it. Again, the digital marketing is a sophisticated strategy that uses a whole arsenal of cutting-edge technologies, such as videotapes, audiotapes, CD-ROM's and even web pages to reach prospects in ways those conventional sales tools could not reach. It is an innovative and cost-effective way to help the business enterprises gain a competitive advantage and increase their profits.

In working with business firms that could sell more by using the testimonials, it occurred to Mr. Aravind that the digital media and the Internet might be the most effective way to go. "I thought, what if I were in the business of selling, say, FMCG supplies, and I could introduce my prospects to 10 or 20 of my best customers? What if I could have people in their own words express the emotions, the results, benefits, and real-life stories of how my product or service has transformed their life or their business? That could be more compelling than any sales presentation. A letter or a brochure could not fully capture the facial expressions or voice inflections or emotions which the video and audiotapes can. They give you a dimension that print media can only suggest.", He says.

Exhibit 1describes the common pitfalls in the present web pages.

EXHIBIT: 1

COMMON PIT FALLS IN THE PRESENT WEB PAGES

✓ Too many user-unfriendly sites, with poor content and awkward navigation;

✓ Sites contain too many images, making them slow to load;

✓ Limited transaction capabilities and product information;

✓ Lack of a proper focus on deepening the customer relationships;

✓ Lack of strategic clarity: should they increase awareness, drive sales or motivate online surfers to visit the real store?

✓ Few luxury brands had integrated their digital channel with their stores and other offline media;

✓ Poorly defined performance indicators, such as sales and margins,

✓ Dearth of robust data or consumer information to create personalised shopping experiences.

Source: In-house study report

Mr Aravind was fully aware of the fact that he was venturing into a revolutionary concept and he wanted to advise his clients to take full advantage of the Internet-based promotions. He then started a new e-firm, 'the myshop.com'. Mr Aravind is a software specialist, and not a marketer, and he was fully aware of his limitation in the required marketing skills that could actually provide the lead inputs for designing the various digital media for his clients. Fortunately, he got the service of Mr David, who was waorking as GM, Marketing, Synergy Communications. David was appointed in the same dsignation at Myshop.com. Aravind was very impressed with David's topnotch professionalism in several professional interactions in the past.

"We're looking for entrepreneurs, business owners and professionals who are totally passionate about their product or service," Aravind says. "They must want their business to be special, different, to stand out in the eyes of their customers and prospects. If you don't think your business is exciting, if you don't think you can add value to your customer's lives, then don't call us."

Unlike a lot of people with a new and promising technique in their repertoire, neither David nor Aravind try to portray the cyber media as silver bullets that could transform a business enterprise overnight. They both believe that in order to make the cyber marketing work, it has to be the part of an overall marketing plan that's carefully designed, properly executed, and constantly monitored.

"You can have the most technically perfect video in the world," says David, "with superb footage and breathtaking testimonials from your customers about why your product or service is the best. But without a comprehensive marketing plan, you won't get very far. You can't just mail your video to a few names on some list and expect miraculous results. You need a master strategy." That's why the Aravind/David alliance is so complimentary: Aravind provides the technical expertise to produce the first-rate marketing materials in cyber and digital format, while David provides the master strategy on deploying the materials in the net.

Aravind, CEO of Myshop.com, started his talk in the brainstorming session of the company explaining the benefits of digital marketing and how it could be boiled down to simple demographics. According to the recent studies, online consumers appear to be a marketer's dream. They are, for example, likely to spend more to get the best, buy from catalogues, and make an effort to utilise the new devices or methods. Most striking, though, is the fact that the people with online subscriptions are up by three-and-a-half times more than the likely to be college graduates. Aravind's discussion served as a blueprint for any company interested in listing via the myshop.com. He posed three main questions:

Who should do the cyber marketing?

What elements should be included in the digital and cyber marketing programme?

How should the cyber marketing organisation be designed?

Mr David expressed his views that the online experience must build traffic and sales in the world. According to him, "most websites are like window shopping after closing time. You can see some things, but not all, and you can't buy them." It is understood very well from the above that, the personalised service and an aura of exclusivity are the online challenges for luxury brands. The trick is to connect the online world with your existing operations. An online customer could browse the products, source information, create a wish-list, send it to the nearest stockist and then visit the store to view, touch and buy the items. Interesting site features, such as 3D imaging, zoom and virtual modelling, are essential for marketing luxury brands, as consumers should feel that they are buying into a dream. Hence Aravind opted the following strategies (Exhibit-2) for the luxury brand e-tailing.

EXHIBIT 2

STRATEGIES FOR LUXURY BRAND E-TAILING

✓ Offer limited edition products

✓ Provide access to waiting lists for hot/high demand products

✓ Create a brand culture or develop celebrity links - for example, jewellery or make-up designed by a well-known personality

✓ Emphasise craftsmanship and quality. Offer free samples, swatches or teasers

✓ Ensure that offline and online offers are consistent

✓ Offer tailor-made products or services

✓ Categorise the products by mood, time or individual choice

✓ Provide the exclusive membership and perks, such as invitations to previews and exclusive events.

He explained the best use of digital channels for building the brand image and their customer relationships based on the fact that e-tailing sites selling luxury goods grew from 20,000 to 50,000 between 1998 and '99. Aravind also suggested additional features like the shopping carts (These are programmes linked to the companies products and services. When a potential client clicks on the link, they are offered an opportunity to purchase that product or service) for wider acceptance and popularity of the site. The features of Myshop.com shopping cart are explained in Exhibit 3.

EXHIBIT: 3

MYSHOP.COM CART'S FEATURES

1. **Product Search Engine**

   With site search feature, a customer could empower the shoppers with the ability to search for specific products based on key words. Additionally, this feature will allow the customer to programme the "hard searches" – the predetermined searches hard coded to a single link

2. **Affiliate Tracking**

   Offer an incentive for other web stores to sell the listed products and services of myshop.com through this capability. When a customer visits the web store by clicking a link on an affiliate's site, the shopping cart tracks that customer from start to finish and lets the myshop.com know from which affiliate that customer was referred.

3. **Discounting**

   The listed firms and their products/services could run sales and promotions just like the regular retail stores. The shopping cart allows each firm to establish quantity discount tiers by product, by order subtotal or both.

4. **Frequent Shopper Points Tracking**

   Just like airlines reward the repeat customers with the "frequent flyer miles", the shopping cart could track the points assigned to products and provide a summary of the order's total frequent shopper points. This allows the customers to accumulate credit or points toward some future reward or incentive.

5. **Real-time Price Recalculation**

The shopping cart also displays price change in real-time, as soon as the option is chosen under bargaining.

6. **Multiple Lay-out Options**

Most shopping carts have a distinctive look and feel about them which reveals their brand identity as soon as the shopping process begins. However myshop.com will be able to customise the cart even for listed stores. The shopping cart's multiple lay-out options provided this option for realising this objective.

7. **Pricing Categories**

The shopping cart's pricing category feature allows all listed products/services to sell the products across different market segments with each one afforded a different pricing structure.

8. **Online credit card and cheque authorisation**

Myshop.com has different online payment service providers directly integrated into payment solutions to allow real-time authorisation of credit cards and checks.

9. **Real-time transportation cost capture from DHL**

When the myshop.com customer chooses a DHL courier option, the shopping cart could communicate directly with the DHL web site to capture the appropriate transportation charge based on the order's total weight and its pin code origin and destination

WHETHER THE MYSHOP.COM SITE LOOK THE SAME AS EVERYONE ELSE'S?

One of the reasons that prompted Aravind to select this cart solution was that his clients could customise their site to be a reflection of their business. Because of the special error checking and order processing scripts that myshop.com-shopping cart utilises, these functions must be added on. The cost of re-writing this functionality into a custom solution would exceed the cost of the actual shopping cart solution. The growing concern about the abuse of information and cheating the customers through this popular medium was a major source of worry for Aravind (Exhibit: 4)

EXHIBIT 4

E-CONSUMERISM

In the informal hierarchy of the information media, the printed word is still considered the most credible. Now it is a fact that the cynical persons tend to believe everything they pick up on the Internet. It is the seemingly reliable news and information sites and their message boards that find the ready believers, however vague their antecedents. Isn't it time we asked how dependable is the medium that has become such an important part of our lives (at least those who are reading this column)? Whether the www enjoy more credibility than it deserves? Why do people believe everything they read on the Net?

On November 4, 2002, two international consumer organisations that had attempted to find answers to the aforesaid questions have released the findings of a survey of 460 web sites conducted with the help of researchers in 13 countries. The Consumers International (a global federation of more than 250 consumer organisations in 115 countries) and the US-based Consumer Webwatch conducted separate studies, which establish what many of us have always suspected - that the information on the Net should be viewed with care and relied upon only after some basic checking. The Consumers International's press release says that half the sites in their survey failed to (a) give warnings about the proper use of the information presented, (b) offer credentials or background on the people dispensing advice on the sites, or (c) to give the sources for advice. The research covered sites providing information on (a) health, specifically breast cancer, prostate cancer and allergies; (b) financial services and products such as mortgages and life insurance; and (c) 'deal-finder' sites which provides the comparitive prices on computers, flights and car rental rates. Broadly, the study reveals that:

✓ Forty nine per cent of health and financial sites failed to give warnings about the appropriate use of their information or say that consumers should consult a professional before acting on their advice.

✓ Half the sites on health and finance failed to provide full information about the authority and credentials of the people behind that advice. But more than half (57 per cent) of general advice sites did quote sources.

✓ Thirty nine per cent of sites that collect personal information had no privacy policy, 62 per cent contained claims that were vague and unspecific while 55 per cent did not bother to say how up-to-date their content was.

✓ Thirty per cent had no address or telephone number listed and 26 per cent were not clear about who owned them.

✓ Sixty per cent of the sites provided no information on whether or not their content is influenced by commercial interests of partners, sponsors and advertisers.

Interestingly, the study by Consumer Webwatch (conducted together with Sliced Bread Design and others) showed that most experts already take care to check the credentials of sites that they rely on and are more comfortable with the web sites that educate consumers and do not nudge them towards their own products. But they seem to be the only ones who show some discernment; the average reader continues to be unconcerned about the credibility of the Net.

The Consumer Webwatch notes that out of the 2,440 comments it analysed about credibility, less than 9 per cent of the readers seemed concerned about the identity of the site or its operator. This was part of an assessment that it made about concerns that participants had raised on their own about the accuracy of information and its reliability. The findings are disturbing. They reveal that none of the participants were worried about the site's record in correcting false and misleading information. Only 7 per cent paid attention to 'customer service' or related policies, while assessing the credibility and less than one per cent mentioned privacy policies in their comments.

Source: Business Standard and www. rediffmail.com

ESTIMATION TO GO ONLINE:

According to Mr Ramesh, the finance director, the cost of developing the software will be around Rs.10,00,000. Moreover, hosting web pages with the facilities for online retailing may come around Rs 20 lakh. Again, myshop.com should go for the connectivity with other leading supermarkets to cater to the needs of the customers. This require an amount of Rs 40 lakh. Therefore if the firm goes online it has to spent at least Rs 160 lakh to become a well-established online retailing firm. The itemwise expenditure is given in Exhibit 5

EXHIBIT 5

EXPENSES AT GLANCE:	
	Figure in Rs
Developing Software	10 lakh
Web page hosting	20 lakh
Recruitment of personnel	10 lakh
Connectivity to other stores	40 lakh
Training the personnel	40 lakh
Investment in computers and other accessories	40 lakh
	Total 160 lakh

PROJECTION OF FINANCIAL PERFORMANCE

The projected turnover per month of the site is expected to be Rs 10 lakh. Once myshop.com becomes an established e-tailor the market share may improve. Also the increase in the Internet users and non-availability of time for shopping add further impetus for online retailing. Moreover the myshop.com facilitates comparison-shopping based on price, nutritional content, fat or calories. By looking into the problem and analysis, Mr. Ramesh concluded that the new generation e-tailor, myshop.com who combines the current market products, rapid expansion, focussed culture, productivity, technology and cost leadership will be a wise choice for the new generation.

1. Analyse the case and give your suggestion to the chief executive of Myshop.com

WEB ANALYTICAL SOFTWARE ILLUSTRATION

The life time value is the current value plus the expected future value of a customer. If you know the likelihood of a customer to respond, what do you know about their future value? A customer who is more likely to respond has a higher future value than a customer does less likely to respond, by definition. Therefore, a business firm could use this scoring technique not only to determine the likelihood to respond, but also to compare the future value of customers. If you can compare the future value of customers, you can organise the business around customer value. You can specifically tie any activity in your business—the ad sources, search terms, products, areas of your site—to future customer value. If the customers coming from one ad have high likelihood to respond scores (high future value), and the customers coming from another ad have low likelihood to respond scores (low future value), which ad is the more profitable ad for your business longer term? If the customers who buy a certain product have high future value, and the customers who buy another product have low future value, which product do you feature? If the customers who frequent one area of the site have high future value, but the customers who frequent another area of the site have low future value, which area do you promote? Which area do you fix? You can use the data customers leave behind through their interactions with you to create likelihood to respond scores, and use these scores to dramatically increase customer marketing profitability.

ASSUME Cost per order (CPO)		$ 10.00	
	The Effect of CR Changes on CPO		
	Change:	CR Increased	CPO
	1.00%	1,515	$ 9.90
	5.00%	1,575	$ 9.52
	10.00%	1,650	$ 9.09
	15.00%	1,725	$ 8.70
	25.00%	1,875	$ 8.00
	50.00%	2,250	$ 6.67
	75.00%	2,625	$ 5.71
INPUT: Average monthly existing customer orders		250	
Average number of orders per month		1,500	
RESULT: Repeat Order Rate (ROR)		16.67%	
INPUT: Average Sales per Month		$ 50,000	

INPUT: Average number of Orders per Month		1,500	
RESULT: Average order Amount (AOA)		$ 33	
	Sales From Increasing Avg. Order Amount		
	Change:	New AOA	Per Month
	1.00%	$33.67	$500.00
	5.00%	$35.00	$2,500.00
	10.00%	$36.67	$5,000.00
	15.00%	$38.33	$7,500.00
	25.00%	$41.67	$12,500.00
	50.00%	$50.00	$25,000.00
	75.00%	$58.33	$37,500.00
Average number of orders per month		1,500	
INPUT: Average number of Visits (Sessions) per month		150,000	
RESULT: Conversion rate (CR)		1.00%	
Average order amount		$ 33	
Average sales per month		$ 50,000	
	Sales Increase From Increasing CR		
	Change:	CR	Per Month
	1.00%	1.010%	$ 500.00
	5.00%	1.050%	$ 2,500.00
	10.00%	1.100%	$ 5,000.00
	15.00%	1.150%	$ 7,500.00
	25.00%	1.250%	$ 12,500.00
	50.00%	1.500%	$ 25,000.00
	75.00%	1.750%	$ 37,500.00
Average sales per month		$ 50,000	
Average number of visits (Sessions) per month		150,000	
RESULT: Sales per visit (SPV)		$ 0.33	

	SPV Increase From Increasing CR		
	Change:	CR	Increase
	1.00%	1.010%	$ 0.34
	5.00%	1.050%	$ 0.35
	10.00%	1.100%	$ 0.37
	15.00%	1.150%	$ 0.38
	25.00%	1.250%	$ 0.42
	50.00%	1.500%	$ 0.50
	75.00%	1.750%	$ 0.58
INPUT: Average monthly marketing Expenses		$ 15,000	
Average number of orders per month		1,500	
RESULT: Cost Per Order (CPO)		$10.00	
	The effect of CR changes on CPO		
	Change:	CR Increased	CPO
	1.00%	1.010%	$ 0.34
	1.00%	1,515	$ 9.90
	5.00%	1,575	$ 9.52
	10.00%	1,650	$ 9.09
	15.00%	1,725	$ 8.70
	25.00%	1,875	$ 8.00
	50.00%	2,250	$ 6.67
	75.00%	2,625	$ 5.71
INPUT: Average monthly existing customer orders		250	
Average number of orders per month		1,500	
RESULT: Repeat order rate (ROR)		16.67%	
Average order amount		$ 33	
	Sales Increase From Increasing ROR		
	Change:	Per Month	Per Year
	1.00%	$ 83	$ 1,000
	5.00%	$ 417	$ 5,000
	10.00%	$ 833	$ 10,000
	15.00%	$ 1,250	$ 15,000
	25.00%	$ 2,083	$ 25,000
	50.00%	$ 4,167	$ 50,000
	75.00%	$ 6,250	$ 75,000

Average number of visits (Sessions) per month	150,000	
Average monthly marketing Expenses	$ 15,000	
RESULT: Cost per visit (CPV)	$ 0.10	
Cost per visit	$ 0.10	
Cost per order	$ 10.00	
RESULT: Order acquisition gap (OAG)	$ (9.90)	
Cost per order	$ 10.00	
Cost per visit	$ 0.10	
RESULT: Order acquisition ratio (OAR)	100	
INPUT: Your average gross margin percentage	50%	
Average order amount	$ 33	
Cost per order	$ 10.00	
RESULT: Contribution per order (CON)	$ 6.67	
Contribution per order	$ 6.67	
Cost per order	$ 10.00	
RESULT: Return on investment (ROI)	67%	

	Week 1	Week 2	Week 3	Week 4	Week 5	Week 6	Week 7	Week 8
CONTENT ANALYSIS: (for commerce analysis see below)- For two months or, 8 WEEKS								
Please INPUT the following values for each week from General Statistics Section								
INPUT: Page views: Document views								
INPUT: Visitor sessions Visitor Sessions								
INPUT: Visitors: Unique visitors								
INPUT: Visitors: visitors who visited more than once From resources Accessed section								
INPUT: Top entry Pages: Home Page								
INPUT: Single access Pages: Home Page From advertising section								
INPUT: Views and clicks: newsletter								
INPUT: Views and clicks: Bookmarks								
INPUT: Views and clicks: downloads from activity statistics section By length of visit								
INPUT: Top line: 0-1 Minute visits								
INPUT: Top line: 0-1 Minute page views								

INPUT: Bottom line: >19 Minute visits								
INPUT: Bottom line: >19 Minute page views								
By number of views **INPUT:** Number of pages viewed: 1 Page								
INPUT: Number of pages viewed: 11 or more pages								

COMMERCE ANALYSIS:

INPUT: The following values for each week								
INPUT: Average sales per month								
INPUT: Average number of orders per month								
INPUT: Average number of visits (Sessions) per month								
INPUT: Average monthly marketing expenses								
INPUT: Average monthly existing customer orders								
INPUT: Average gross margin percentage								
RESULT: Scanning visitor volume								
Commerce Metrics: Converting Activity into Profits. (All results will be automatically here are few)								
RESULT: Average order amount (AOA)								
RESULT: Conversion rate (CR)								

RESULT: Sales rer visit (SPV)								
RESULT: Cost per order (CPO)								
RESULT: Repeat order rate (ROR)								
RESULT: Cost per visit (CPV)								

Sources: www.jimnovo.com and Drilling Down project with permission: validation of result is possible only with input data. Data structure is devised in simple excel format compatible with all PC operation systems

APPENDIX 2

FAMILIARISATION OF TERMS USED IN CONTENT METRICS

Take Rates Newsletter, bookmarks, and downloads.

This is a measure of how compelling a company's offerings are to the audience that it receives at the site, and how well the company is equipped in marketing to them.

Repeat Visitor Share This is a measure of how compelling the company's content is to visitors and how easy it is for them to find what they want. Are you giving them a reason to come back?

Heavy User Share Percentage of visits involving very high page view counts; these are the heaviest users in terms of pages viewed.

Committed Visitor Share Percentage of very long visits, similar in nature to heavy penetration above, only using the time-based visits instead of page views. Depending on the purpose of your site, you can use either, just one, or both of these metrics.

Committed Visitor Index Average page views per visit for only very long visits, a very important metric for most sites because it combines page views and timer.

Committed Visitor Volume Percent of total page views on the site viewed by visitors with very long visit behaviour.

Visitor Engagement Index This is a average sessions per visitor, indicating the tendency for multiple sessions on the part of users.

Reject Rate : All Pages Per cent visits where only one page was viewed and then the visitor left; this metric frequently ties to broad navigation or design issues.

Reject Rate : Home Page This is the percentage of visits where the only page viewed was the home page. If you can't get them past the home page, you have a problem.

Scanning Visitor Share This is the index of average pages scanned in a one minute or less visit.

Scanning Visitor Volume This is the per cent of total site page views completed in visits of one minute or less.

COMMERCE METRICS : CONVERTING ACTIVITY INTO PROFITS

Average Order Amount (AOA) This can be used as a measure of how well your site up-sells & cross-sells.

Conversion Rate (CR) This is the ratio of total orders, the number of visits and is one of the most important metrics you can track. It is also called the sales closing rate or sales closing ratio, and is a measure of how well the website of a firm could make a sale to a shopper.

Sales per visit (SPV) This is another way of measuring the company's marketing efficiency.

Cost per order (CPO) This is the cost that the business will have to expend to generate an order.

Repeat order rate (ROR) This measures the ability of the firm's site to generate repeat business; the share of total orders placed by existing customers.

Cost per visit (CPV) This is a very useful way to measure the cost of net traffic. It is a simple calculation to get an important number that cannot be overlooked.

Order acquisition gap (OAG) This is a marketing efficiency measure, and represents the value of the mismatch between visitors you are generating and the visitors you are converting.

Order acquisition ratio (OAR) This is another marketing efficiency measure that may be easier to communicate to senior management because it is a ratio rather than a currency per order.

Return On Investment (ROI) The ROI is a measure of how well the marketing campaigns are utilising the money being allocated to them.

Source: www.jimnova.com and Drilling Down project with permission

APPENDIX 3
GLOSSARY OF INTERNET TERMS

Affiliate programme   A revenue-sharing programme where the affiliate web site drives the traffic to the merchant site and in doing so receives a bounty or other incentive for the user's purchase membership signups, click through, etc. on the merchant site through that link or banner. This is also known as the "pay for performance" programme. The Amazon.com Associates programme is one of the most famous affiliate programme in this regard.

Boolean logic   Useful in refining search engine queries such as when using Deja News. Examples include "and," "or," and "not."

Chat   An environment where the Internet users can gather in public and/or private "rooms" and discuss the topics in real time. Each participant can see what the other participants type as they type it.

Collaborative filtering   A virtual environment where users with similar tastes and psychographics make intelligent recommendations to each other. Users rate the degree to which they like or dislike specific things such as the artists, authors, movies, books, restaurants or music CDs. The collaborative filtering software (Firefly, for example) then finds the user's "nearest neighbors" and recommends these users' favorite artists, authors, etc. to that user.

Conditional includes   An "if-then" programming statement, the results of which are displayed on a dynamic web page; mostly used in "rules-based" personalisation.

Cookie   An identifier stored in a file on your hard drive by a web site via the web browser. This identifier is used to track the user (actually it can only identify the computer and not the individual user) during the visit and to recognise that user on subsequent visits. A cookie is only a digital tag; it cannot by itself give the web server the email address, name, or other identity information. However, if at some point in your visits to the site fill out a form giving your name or email address, it is then possible for the web server to associate this information with your cookie.

Email list (listserv)   An online discussion group conducted over email. Posted messages to a list are received by participants in their email box, which is known to potentially yield untidy, overflowing email boxes. The posted messages do not get deleted automatically (as is the case for a newsgroup); instead they collect in your mailbox until you delete them. Has the benefit over newsgroups and web-based discussion groups of being on a ubiquitous system, i.e. nearly all Internet users have email access, whereas only a portion of them have access to the web or use net. To locate an email list on a particular topic of interest, check out the fairly comprehensive list of email mailing lists at http://www.neosoft.com/internet/paml

Email notification service An email announcement or reminder, often times personalised to the individual recipient. For example, the Amazon.com will notify you by email when a new book comes out by one of your favorite authors or in a genre of interest to you.

Encryption A security mechanism that codes web and/or email transmissions. Most web browsers and servers use a type of web site encryption called SSL (secure sockets layer). The email communications could be encrypted using PGP (pretty good privacy), for instance.

Extranet An access-restricted web site similar to an Intranet, but opened up to additional business partners, such as customers, distributors, and/or suppliers.

FAQ A compendium of frequently asked questions with answers. Such a document or series of documents is meant to reduce the amount of repeatedly asked questions on newsgroups, email lists, and the web sites. Not all newsgroups have a FAQ, although great many do. The newsgroup FAQs are posted periodically in the corresponding newsgroup and in the newsgroup news. answers (news:news.answers). You can search through most FAQs by visiting the Infoseek web site at http://www.infoseek.com; once there, just select "web FAQs" from the pulldown menu and type a keyword.

Flaming A countermeasure frequently used by irate recipients of spams. Hate emails, sometimes a barrage of them, are sent to the guilty spammer.

Intranet An internal web site for employee purposes. A typical Intranet might support the electronic submission of vacation request forms and other HR forms, as well as viewing and searching the employee handbook, employee directory, competitive intelligence information, customer lists, etc.

IP address An "Internet phone number," so to speak. Each computer on the Internet has its own unique IP address, although typically with "dial-up" Internet accounts through an ISP (Internet Service Provider), that address is usually different each time the connection to the ISP is made.

IP authentication A security mechanism that allows access to a Web site or Internet service based on the user's IP address.

IP blocking A security mechanism that refuses access to a web site or Internet service based on the user's IP address.

IRC Internet Relay Chat. Separate from the Web, the IRC offers public and private "rooms" where users can gather and type text messages to each other in real time.

Meta-search engines A search engine of multiple web sites or multiple search engines. The search engine is created by sending a "web crawler" or "spider" to explore and index entire web sites, thus creating a full-text search engine of a group of other sites out on the Net. It can also be used to search your competitors' sites, relevant industry sites, suppliers' sites, etc.

META tag The hidden information (HTML code) about a web page, such as keywords or a description, that is picked up by search engines (such as Infoseek) and used in ranking pages in the search engine.

Moderated A discussion group (either newsgroup or email list) where all messages must be approved by the moderator before getting posted to the group. A moderated discussion group can be a welcome break from the spamming (see below) that is running rampant on Usenet and email.

Netiquette An unspoken set of rules (guidelines) on how to market by email and Usenet. It includes adding value and refraining from blatant advertising. And spamming is definitely at the top of the list of no-no's!

Newsgroup An online discussion group in a part of the Internet called the Usenet. Separate from the world wide Web and email, Usenet offers over 50,000 of these newsgroups, all on distinctly different topics, ranging from downhill skiing, to French culture, to computer graphics software, to marketing, and much more. To access Usenet newsgroups, select "Netscape News" under the Window menu, then "Show All Newsgroups" under the options menu, and finally click on a newsgroup name that may be of interest to you from the hierarchically organised list. Or if you already know the name of the newsgroup, you may subscribe to it by choosing "Add Newsgroup" from under the file menu in Netscape and typing the name in when prompted. Or, type "news:

{newsgroup-name}" as the location (web address) in your web browser (e.g. "news:rec.travel.bed+breakfast").

Messages older than several weeks get deleted automatically, so you'll need to access your newsgroups of interest fairly frequently in order not to miss anything. Searchable archives of all the postings to all the newsgroups are offered for free on the DejaNews Web site at http://www.dejanews.com. DejaNews also allows you to locate newsgroups on particular topics of interest.

Offline browser A software product that downloads the entire web sites for later viewing offline. Some offline browsers can be set up to download a competitor's web site every night (or week, or other interval) and compare this with the previous night's version to identify and flag pages which have been added, changed, or deleted.

Personal agent A programme installed on the Internet user's local hard drive that queries and surfs the web for information of possible interest to that user.

Personalisation Tailoring the content of a web site based on the user's profile, surfing patterns, buying patterns, or other variables. "Mass customisation." Several types of personalisation exist: rules-based personalisation which is based on conditional includes, and collaborative filtering

Ping A command that sends "packets" of test data to a particular machine on the Internet to determine if that machine is "alive" on the Internet. Pinging, the act of querying a machine to determine if it is "alive," should not be confused with the hacker activity of "pinging" (waging a "denial of service" attack on a server, i.e. attempting to crash the server).

Push Instead of the user pulling information from the Web, information is "pushed" or broadcast to the user. The users can subscribe to "channels" that they receive with a push client, such as the Point cast.

Reverse DNS lookup A command that takes an IP address and looks up its associated domain name.

Spamming The unscrupulous tactic of sending unwanted and irrelevant messages to newsgroups email lists and individuals' email boxes i.e. junk e-mailing. The messages themselves are referred to as "spams". Spammers often get flamed (see below).

Spider A search engine that indexes one or more web sites, exploring all the links local to the site starting from the main page. (See metasearch engine)

Traceroute   A command that traces a "packet" of data as it travels across the Internet.

Web forum   An online discussion group conducted over a Web site. The viewing and posting of messages is done on the Web site, rather than via email or Usenet.

Whiteboarding application   A programme that allows a group of Internet users to draw diagrams, make notes, etc. on a communal whiteboard that all the participants can see.

Whois   A command that queries the domain database that Inter NIC administers. A whois query can display whether a particular domain name is available, and the owner of the domain name along with contact information. It can also display a list of domains owned by a particular organization

Source: www.jimnova.com and Drilling Down project with permission

FAMILIARISATION OF CASE ANALYSIS

A case is a written description of an organisation (or any of its parts) covering all or some of its aspects for a certain period of time. It sets forth events and organisational circumstances surrounding a particular managerial situation. Despite its known deficiencies, the case method is widely used by universities and professional institutes throughout the world, especially for imparting knowledge and developing skills in the area of services marketing. The goal of case analysis is not to develop a set of "correct" facts, but to learn the reason well with the available data. The cases mirror the uncertainty of the real-world managerial environment in that the information present is often imprecise and ambiguous. You may perhaps be frustrated that there is no one right answer or correct solution to any given case. Instead, there may be a number of feasible strategies that the management might adopt, each with somewhat different implications for the future of the organisation, and each involving different trade-offs.

The service managers cannot afford to delay making decisions until they are satisfied with the quality and quantity of available information. Such a time perhaps may never arrive. Like a real world manager, a student of service marketing must make a decision, making best use of whatever information is available and making assumptions about whatever is unknown or is not available. If you are using this book in a course or seminar, you will be exposed to a wide range of different management situations within a relatively short time. As a result, the cases presented in this book will collectively provide a much broader exposure to service marketing problems than most managers experience in many years on the job. Recognising that managerial problems are not unique to a particular institution (or even to a specific service industry) forms the basis for developing a professional approach to management.

OBJECTIVES OF CASE METHOD ANALYSIS

The objectives of the case method analysis are to:

➢ help acquire the skills of putting text book knowledge about management into practice. Managers succeed not so much because of what they know but because of what they do.

➢ get you out of the habit of being a receiver of facts, concepts and techniques and get into the habit of diagnosing problems, analysing and evaluating alternatives, and formulating workable plans of action.

➢ train you to work out answers and solutions for yourselves, as opposed to relying upon the authoritative crutch of the teacher/counsellor or a text book.

➢ provide your exposure to a range of organisations and managerial situations (which might take a life time to experience personally), thus offering you a basis for comparison in your working as a career manager.

ADVANTAGES AND DISADVANTAGES

It's important to recognise that even though case writers try to build realism into their cases, these cases differ from the real-world management situations in several important respects. First, the information is prepackaged in written form. By contrast, the managers accumulate their information through memoranda, meetings, conversations, research studies, observations, news reports, and other externally published materials and, also by rumour.

Second, the case tend to be selective in their reporting because most of them are designed with specific teaching objectives in mind. Each must fit a relatively short class period and focus attention on a defined category of management problems within a given subject area. To provide such a focus and to keep the length and complexity of the case within reasonable bounds the writers should omit information on problems, data, or personnel that are peripheral to the central issues in the case. In the real world, management problems are usually dynamic in nature. They call for some immediate action, with further analysis and major decisions being delayed until some later time. Managers are rarely able to wrap up their problems, put them away, and go on to the next "case". In contrast, discussing a case in class or writing an analysis of a case is more like examining a snapshot taken at a particular point in time - although sometimes a sequel case provides a sense of continuity and poses the need for future decisions within the same organisations .

A third, and final, contrast between the case analyses and real-world management is that participants in case discussions and authors of written case reports aren't responsible for implementing their decisions, nor do they have to live with the consequences. However, this doesn't mean that you can be frivolous when making recommendations. Instructors and classmates are likely to be critical of contributions that aren't based on careful analysis and interpretation of the facts. The pedagogical objective of case method is very much different from the usual teaching in the class room Instead of the professor/ instructor/ counsellor, it is the students who do most of the talking. The counsellor/instructor's role is to solicit student participation and guide the discussion. Since a case assignment emphasises student participation, it is obvious that the effectiveness of the class discussion depends upon each student having studied the case before hand. A case assignment therefore requires conscientious preparation before class. The case analysis and discussion help the students in developing analytical, communication and interpersonal skills which are vital for success in management. The method also provides some opportunity to the students to relate their viewpoints with those of the others. While defending his own viewpoint, a student has also to develop an appreciation for the viewpoints held by others.

PREPARING A CASE

In the case study method, issues are discussed and various alternatives and approaches are evaluated in detail. Usually, a good argument can be made for more than one course of action. The important thing that should be kept in mind regarding the case analysis is the exercise of *identifying, diagnosing* and *recommending* that counts rather than discovering the "right answer". The essence of case analysis is to become skilled in the process of designing workable action plans through evaluation of the prevailing circumstances. Just as there is no one right solution to a case, there is also no single correct way of preparing a case. However, the broad guidelines outlined in "Preparing a Case" may help familiarise you with the job of case preparation.

A case may be prepared for:

➤ Oral analysis for discussion (by individuals)

➤ Oral analysis for discussion (by groups)

➤ Written analysis (by individuals)

➤ Written analysis (by groups)

➤ Oral/written analysis and presentation (by individuals/groups).

What particular method would be followed in the counselling sessions would depend upon the thinking of the counsellor and other factors, including the nature of the company and the length of the case. However, with practice, you should be able to establish a working style with which you feel comfortable.

INITIAL ANALYSIS

A case is a technical paper. As such it deserves careful reading. A good approach is to read the case three times: once rapidly, scanning quickly any exhibits; a second time thoroughly and slowly, putting careful attention to the exhibits and making some notes about apparent organisational objectives, strategies, symptoms of problems, root causes, unresolved issues and the role of key individuals; and a third time rapidly again to reinforce the main points.

First, it's important to gain a feel for the overall situation by skimming quickly through the case.

Then ask yourself:

➤ What sort of organisation does the case concern?

➤ What is the nature of the industry (broadly defined)

➤ What is going on in the external environment?

➤ What problems does management appear to be facing?

While no standard procedure could be laid down, the following successive steps will help while analysing the case (whether for oral discussion or written presentation):

➤ Know the facts

➤ Understand the environment of the organisation (external and internal)

➤ Gather relevant information from outside sources, if necessary

➤ Appraise and evaluate the environment

➤ Consider and keep in mind the mission of the organisation, while making recommendations.

➤ As you proceed the case further, try to make notes in response to such questions as:

➤ What decisions need to be made, and who will be responsible for making them?

➤ What are the objectives of the organisation itself and of each of the key players in the case? Are these objectives compatible? If not, can be problem be reconciled, or will it be necessary to redefine the objectives?

➤ What resources and constraints are present that may help or hinder attempts by the organisation to meet its objectives.

You should make a particular effort to establish the significance of any quantitative data presented in the text of the case or, more often, in the exhibits. See whether the new insights could be gained by combining and manipulating data presented in different parts of the case. But the data should not be accepted blindly. In the cases, as in real life, not all information is equally reliable or equally relevant. On the other hand, case writers won't deliberately misrepresent data or facts to try to trick you.

DEVELOPING RECOMMENDATION

Once you have thoroughly diagnosed the company's situation and weighed the pros and cons of various alternative courses of action, you may decide on what the company should do to tackle the problems or improve its performance. Draw up your set of recommendations and prepare an "action agenda". This is the most crucial part of the analysis. Bear in mind that proposing realistic, workable solution is not the same as offering a hasty, or not a properly conceived possibility. Do not recommend anything you would not be prepared to do yourself if you were in the shoes of the decision maker. Your recommendations won't be complete unless you give some thought to how the proposed strategy should be implemented.

> What type of resources, whether human, financial, or other, will be required?

> Who should be responsible for implementation?

> What time frame should be established for the various actions proposed?

> How should subsequent performance be measured?

In other words, offer a definite agenda for action, stipulate a time-table and sequence for initiating actions, indicating priorities and suggesting who should be responsible for doing what.

WHAT AN EVALUATOR LOOKS FOR IN A CASE ANALYSIS

The important elements that a counsellor (or evaluator) would generally look for in a case analysis are:

> care with which facts and background knowledge have been used

> ability to state problems and issues clearly

> use of appropriate analytical techniques

➢ evidence of sound logic and arguments

➢ consistency between analysis and recommendations.

➢ ability to formulate reasonable and feasible recommendations for action

In short, both future managers as well as the present managers can make use of the case study method for developing a sense of responsibility, commitment and commonsense while taking decision in modern business environment. Efforts have been taken by the author for simulating most of the service marketing problems while marketing / developing organisational products/services in the present context.

SUBJECT INDEX